BRITISH THEATRE AND YOUNG PEOPLE

British Theatre and Young People gathers together new and original studies on the issues, theories, practices and perceptions which characterize British theatre about, for, by and with young people in the 21st century.

Interrogating the critical relationship between theatre and young people today, the book brings together perspectives on theatre about, for, by and with young people and presents it as an art form in its own right. The first part of the book focuses on applied and socially engaged theatre practice with young people, illustrating the ways in which theatre can highlight inclusivity, well-being, community and politics among young people. Part 2 presents essays on adaptation and appropriation, generally looking at how classic texts have been adapted for young audiences. Finally, the last part of the book looks at the ways in which British Youth Theatre and practice in the UK has impacted regional and national theatre scenes. Highlighting this rich and active community and practice, this edited collection paints a picture of the state of theatre for and by young people in the UK today.

British Theatre and Young People is ideal for undergraduate and post-graduate students of theatre studies and applied theatre with an interest in British theatre.

Uğur Ada is currently working as Assistant Professor Doctor at Tokat Gaziosmanpasa University in Türkiye. He holds a Ph.D. degree and his dissertation is entitled "Theatre in Education and the Analysis of Edward Bond's Big Brum Plays within the Context of Theatre in Education". His research areas are Contemporary British Theatre, Applied Theatre/Drama, In-Yer-Face Theatre, and Theatre and Young People. His recent book publications include *Eğitimde Tiyatro/Theatre in Education (TiE)* (2021) and *Edward Bond: Bondian Drama and Young Audience* (2023).

BRITISH THEATRE AND YOUNG PEOPLE

Theory and Performance in the 21st Century

Edited by Uğur Ada

Routledge
Taylor & Francis Group

LONDON AND NEW YORK

First published 2025
by Routledge
4 Park Square, Milton Park, Abingdon, Oxon OX14 4RN

and by Routledge
605 Third Avenue, New York, NY 10158

Routledge is an imprint of the Taylor & Francis Group, an informa business

British Library Cataloguing in Publication Data
A catalogue record for this book is available from the British Library

ISBN: 978-1-032-74688-3 (hbk)
ISBN: 978-1-032-74687-6 (pbk)
ISBN: 978-1-003-47043-4 (ebk)

DOI: 10.4324/9781003470434

Typeset in Times New Roman
by Taylor & Francis Books

CONTENTS

To my beloved family, Ayşe Derya Aksoy Ada and Deniz Kağan Ada for their love and support
and
Mustafa Kemal Atatürk, the foremost leader of the Republic of Türkiye.

CONTRIBUTORS

Uğur Ada is currently working as Assistant Professor Doctor at Tokat Gaziosmanpasa University in Türkiye. He holds a Ph.D. degree and his dissertation is entitled "Theatre in Education and the Analysis of Edward Bond's Big Brum Plays within the Context of Theatre in Education". His research areas are Contemporary British Theatre, Applied Theatre/Drama, In-Yer-Face Theatre, and Theatre and Young People. His recent book publications include *Eğitimde Tiyatro/Theatre in Education (TiE)* (2021, Pegem Akademi) and *Edward Bond: Bondian Drama and Young Audience* (2023, Vernon Press).

Ben Ballin has been an Educationalist and Project Worker at Big Brum since 2012, coordinating and developing creative projects with partners in the UK and internationally and contributing to its publications. He has recently taken in additional coordination responsibilities as part of the company's commitment to young people in North Solihull. Prior to that, he has worked for a wide range of socially-committed organisations on educational projects and publications.

Ajda Baştan is a full-time Assistant Professor at Sivas Cumhuriyet University in Türkiye. She holds a Ph.D. in English Literature and her dissertation is entitled "Women and violence in Caryl Churchill's plays". Her research interests include post-modernism, feminism, violence, British women writers and post-war playwrights. She has published about 20 articles and a book entitled *Violence in British Theatre*. She is also the editor of *Shakespeare's Sonnets* translated and published in Turkish. Her most recent studies are on intertextuality and social learning theory in contemporary British plays.

Pilar Botías Domínguez is Assistant Professor at Universidad de Córdoba, Spain (Department of English). She holds a B.A. degree in English Studies (University of Córdoba, 2011–2015). She completed the final year at Oxford Brookes University (Erasmus+) and The Oxford Academy (UK). She holds an M.A. in English Literature and Linguistics (University of Granada, 2015–2016) and she also holds a Certificate of Proficiency in English from Cambridge University Assessment (2016). She has a Ph.D. in English Literature (International Ph.D. Mention, University of Córdoba 2022). In 2019 she was a Recognised Student (Doctoral Researcher) at the University of Oxford (UK). Her main field of research is Restoration and Eighteenth-century England, particularly the novel. Furthermore, she has published papers on literary translation (novel, drama and poetry).

Richard Holmes has been Artistic Director at Big Brum TIE since 2016, leading the company's artistic and theoretical development, directing its plays and TIE programmes and contributing to its projects and publications. Prior to that, he was lead Actor Teacher at Big Brum, leading the touring company in its work with schools and universities and supporting a youth theatre. Before joining Big Brum in 1996, he was a member of the Actors' Group and an active member of the seminal Standing Conference in Young People's Theatre (SCYPT).

Xiaolin Huang is currently a visiting academic scholar at the Royal Central School of Speech and Drama, University of London, UK. She is a doctoral candidate at the Central Academy of Drama in China. She is also a freelance director, theatre and film actress. Her research focuses on Inter-Cultural Theatre Study, Performance Studies, Musical Theatre and Applied Theatre Study.

Ava Hunt has been a practitioner in the field of applied theatre for 40 years. She trained with Boal, Heathcote in Mantle of the Expert practice and is a Programme Leader on the M.A. in Applied Theatre & Education at the University of Derby, UK. Her published Ph.D. explores the Activation of the Role of the Bystander and Tritagonist Theatre. She has published articles on the effect of artists using drama following the COVID pandemic. She has performed and presented research in Sri Lanka, the Soviet Union, the USA, the Czech Republic, Palestine, Romania, Australia, New Zealand, India, Canada and across Europe.

Zoe Katsilerou is a senior lecturer, performer and maker, with a background in dance theatre, devised theatre, voice coaching, polyphonic singing, musical composition and improvisation. She is a Senior Lecturer in Performing Arts at Leeds Beckett University, UK (part-time) and works as a visiting lecturer for institutions across the UK. She is a creative associate artist with SBC

Theatre Company and Leeds Playhouse, and Artistic Director of the improvisation collective ICEBERG. Zoe is a member of The Work Room (Glasgow), The Natural Voice Network (Sheffield), and of the artistic committee of The Makings of The Actor.

Leonard Love has been writing and directing theatre productions for young people for nearly 20 years. He has a keen interest in popular theatre and entertainment, which he has also written and performed in through various forms and venues. Most recently he has collaborated with young performers and directed Shakespearean adaptations such as *Rockbeth, Romeo & Jools, A Mid-80's Nights Dream, The Tempest* and *12th Night: All Inclusive*.

Rosie MacPherson is Artistic Director and Joint CEO of Stand & Be Counted, the UK's first and leading Theatre Company of Sanctuary. She oversees the artistic and community strands and is heavily involved in local and national activism, a driving mechanism within the charity. A passion for politics and social justice ensures SBC are up to date on current policies affecting our participants and the support networks available to them. She is a critically acclaimed playwright & award winning actor; she writes and directs for SBC with a focus on developing first commissions and productions alongside its associate artists and participants. She leads on SBC's sector support strategy, ensuring a wider range of organizations and practitioners are prioritizing the needs of people seeking sanctuary.

Ester Díaz Morillo is a Ph.D. Fellow in English Literary Studies at the Universidad Nacional de Educación a Distancia (UNED), Spain, where she holds a FPI grant. Her doctoral research focuses on the study of the poetic language and how it can be adapted and transferred to other artistic means such as painting and music. Her main research interests include transmediation, adaptation and translation studies, as well as the sisterhood of the arts. She is a member of the Pre-Raphaelite Podcast of the Pre-Raphaelite Society. She works as an Editorial Assistant for the PopMeC Association for US Popular Culture Studies.

Rachael Newberry is a Senior Lecturer in the Department of Theatre and Performance at Goldsmiths College, University of London, UK. She teaches across a range of specialisms from Shakespeare and theatre history through to post-war British theatre, and post-modern and avant-garde dramatic texts. She has published in the areas of theatre-fiction, in-yer-face theatre, and gastro-criticism. She is the director of the degree programme Drama and Theatre Arts, and Chair of Learning and Teaching. She is a champion of teaching excellence and widening participation. Rachael's research interests are in the fields of feminist and critical theory, eco-criticism, the body, and themes of consumption and self-denial.

James Peachey-Baker has been a Senior Lecturer in the Department of Theatre at the University of Chichester, UK, since 2009. He is programme coordinator for the Drama & Theatre programme and also a practising artist and trained theatre performer/director. He has also been a Lecturer in Performance at Solent University since 2019. His particular interests are in children's theatre, durational work, endurance, one-offs, walking, space and travelling. These interests have been nurtured whilst working with Bootworks Theatre, the company where he has been a Co-Artistic Director since 2007; its work is award-winning, tours internationally and is supported by The British Council and Arts Council England. His work has been performed in a variety of non-traditional spaces; from an orphanage in Cairo to the middle of a lake in Kochi, Japan.

Susana Nicolás Román is a Senior Lecturer in the English Department at the University of Almeria (Spain). Her research areas principally focus on the connection between theatre, violence, precarity and vulnerability. She has published extensively on educational and social drama. She is an active collaborator in theatre and research projects in Spain.

Yiming Wang is a theatre director, playwright and dramaturg. He co-founded the Dionysuscat Theatre Company in London and has collaborated with the Royal Court Theatre and Shakespeare's Globe. His works have been staged in various fringe theatres and theatre festivals. He is holds an M.A. in Text and Performance at RADA and Birkbeck. His current Ph.D. on scholarship at the Central Academy of China focuses on contemporary intercultural theatre studies.

James Woodhams is researcher, theatre-maker, community-applied theatre producer and puppeteer. Based in Plymouth, United Kingdom, James has built a career that spans multiple artistic disciplines, with a particular focus on Theatre for Young Audiences (TYA). His research interest lies in exploring the intersection of space and theatrical engagement, investigating how different environments can shape, enhance and reach new audiences' experiences. His work also includes an exploration of children's creative engagement online, the intersections of theatre in unconventional sites, barriers to access in the arts and adapting business models within the industry. He currently works as a Commercialisation Manager for the Humanities, Arts, and Social Sciences (HASS) faculty at the University of Exeter, helping turn research outputs into sustainable impact.

PREFACE

Young people are traditionally accepted as the future of the world, a notion that has consistently occupied the thoughts and conversations of society. As the forthcoming generation, they are expected to navigate the responsibilities of adulthood, which might include securing employment, starting a family, or taking on leadership roles within their communities and nations. These normative experiences are not left to chance but are meticulously shaped by various societal structures, including schools, families, institutional policies, media and technology. Schools provide education and socialization; families offer foundational values and support; and media and technology influence perceptions and behaviour. Institutional policies further guide and regulate these processes to align with broader societal goals. Through both direct and indirect means, these entities work to ensure that essential values and skills are passed down from one generation to the next.

Although this ongoing reproductive process of societal norms and expectations highlights these institutions' critical role in shaping the future, the effectiveness of these practices in preparing young individuals for the future – despite the meticulous planning and efforts involved – remains a topic of ongoing debate and adjustment. Today's world is in chaos, facing global problems that are deepened from past to present, including climate change and environmental crisis, economic uncertainty, social inequality, political instability, global migrations, refugee crises and cultural and identity issues. The future is not progressing in a good way anymore, and young people will soon inherit the large-scale violence, droughts, famine, discrimination, pandemics, insecurity and so forth, of the present-day.

While adults – perpetrators the future – control the discourse and actions concerning what lies ahead, young people, victims of these future conditions, lack the authority to influence or predict the world's future. The media, academic courses, policies and books predominantly reflect the perspectives of today's adults. Ironically, young people must eventually grow up to gain the authority to raise awareness about future issues or to be taken seriously. Their views and actions, whether marked by innocence or the turbulence of adolescence, are often dismissed as naive, simplistic or idealistic by the adult world, with the exception of their value in theatre.

The relationship between theatre and young people has a long and evolving history, which materializes a variety of theories and performances that place children and youth as the main focus of theatre art, with diverse responsibilities such as audience, playwright, facilitator, critic, performer and so on. In the 21st century, theatre *about, for, by* and *with* young people is an art form in its own right and plays a significant role in both the creative arts industry and contemporary society. Despite the most recent local and global problems such as funding cuts and the closing of performance venues during the coronavirus pandemic, it is still one of Britain's most innovative and flourishing fields of contemporary theatrical practice. Local and mainstream theatre companies are finding new ways to reunite with young people who are still drawn to the immediacy of the dramatic experience despite the many distractions such as social media and others.

This book gathers together new and original work on the issues, theories, practices and perceptions which characterize British theatre *about, for, by* and *with* young people in the 21st century. It does not focus on the history of the relationship between theatre and young people, the instrumental, aesthetic or educational value of theatre as an art for young people, nor the place of theatre *about, for, by* and *with* young people among other theatre practices. Instead, the breadth of focus aims to manifest the diverse and compelling performances of British theatre that create a broader awareness of diverse issues from the perspective of young people. The book goes beyond academic discourse, including chapters offering critical reflections and local, national and international practices. Rather than providing certain chapters on one particular topic or practice from a specific perspective, its structure is divided into three sections. In arranging the chapters and sections, the editor brings together researchers, facilitators, performers and others who are deeply committed to the field.

The first section, "Socially Engaged Performances", consists of five chapters which provide critical reflection and analysis of wide range of different social issues that engage with the common challenges of young people. The chapters focus on gender and sexuality (Uğur Ada), parentification and dependency (Ajda Baştan), precarious conditions intersecting with cruel optimism (Susana Nicolás Román), climate activism and awareness (Rachael Newberry), censorship and sex (James Peachey-Baker).

The second section, *Adaptation and Appropriation,* includes four chapters that interrogate the issues and practices that are based on adaptation and appropriation as a concept and performance that characterizes British theatre *about, for, by* and *with* young people in the 21st century. The chapters comprise of an adaptation of Christina Rossetti's poem *Goblin Market* for a young audience (Ester Díaz Morillo), Zadie Smith's theatrical adaptation of Geoffrey Chaucer's *The Wife of Bath* (Pilar Botías Domínguez), William Shakespeare and young people (Leonard Love) and a case study on *Cloud Man* and the Chinese youth theatre market (Xiaolin Huang and Yiming Wang).

The third section, *Local, National and International Voices*, comprise four chapters that feature practices of theatre *about, for, by* and *with* young people with the dedication of stakeholders with diverse backgrounds. The chapters introduce Big Brum Theatre in Education Company (Richard Holmes and Ben Ballin), Destinies, a co-creation theatre project (Ava Hunt), Stand & Be Counted Theatre and sanctuary youth groups (Rosie MacPherson and Zoe Katsilerou) and Theatre Bath Bus and mobile space (James Woodhams).

I hope this book will capture the interest of artists, playwrights, theatre companies, researchers, facilitators and practitioners, inspiring them to continue their work in theatre *about, for, by* and *with* young people. I am deeply thankful to the researchers, practitioners and colleagues who contributed their time and effort to this project; their trust and support have been invaluable. I also extend my gratitude to the Routledge editorial board, particularly Claire Margerison and Tassia Watson, for their time and support throughout the development and completion of the book. I also really appreciate the encouragement of a close friend and scholar, Associate Professor Dr Juan de Dios Torralbo Caballero (University of Córdoba, Spain), who would have been one of the contributors to this book. Unfortunately, he passed away at the beginning of the project. His generosity and kindness were truly inspiring for me and my family.

Uğur Ada
Türkiye, September 2024

PART 1

Socially Engaged Performances

1

"GROWING SIDEWAYS" IN MARK RAVENHILL'S PLAY FOR YOUNG PEOPLE, *CITIZENSHIP*

Uğur Ada

Introduction

While the draft of this chapter was still incomplete, Edward Bond – widely known as one of the United Kingdom's most influential playwrights[1] – passed away at the age of 89 on 3 March 2024. As one of the witnesses of World War II in his childhood years, the playwright always underlined the trauma and sorrow as a result of devastating worldwide violence during his lifetime. Peculiarly in his last plays, he drew attention to today's world which is under the influence of the first shock waves of *The Third Crisis* (Bond, 2013). Unfortunately, the beginning of the 21st century or the third millennium has confirmed that statement, with unprecedented threats and dramatic disasters to human beings in a very short time. In its 24 years it has experienced Coronavirus disease (Covid-19), the war between Ukraine and Russia, war between Palestine and Israel, revolts in Iran, large-scale migration flows , terrorist groups such as ISIS, environmental and ecological damage, the 9/11 attacks, the Afghanistan and Iraq wars, economic recession and natural disasters such as high magnitude earthquakes. Moreover, the aftermaths of these shock waves are rendered more visible and pathetic all around the world due to globalization.

Vicky Angelaki (2017) mentions, in parallel with Bond's views, that *crisis* has been a recurring term in the post-2000 period and a buzzword (p. 1) "teetering at the edge between improvement or decline, salvation or catastrophe" (p. 2). The dichotomy of the blurring boundaries, which marks both the sorrow of the past and present days and an optimistic belief for the future, has soon revealed a generation of new writing. Although still new, theatre plays for adults devote close attention to this new century's social, economic and political landscape. A thorough examination of these issues

DOI: 10.4324/9781003470434-2

and conflicts has produced mainstream and radical theatre plays such as *Jerusalem* (2009) by Jez Butterworth, *London Road* (2011) by Alecky Blythe, *An Oak Tree* (2005) by Tim Crouch, *The Wonderful World of Dissocia* (2007) by Anthony Neilson, *Scarborough* (2008) by Fiona Evans, *Grasses of a Thousand Colours* (2009) by Wallace Shawn, *Cruel and Tender* (2004) by Martin Crimp, among others. "These representative plays and playwrights who have stood out in the UK and internationally in the post-recession era, delivering theatre that in the process of being truthful to the contemporary experience has also redefined theatrical form and content" (Angelaki, 2017).

In contrast to adult theatre, theatre for young people is still preserving a safe ecology and grounded in protecting children and teenagers from confronting challenging issues even in the turbulent 21st century. Shifra Schonmann (2022) underlines that theatre for young people has been entangled with education concerns, particularly in schools, and the idealized portrayal of a pure and innocent child. Although there is a great variety of issues relating to the world which will be inherited by the young people, theatre for young people "seems to be stuck in the capsule of content" which "is misleading, hindering us from seeing that the theatre for young audiences is faltering, following in the footsteps of the commercial theatre for adults" (p. 238). On the 21st century common "teen boom" (Sierz, 2011) of British theatre, Erkinovna and Bahodirovna (2023) underline that:

> the growth of dramatic children's characters once again actualizes the cruelty of the characters, their tendency to rebellion and violence, although the cruelty and inconsistency of modern teenagers increasingly appear in the form of violence in the texts and stage changes – passive and verbal aggression, communicative violence and a tendency to escapism. And in a broad framework, the performances presented in various children's dramas about adolescent conflicts and ways to overcome them are united by the general approach of playwrights to the character of a child hero. As a regularity factor, one can define a line, a certain contraction of the symbol.
>
> *(p. 100)*

Nevertheless, the poetics and aesthetics of theatre can still give voice to the current generation of young people to enable a "third space" (Woodson, 2015) for considering personal and social experiences and may create "an interaction that is open to the diverse experiences, and multifaceted discourses of artists from different worlds and their different artistic understandings: radical artistic activity engages with deeply contentious issues … all of which are political in the broad sense" (Schonmann, 2022, pp. 237–238). The artistic and aesthetic experience of theatre for young people may create a liminal space, a transitional, unlimited space that is part of the change from one state to another, a space of ignorance, confusion and uncertainty in which old truths have been abandoned and new ideas have not yet emerged.

(*ASSITEJ Artistic Gathering 2023*)

According to ASSITEJ (2023), the transitional space mentioned above "often begins with … *crisis*" in which "process we *need to* [2] give up the old meanings and enter the marginal space in which new ones have not yet been created." The current problems related to cultural exchange, migration, diversity, mobility, identity and changing norms, interconnectedness, and so on, are increasingly demanding more space for aesthetic expression, where young people worldwide can benefit from the arts as a catalyst for creative change. "The provision of this space … may bring the untold stories and situations of young people to the stage and sharing them within and beyond those communities" (Lane, 2010, p. 137).

The alerts on *crisis* and the desire for *space* in return – to meet with today's stories from young people's perspectives – have urged some of the stakeholders of British theatre to promote the role of children and teenagers as engaged contributors and decision-makers in theatrical activities. In Britain, the "National Theatre's Connections Scheme offers a unique opportunity for youth theatres and school theatre groups to stage new plays written for young people by some of the most exciting playwrights, and to perform in leading theatres across the UK" (National Theatre Connections – Gulbenkian Young Company, 2023). Every year, the Connections Scheme commissions ten plays with an "access to high quality theatrical writing, and directing and professional theatre spaces" (Busby, 2019, p. 118). It is a "nationwide youth theatre festival" with a history of 30 years and "open to any company of young people aged 13–19, and up to 26 years old for groups with additional needs" (Connections, 2024). The Connections plays which directly engage with thousands of young people across the UK have been staged in 33 venues all around the UK in collaboration with nearly 270 youth theatres and schools in 2024.

"The *modus operandi* of Connections might seem very much to propagate young people as an expedient category, yet another user or client group" (Deeney, 2007, p. 333). The scheme aims not to directly promote educational values for a change. Instead, the long-term production process encourages young people to go beyond the boundaries of their natural environment and enables creative space for questioning hidden or explicit narratives. The scheme has allowed their perspective on the world to be heard with high-quality new playwriting that has "presented young people as their protagonists, apparently speaking directly and for themselves, in ways rarely heard before in mainstream theatre space" (Inchley, 2012, p. 329), which is also mediated through the collaboration of divergent playwrights. Watt underlines that:

> The diversity of our Connections writers is a huge consideration; we also have a combination of male and female voices ... because we are working with young people, we're inspiring and creating role models; we show them videos of our writers to break down that it's not all older white men.
>
> *(as cited in Busby, 2019, p. 122)*

Mark Ravenhill is one of the award-winning British playwrights commissioned for the Connections Scheme. Although Ravenhill has gained reputation with controversial plays for adults such as *Shopping and F***ing*, the famous playwright has written a series of plays for young people: *Scenes from Family Life* (2007), *Totally Over You* (2003) and *Citizenship* (2005). Unlike the first two, *Citizenship* was also premiered with a professional production at the National Theatre in 2006. Along with the desire of local theatre companies such as the King's Head Theatre and the full support of the National Theatre, Ravenhill's experience as an administrative assistant, drama teacher, actor, director and playwright began an appreciable collaboration for, with and by young people, which they can fulfil diverse responsibilities and be spokespersons for their narratives.

Mark Ravenhill and the Younger Generation

Since his first debut play, *Shopping and F***ing*, in 1996, Mark Ravenhill's trajectory in playwriting has revolved around the implications of the younger generation in British theatre. Born in 1966, Ravenhill emerged as one of the central young figures – with other young playwrights such as Sarah Kane, Martin McDonagh, Patrick Marber – in the new writing of the 1990s which is widely recognized as in-yer-face theatre.[3] "For a few heady years" when "theatre was the new rock 'n' roll – a real cool place to be" (Sierz, n.d., para. 1), his intense, influential and provocative in-yer face plays scrutinize the struggles of youth, exploring the interplay between daily societal pressures and personal turmoil, from consumerism to technology's ethical dilemmas. Coupled with his close observation of societal shifts, the playwright not only has desired to capture the essence of his generation's experiences but also "identified the contradictions that arise in the youth community as a source of real dramatic conflicts" by "focusing on the representatives of the younger generation" (Erkinovna & Bahodirovna, 2023, para. 2). As Michael Billington (1996) mentioned, Ravenhill was one of "so many exciting dramatists in the twenty something age-group: what is more, they are speaking to audiences of their own generation."

In this newly built-up theatre society created by younger counterparts, one of the starting points of Ravenhill's dramatic writing was triggered by the death of James Bulger.[4] The real tragedy involving young individuals both as victims and perpetrators transformed his interest in theatre – since the very early age of ten to sixteen – into "challenging the boundaries of what is acceptable … questioning current ideas of what is normal, what it means to be human, what is natural and what is real" (Sierz, 2001, p. 5). His oeuvre serves as a mirror to the contemporary society of young characters "that's without politics, without religion, without family, without any kind of history, without structures or narratives, and as a consequence they have to build up their own structures" (as cited in Monforte, 2007, p. 93). Through his sense of the world devoid of traditional sentiments, the playwright reflects a generation's ironic and cynical comprehension. According to Ravenhill (2004)

> Nobody in … [his] plays is fully adult. They are all needy, greedy, wounded, only fleetingly able to connect with the world around them. Consumerism, late capitalism – whatever we call it – has created an environment of the infant "me", where it is difficult to grow into the adult "us".
>
> *(pp. 311–312)*

Epitomized by more than 20 plays, these children, teenagers, youngsters and "adult children" (as cited in Kan, 2015a, p. 1018) are generally "semi-homeless, parentless, unloved, confused" characters "that live without political ambitions" (as cited in Liu, 2020, p. 151). They are neglected and labelled as "hoodies" and "chavs" (Inchley, 2015, p. 101) by a large segment of modern society. Without any help, they are trying to explore new power dynamics and struggle for autonomy which often leads to a re-evaluation of self and societal structures. "Feeling lost in capitalist modernity and nostalgic for grand narratives" (as cited in Liu, 2020, p. 122), they are trying to create their own stories in – as Zygmunt Bauman (2000) identifies as – a phase of liquid modernity:

> in which all social forms melt faster than new ones can be cast. They are not given enough time to solidify, and cannot serve as the frame of reference for human actions and long-term life-strategies because their allegedly short life-expectation undermines efforts to develop a strategy that would require the consistent fulfilment of a "life-project".
>
> *(p. 303)*

In the midst of personal, societal, cultural and political instability, Ravenhill's narratives highlight the evolving nature of taboo related to omnipresent sexual transitions. Most of his plays are about "young, queer, defiant characters" (Svich, 2011, p. 404) in conflict with traditional ideologies, and embrace uncertainty and boundlessness as essential components of modern existence. These characters are not marginalized identities confirming the status of disadvantaged young people in contemporary society. The audience witnesses the growth of characters – traditionally predetermined by capitalist society – "from sexual repression to triumphant enlightenment" (p. 114). His dramaturgy aims "not to offer judgement or criticism, but to build the context of each individual being aware of their own identities and how they differ from the dominant identification of the society they live in" (p. 122).

Ravenhill's reflections on his identity as a playwright add depth to his portrayal of queer young characters. He distances himself from the etiquette of a gay playwright, preferring to depict gay and lesbian characters as a natural reflection of his own experiences rather than as a deliberate artistic statement. His reluctance to conform to a specific "gay aesthetic" (Monforte, 2007, p. 91) underscores his commitment to portraying characters authentically rather than pandering to a particular audience. His queer or post-gay writing "provides a particular dialectical comparison to present a more complex and detailed observation" (Liu, 2020, p. 123). Ravenhill conveyed the authenticity of his writing:

> Any specific politics of representing gay identity and narratives had been done before I came along …. There are plenty of gay narratives around, because in many ways the gay condition is something that all of society aspires to. There's a hedonistic, materialistic, selfish disposition in contemporary gay culture that all of contemporary Britain desires …. they're the ultimate definition of a hedonistic, materialistic society. They are metaphors for a wider society, but I'm not interested in writing plays that affirm that gay people exist and that their narratives exist. That's everywhere; we have reached saturation point.
>
> *(Monforte, 2007, p. 92)*

In Ravenhill's dramaturgy, the queerness of young characters is not the confirmation of gay/lesbian theatre for a specific audience and also not a stance against heterosexuality. Yung-Chen Liu (2020) describes the linear process of his narration of young people as "the queer's journey" which "begins with some characters that cannot be defined in the capitalist society, who are excluded from routine and norms" (p. 106). Within this context, Ravenhill explores a teenager's journey of growing up in a queer manner on the disposition of sexual identity in today's society in *Citizenship* – his last play written for young people. The lonely journey of a teenager in the play mirrors the complexities of daily life, where sexual identity intersects with broader social and political landscapes. As "a subversive social and political commentator" (Billingham, 2007, p. 135) of British theatre, the playwright invites audiences of various ages to confront uncomfortable truths and reconsider their preconceived notions about sexuality and societal norms from the perspective of the younger generation.

Citizenship

Produced as part of the National Theatre's 2005 Connections programme, *Citizenship* is a nine-act play characterized by humour, fast-paced action and ravenous use of language with a duration of 50 minutes. The play adopts a dramaturgy with limited playwright notes and features a minimalist stage-setting and scenery but a large cast including nine British school students (Tom, Amy, Gary, Ray, Stephen, Kerry, Chantel, Alicia, Melissa), a teacher (De Clerk), Tarot Reader, Baby and a boyfriend (Martin). The play's tittle resonates with Citizenship classes – introduced into the National Curriculum in 2002 – which creates a sense of the clichéd exploration of complex relationships between young British students based upon issues such as multiculturalism and so forth. Conversely, it is "something of an ironic title" (Deeney, 2007, p. 340) which "contains a direct response to New Labour's attempts to use the education system as a means to instil its ideologies into the young" (Inchley, 2015, p. 333). Dan Rebellato (2015) notes in his introduction to the play that

> Ravenhill recalls that after his first Connections play, he was contacted by a teacher who, rather earnestly, asked if he would write a play to illustrate the Citizenship classes he was teaching. Anyone familiar with his work would know how uninterested he seems to be in this kind of issue-based drama. Instead, he has written something much more ambivalent: a play for schools that is designed both to embody and critique, help and disrupt the Citizenship project, by turning teenagers, through a strategic act of theatre, into radical citizens.
>
> *(p. 15)*

Citizenship delves into a politically ambiguous and somewhat subversive critique of societal efforts – to shape ideal future citizens – that leads to a "valueless, liberal, postmodern consensus of the adult world" (Inchley, 2015, p. 333). The play challenges the conservative notion of citizenship by questioning "the emergence of new problems and cries which are acutely felt by the younger generation, which has stepped on the path of the search for social, cultural and gender identity" (Erkinovna & Bahodirovna, 2023, para. 1). Throughout its narrative, the teenagers' struggle for identity amidst societal shifts becomes a bitter exploration of growing up and self-discovery. The absence of family support and the *necessary* guidance of the school in everyday life – apart from curriculum topics and institutional policy – result in teen pregnancy, passive and verbal aggression, self-harm, internal dissonance, drug use, peer pressure, fragile wellbeing, porn addiction, and so on. This realistic depiction of teenage life through a critical examination in "a non-judgemental way" (Mulligan, 2005, para. 3), highlights the dangerous realities and social oppression faced by young people, that "either adults disapprove of or pretend do not happen" (para. 3) today. Ravenhill commented that

> I wasn't quite sure what they would make of it because sometimes young people can be quite conservative and prudish and I was worried they might reject it, but actually they were really animated by it and talked about it for hours. They were really fired up by it so I realised I was on to a good thing.
>
> *(as cited in Mulligan, 2005, para. 2)*

The fears, desires, failures and struggles of young people the audience is invited to witness with tolerance and understanding are centred on an exploration of "growing up, purity and impurity, about the child's search for sexuality and discovery of his own identity" (as cited in Erkinovna & Bahodirovna, 2023, para. 4). Throughout the play, this is represented by the journey of Tom, who is uncertain about his sexual orientation and feels pressured to make a decision quickly. As a teenager who is on the verge of "taking the first step into adult sexuality" (as cited in Rebellato, 2015, p. 11), he portrays a complicated exploration of adolescence and his place in society "with a realisation of the inadequacy of the narrowly defined restrictive labels which didn't describe him, coupled with his growing confidence and expression of his sexuality" (Citizenship review, 2018, para. 6).

Ravenhill introduces the confused young protagonist, as of the play's first scene, with a confession while having his ear pierced by his friend Amy. Rather than having professional care, Tom relies on Amy to fulfil his desire to have an earring. They have all the supplies – Nurofen, Dettol, vodka, needle and so on – except for his decisiveness. Amy's effort to "push the needle into his ear" (Ravenhill, 2015, p. 21) ends in Tom bleeding from his ear, insulting her, fainting and leaving Amy in a state of panic. After regaining consciousness, Tom's words and gestures meant to relieve his friend encourage Amy to kiss him, leaving Tom uncomfortable. Tom tries to explain why he feels unready for his first intercourse by sharing a significant truth about his life:

> I have this dream. And in this dream I'm kissing someone. Real kissing. Tongues and that. But I can't see who I'm kissing. I don't know if it's a woman. Or a man. I try to see the face. But I can't.
>
> *(Ravenhill, 2015, p. 24)*

Tom's fantasy is a site of discovery throughout the unstable selfhood of adolescence, which is structured as the crucial period when youngsters begin to form their gender identity. In this transition period of life, Tom is caught between childhood, in which sexuality is identified as non-existent (Robinson, 2012, p. 115), and adulthood, which is associated with traditional gender archetypes and sexual-sociocultural norms. As "not yet grown up" (Kristeva, 2024) but who is supposed to have reached a state that is natural, stable, coherent and decided, Tom confronts the contradictions and uncertainties about discovering his gender, an instinctive component of his identity.

Amy's initial reaction to Tom's struggle to clear up his confusion on gender is, "Don't waste yourself" (p. 25). In contrast to her awareness of gender-creative terms such as gay and bisexual, her advice corresponds to a perspective deeply rooted in Western psychological development from humanist modernist frameworks, which often views gender exploration during adolescence as a phase to be outgrown (Robinson, 2012, p. 13). As Derritt Mason (2021) notes, male, heterosexual adulthood is considered the ultimate goal of this developmental trajectory (S. 10). This framework tends to distance and minimize non-normative gender experiences of adolescence or use other terms such as *developing child* (as cited in Owen, 2020, p. 32), reflecting a broader societal tendency to view such deviations as mere phases rather than legitimate aspects of human diversity (p. 95).

It is evident in the play that Tom's "supposedly blissful promise of adult heteronormativity" (Bruhm & Hurley, 2004, p. ix) is delayed by the question of "What you are?" (Ravenhill, 2015, p. 25). Kathryn Bond Stockton (2009) argues that "delay is said to be a feature of … growth and is seen as a friend" (p. 62). She theorizes in *The Queer Child, or Growing Sideways in the Twentieth Century*, that "the point of delay as a boon is to shelter children" (p. 62) from "feeling a frightening, heightened sense of growing toward a question mark or growing up in a haze" (p. 3). For Stockton, this gradual growth with temporality is attributed to Jacques Derrida's *différance*, which she underlines as

> the inescapable effect of our reading along a chain of words, where meaning is delayed deferred exactly because we read in sequence, go forward in a sentence … while we must take the words we have passed with us as we go, making meaning wide and hung in suspense.
>
> *(p. 4)*

Stockton benefits from the idea of *différance* to disrupt the conventional narratives about growing up which are linear and goal-oriented, implying a progression from immaturity to maturity, with each stage having a clear endpoint or purpose, which is "figured as vertical movement upward toward full stature, marriage, work, reproduction, and the loss of childishness" (p. 6). She highlights that the intrinsic value of latency may change the orientation of growth from horizontal progress to sideways growth. Growing sideways due to the surviving curiosities related to the unresolved realms of sexuality throughout adulthood may be identified as queer. As Stockton describes, "If you scratch a child, you will find a queer in the sense of someone gay or just plain strange" (p. 1). "They are seen as normative but also not like us at the same time" (p. 31).

This in/visible duality of growing sideways is deceptive and may create peculiar dangers despite its sheltering opportunity. Queer youth frequently face problems due to the normative nature of sex categories, which govern their common activities and create pressure on their internal sense of gender identity. It is evident in the second act of the play that Tom's sex small talk with the other boys on last night with Amy suddenly turned into verbal abuse, fights, and then fake confessions. Gary's request for respect for girls as opposed to vulgar language including "jiggy-jiggy", "riding like a bitch" (Ravenhill, 2015, p. 26) costs him to be accused of effeminate behaviour. The collective attitude against Gary creates a frightening effect on Tom and urges him to charge Gary with being gay and punch him in the stomach very hard with the support of other boys. Under the pressure of his contradictions on self-determination, Tom continues to "follow the leader" (p. 29) – as Gary mentions – and lies that he has had sex with Amy. The heightened sense of the normative sexual conversation, which stigmatizes growing sideways even hinders him from telling the truth about his bleeding ear, which Ray says, "Thass the gay side. Shit. You was doing an earring in the gay side. Shit" (p. 32). In order not to feel excluded like Gary, – even if he is not queer – Tom is "self-ghosting" (Stockton, 2009, p. 3) himself and chooses to "belong to society's shadow" (Foucault, 1975, as cited in Huffer, 2009, p. 23). Doing an earring is transformed into another lie, love-biting, "to be like everyone else" (p. 23). Because "if you are not like everyone else, it's because you're abnor-mal" (p. 23).

Ravenhill benefits from Tom's confusion about growing "as a conduit of cultural anxiety" which is "the persistent … threat perceived by society in homosexuality" (Inchley, 2012, p. 334). This unintentional drive of Tom's peers to enforce and uphold normative gender labels to shape and judge young people's self-image and behaviour, along with the associated stigmas (Goffman, 1961), is also concealed within official narratives and spaces which create a rationale for the surveillance and control of young people. As a student, Tom seeks guidance from his Citizenship teacher, Mr De Clerk, during their meeting on the problem related to his homework project, "What Does Multicultural Society Mean to Me?" Since there is blood on his Citizenship coursework, Tom has to copy it as soon as possible because of an inspector's visit to the school the following day. As De Clerk complains about the stress and demands of his workload, Tom attempts to change the conversation to personal topics like marriage, clothing, and the gym, and even offers to give De Clerk a shoulder and neck massage.

It becomes clear that it is not only because De Clerk is his Citizenship teacher that Tom hopes he may get some crucial advice and help. Tom suspects, almost certainly correctly although the play interestingly never confirms this, that his teacher is gay.

(Billingham, 2007, p. 156)

Tom has a possible closeness with his teacher and tries to discuss his sexual dream and seek advice from him. However, De Clerk harshly dismisses Tom's attempt and suggests he should talk with the form tutor. In order to end the conversation quickly and send Tom home, he decides to explain the blood stain on the homework to the inspectors. In his interview with Peter Billingham (2007), Ravenhill clarifies the illusion behind the politics of education and its implementation at schools:

it's one of the things that I wanted to write about in *Citizenship* because the kids and the teachers exist in that environment where that form of liberalism is especially evident in the school environment. ... the kids become very literate in that form of liberalism and so in the classroom, talking to teachers, they can absolutely speak the language of "diversity and equal opportunities" and all that stuff. Yet in the playground there are all codes of other language and as much as a school might try to instil a liberal environment, it's still incredibly hard for the teacher that is gay to talk honestly about their sexuality because there are both parents and kids who couldn't handle it. Therefore, there's all sorts of gaps between the liberal vision that the school aspires to be and the reality.

(p. 131)

In 2002, Citizenship was introduced into the curriculum to promote a sense of nation with responsible citizens who recognize the diversity in British society, including religion, gender, culture, disability, age, sexuality, and so on. In order to create a collective British identity, teenagers should recognize different values and attitudes in schools that represent in part society enriched with differences. Conversely, the institutions develop elaborate means of rearranging or avoiding the kinds of affirmations about diversity and inclusion teenagers are supposed to have. Teenagers "are left in the unsatisfactory position of citizen-in-making" (as cited in Rebellato, 2015, p. 8) that cannot reply to controversial questions but may "celebrate the difference" (Ravenhill, 2015, p. 41) with a watchful and guided upbringing:

DE CLERK: You know the school policy. ... You report bullies. Everything is okay. You're okay.
TOM: I don't feel okay.
DE CLERK: Well – You should do.

(Ravenhill, 2015, p. 41)

In parallel with Stockton's theory (2009) on queerness, Tom's formal upbringing at school is one of "the ways of growing that are not growing up" (p. 11). Tom's questions or curiosity about himself are not connected to the values that need to be challenged. During "his advance to adulthood until the authority says it's time" (p. 6), his education should be grounded in being a responsible citizen rather than the issues "personally related with whether he feels whole, or happy, or spiritually enlightened" (Owen, 2020, p. 6). For this reason, De Clerk's attitude forces Tom to return to his friends to seek at least an answer to his questions. On his visit to Gary to smoke a joint, their conversation on "brother love", "many types of loving" and Gary's gentle behaviour make a false impression on Tom. He is encouraged to kiss Gary on the lips, but is turned down in a friendly manner. Instead, Gary suggests he explore the internet for answers. He also has a website sharing explicit content and his fantasies with the world, which are totally in contrast to his publicly accepted character. He admits that he "can't help what's in his head. ... searching, chatting, message boards, stuff. You can try everything online" (Ravenhill, 2015, p. 47). Gary's concealment of his sexual preference illustrates the difficulty teenagers face in discussing gender identity openly in society, while the performance of gender remains a prevalent aspect of daily life through technology:

> Pornographic images are actually representations, or imitations; however, they are not experienced as representations signifying an original, they are experienced as real. The image once again surpasses reality in itself and becomes the only reality known. ... Through pornography, sex becomes another commodity marketed legally to the masses; it is turned into becoming a necessity, a natural need for people. The massive market share of pornography which proves the (re)definition of pornography as a natural need in the contemporary world (Kan, 2015b, p. 55).

Tom declines Gary's offer but turns to the Tarot Reader for assistance, as suggested by Amy. Using nine tarot cards spread out in a fan, they have a conversation on Tom's "unstable emotions" and "a moment of great decision" (Ravenhill, 2015, p. 55). Despite the cards seemingly presenting him with clear options, he still feels unsure about making a decision. The Tarot Reader draws a final card, The High Priestess, which resonates with Tom. He interprets this as indicative of his future choice, because "It's a woman letting Tom into her ... That's a woman" (p. 55). Tarot Reader warns him on his hasty decision on a clue to realize true choice and instead suggests that he should watch, wait and listen patiently to the cards. Tarot Reader notes that "It's more complicated than that" (p. 55) and explains that the cards now represent "masculine and feminine energies" rather than strictly male or female figures. The High Priestess may also symbolize "a woman or a man with a feminine energy" (p. 55). At a younger age, Tom has to face "'the long crisis of modern sexual definition', in other words, the heterosexist system's tendency to accept 'gender of choice' as the main criteria [sic] for determining one's sexuality" (Kılıç, 2018, p. 153). As Butler (2004) explains;

> Gender is not exactly what one *is* nor is it precisely what one *has*. Gender is the apparatus by which the production and normalization of masculine and feminine take place along with the interstitial forms of hormonal, chromosomal, psychic, and performative that gender assumes. To assume that gender always and exclusively means the matrix of the *masculine* and *feminine* is precisely to miss the critical point that the production of that coherent binary is contingent, that it comes at a cost, and that those permutations of gender which do not fit the binary are as much a part of gender as its most normative instance.
>
> *(p. 42)*

Influenced by the last tarot card, The High Priestess, Tom decides to address his dilemma with Amy. He finally decides to engage in a sexual relationship with her, and despite his admission that she is not the person he kisses in his dreams, Amy accepts his offer. Ravenhill employs postdramatic time in this act and benefits from De Clerk to "deconstruct linear time" (Lehmann, 2006) in the play. De Clerk's magical entrance through the wall creates an alternative reality that allows "an unguarded conversation" (Deeney, 2007, p. 338) between them. "Disintegration of time as a continuum" (Lehmann, 2006, p. 155) enables an asynchronous moment that reveals generational tension based on growing sideways:

DE CLERK: And what would you prefer?
TOM: Someone to tell me what to be.
DE CLERK: No one's going to do that.
TOM: I wish they would.
DE CLERK: When I was growing up: everyone told you who to be. They told you what to do. What was right and what was wrong. What your future would be.
TOM: I'd like that.
DE CLERK: No. It made me very unhappy.
TOM: I'm unhappy – too many choices. You were unhappy – no choices. Everyone's unhappy. Life's shit, isn't it, sir?

(Ravenhill, 2015, p. 61)

Within the context of Stockton's theory (2009), the contradiction in the above dialogue is bringing De Clerk and Tom "the ghostly gay child" (p. 17) into the lateral contact of growing sideways which is "like a jigsaw that's never going to be finished" (Ravenhill, 2015, p. 61). De Clerk is "the grown homosexual" (Stockton, 2009, p. 22) who couldn't find any opportunity to define his gender identity because "we do presume every child to be straight" (p. 6) and all the steps of growing are constructed according to "certain linguistic markers" (p. 6) without any doubt. For De Clerk, the past "is precisely who we are not, and in fact, never were. It is the act of adults looking back" (p. 5). The questions, "when did you know?, did you know as a kid?" (p. 2), can be answered so conceptually in the memories that are constructed retrospectively. The reminiscences of queerness can be recalled when the straight child dies and becomes the grown homosexual.

On the other hand, today is different from the past in some ways, as Tarot Reader also mentioned before. Tom, the ghostly gay child, is "in a privileged position because he can decide who he is and there haven't been that many periods in history when kids could decide that" (as cited in Mulligan, para. 5). While growing sideways at a younger age, he observes "the width of a person's experience or ideas, their motives or their motions" (Stockton, 2009, p. 11) such as kissing Gay Gary, trying to take help from his teacher, consulting a Tarot Reader and having sex with Amy. Additionally, he has a relationship with a 22-year-old boy, Martin, whom he talks to in the chatroom. He is still not sure about his new attempt and is trying to reach a decision by asking Martin whether he is content with his boyfriend, job and life. He cannot attain the expected answer but thinks Martin is happy, and then has sex with him. His first queer relationship continues for a while at Martin's home, which is a kind of "queer heterotopia" where he can "challenge the heteronormative regime" (Jones, 2013, p. 3). As Foucault mentions in *Of Other Spaces*:

> In everyday life escaping repression requires the creation of heterotopic spaces, where individuals can celebrate their difference. Unlike utopias, heterotopic spaces can be created in reality … They are sites where actors, whether academics or activists, engage in what we might call a radical politics of subversion, where individuals attempt to dislocate the normative configurations of sex, gender, and sexuality through daily exploration and experimentation with crafting a queer identity.
>
> *(as cited in Jones, 2013, p. 3)*

In the last act of the play, the playwright brings together the newly graduated high school students, Tom, Amy and Gary, and then Martin to showcase their latest relationship status to the audience. With a surprise for Tom, Amy and Gary are together. They share the responsibility of raising a baby, whom Amy has now given birth to since Tom did not take into account the only advice of De Clerk, "use protection" (Ravenhill, 2015, p. 62). She postpones going to college until the baby is a bit older and sometimes receives babysitting help from Kelly, with whom she practised in a "Life Skills" course at school (p. 22). Gary has quit smoking and is pleased to father a baby with care. Meanwhile, Tom's only benefit from his relationship with Martin seems to be sex (Mulligan, 2005, para. 9). Frustrated by Martin's excuses for not leaving his boyfriend, Tom admits that he thinks of Amy when kissing Martin, but Amy rebuffs him, declaring that "You can't have it both ways" (Ravenhill, 2015, p. 71). He is not allowed to pick up his baby and yearns for Martin's affection, feeling dissatisfied with merely "moneysexfun" (p. 74):

MARTIN: Fuck's sake. Why can't you ... moneysexfun?
TOM: Because I want more. I want everything. I want ...
MARTIN: Yes?
TOM: I want everything. I want ... I want ... I want to find out everything.
(p. 74).

Tom's desire at the end of the play is an existential crisis throughout the play. It is not resolved yet, since "there's no right or wrong in this play" (as cited in Mulligan, 2005, p. 11). It is a journey alone "in a shapeless, formless world" (p. 11) and Tom cannot be seen as a victim of his search. The sufferings are his own choice and cannot be healed painlessly. Without the absence of family and school support, he creates authentic "little stories", affording him time – adolescence – to gradually grow sideways (Stockton, 2009, p. 40). By follow-ing his own path, he challenges the time constructed under the influence of authority and in this way "reaches adulthood ... with achieving the status of human" (Hall, 1904; as cited in Owen, 2020, p. 71):

MARTIN: You're a baby. Treat you like a baby.
TOM: No. Not any more. No.
(Ravenhill, 2015, p. 74)

Conclusion

Mark Ravenhill's *Citizenship*

> is not gesture of goodwill or as a charitable social act. The urge to write them sprang directly from *his* artist's ego and the wish that *his* plays have the biggest possible impact on the biggest possible group of people.
> *(Ravenhill, 2010, p. x)*

With *Citizenship*, Ravenhill captures "the right story, creates the right char-acters and finds the right language that a play will have a profound effect upon a teenager" (p. x). With the support of local theatre companies and the National Theatre's Connections Scheme, the playwright has given life to a play that makes sense to young people with a challenging modern-day issue and is intended entirely for performance with the requirement of minimal budget, not much unique costumes or scenery and the cast size right for the average drama class (p. xi).

Citizenship marks the journey of a teenager, Tom, to decide his sexual identity in his turbulent years. Ravenhill uses Tom's dream as a reference to explore the issues based on gender and scrutinize the role of institutions, the absence of parents in modern life, peer pressure and the effects of media. As a queer teenager, Tom needs to create his own narrative to "grow sideways" (Stockton, 2009) because of the presuppositions of his friends, the school's so-called principles of diversity, no family help and online fake adult content. In contrast to modern-day reality that seems to support liberal thinking and multiculturalism, Tom faces the challenge of making decisions largely on his own. The play reveals that it is not easier for him to follow the paths of horizontal routes of growing instead of choosing the vertical way which represents the heteronormative practices of life (Stockton, 2009). Although Tom requires answers to the question, "What you are?" (Ravenhill, 2015, p. 25), throughout the play, the playwright does not provide him with any particular solution. Instead, he prefers highlighting Tom's experiences during his journey to challenge the underlying conservative realities of everyday life. This does not imply a hopeless end for either Tom or the audience. With *Citizenship*, Ravenhill re-questions contemporary norms from the perspective of young people to create an awareness of gender and sustain a humanizing process of growing sideways within the individual values and social order of the adult world for the future.

Notes

1 For a detailed discussion on the issue, see: Ada, U. (2023), *Edward Bond: Bondian drama and young audience*. Vernon Press.
2 The author's own words.
3 For a detailed discussion on the issue, see: Sierz, A. (2001), *In-Yer-Face theatre: British drama today*. Faber & Faber.
4 In 1993, James Bulger, a toddler of three years, was kidnapped from a shopping mall by two ten-year-old boys and left on railway tracks to die.

References

Angelaki, V. (2017). *Social and political theatre in 21st-century Britain*. Bloomsbury.
ASSITEJ Artistic Gathering 2023 (2023, 12 Oct). ASSITEJ International. https://assitej-international.org/assitej-artistic-gathering-2023/.
Bauman, Z. (2000). *Liquid modernity*. Polity Press.
Billingham, P. (2007). Mark Ravenhill. In P. Billingham, *At the sharp end* (124–162). Bloomsbury.
Billington, M. (1996, 13 Mar). Fabulous Five. *The Guardian*.
Bond, E. (2013). The third crisis: The possibility of a future drama. *JCDE*, 1(1), 13–21.
Bruhm, S. & Hurley, N. (2004). *Curiouser: On the queerness of children*. University of Minnesota Press.

Busby, S. (2019). "The biggest youth theatre on planet": National Theatre Youth Connections. In M. Finneran & M. Anderson (Eds.), *Education and theatres: Beyond the four walls* (115–130). Springer.

Butler, J. (2004). *Undoing gender.* Routledge.

Citizenship review (2018, 3 Nov). Citizenship review: "Witty, thoughtful and true-to-life". https://cherwell.org/2018/11/03/citizenship-review-witty-thoughtful-and-true-to-life/.

Connections. (2024, 1 June). Connections. How it works. https://www.nationaltheatre.org.uk/learn-explore/young-people/connections/.

Deeney, J. F. (2007). National causes/moral causes? The National Theatre, young people and citizenship. *Research in Drama Education*, 12(3), 331–344.

Erkinovna, M. N. & Bahodirovna, A. M. (2023). *The principles of displaying the aesthetics of cruelty in children's dramas of the 21st century.* International Conference on Agriculture Sciences, Environment, Urban and Rural Development, 99–101. https://www.conferenceseries.info/index.php/morocco/article/view/1308.

Goffman, E. (1961). *Asylums.* Doubleday.

Hall, G. S. (1904). *Adolescence: Its psychology and its relations to physiology, anthropology, sociology, sex, crime, religion, and education.* D. Appleton and Company.

Huffer, L. (2009). *Rethinking the foundations of queer theory.* Columbia University Press.

Inchley, M. (2012). Hearing young voices on the London stage: "Shit bein' seventeen int it? never take us serious". *Contemporary Theatre Review*, 22(3), 327–343.

Inchley, M. (2015). Sending up citizenship: Young voices in Tnaika Gupta, Mark Ravenhill and Enda Wash. In M. Inchley, *Voice and new writing, 1997–2007* (101–118). Palgrave Macmillan.

Jones, A. (2013). Introduction: Queer utopias, queer futurity, and potentiality in quotidian practice. In A. Jones, *A critical inquiry into queer utopias* (pp. 1–17). Palgrave Macmillan.

Kan, A. (2015a). Violence not on body but through body-image: Mark Ravenhill's Some Explicit Polaroids. *International Journal of Social Sciences and Education Research Online*, 1(4), 1017–1023.

Kan, A. (2015b). Violence and sexuality in in-yer-face drama: Sarah Kane's *Phaedra's Love*, Mark Ravenhill's *Some Explicit Polaroids*, and Anthony Neilson's *Penetrator*. (Publication No. 492346). M.A. dissertation, Boğaziçi University.

Kılıç, H. D. (2018). The changing portrayals of gay and queer identitites in Julian Mitchell's *Another Country*, Jonathan Harvey's *Beautiful Thing* and Mark Ravenhill's *Mother Clap's Molly House*. (Publication No. 399340). Ph.D. dissertation, Hacettepe University.

Kristeva, J. (2024). *New maladies of the soul.* Columbia University Press.

Lane, D. (2010). *Contemporary British drama.* Edinburgh University Press.

Lehmann, H. T. (2006). *Postdramatic theatre.* Routledge.

Liu, Y.-C. (2020, 29 Sept). In-Yer-Face in Taiwan: Mark Ravenhill and contemporary Taiwanese political playwriting. Ph.D. thesis, University of Bristol.

Mason, D. (2021). *Queer anxieties of young adult literature and culture.* University Press of Mississippi.

Monforte, E. (2007). Mark Ravenhill. In M. Aragay, H. Klein, E. Monforte & P. Zozaya, *British theatre of the 1990s: Interviews with directors, playwrights, critics and academics* (pp. 91–103). Palgrave Macmillan.

Mulligan, J. (2005). A zigzag path towards some idea of who you are: Interview with Mark Ravenhill. https://www.jimmulligan.co.uk/interview/mark-ravenhill-citizenship.

National Theatre Connections – Gulbenkian Young Company. (2023, 16 Nov). Gulbenkian Arts Center. https://thegulbenkian.co.uk/project/national-theatre-connections/.

Owen, G. (2020). *A queer history of adolescence.* University of Georgia Press.

Ravenhill, M. (2004). A tear in the fabric: The James Bulger murder and new theatre writing in the nineties. *New Theatre Quarterly,* 20, 305–314.

Ravenhill, M. (2010). Introduction. In M. Ravenhill, *Plays for young people* (pp. ix–xi). Bloomsbury Methuen Drama.

Ravenhill, M. (2015). *Citizenship.* Bloomsbury Methuen Drama.

Rebellato, D. (2015). Introduction. In M. Ravenhill, *Citizenship* (2–17). Bloomsbury Methuen Drama.

Robinson, K. H. (2012). Childhood as a queer time and space: Alternative meanings of normative makers of gendered lives. In K. H. Robinson & C. Davies, *Queer and subjugated knowledges: Generating subversive imaginaries* (pp. 110–139). Bentham Science Publishers.

Schonmann, S. (2022). The ecology of theatre for young audiences: Is radical theatre possible for children today? *RIDE: The Journal of Applied Theatre and Performance,* 28(3), 237–252.

Sierz, A. (2001). *In-yer-face theatre: British drama today.* Faber and Faber.

Sierz, A. (2011). *Rewriting the nation: British theatre today.* Methuen Drama.

Sierz, A. (n.d.). In-yer-face theatre: Introduction. https://inyerfacetheatre.com/intro.html.

Stockton, K. B. (2009). *The queer child, or growing sideways in the twentieth century.* Duke University Press.

Svich, C. (2011). Mark Ravenhill. In M. Middeke, P. P. Schnierer & A. Sierz, *The Methuen drama guide to contemporary British playwrights* (pp. 403–424). Methuen Drama.

Woodson, S. E. (2015). *Theatre for youth third space.* Intellect.

2

POLLY STENHAM'S *THAT FACE:* A PORTRAIT OF PARENTIFICATION AND DEPENDENCY

Ajda Baştan

Introduction

In the landscape of 21st century British stage plays, a detailed exploration of the problems and intricacies faced by young people in contemporary society expands through the adept storytelling of playwrights like Polly Stenham, Lucy Prebble and Jez Butterworth. Their masterful narratives not only captivate audiences but also evoke proper empathy and self-examination. In this context, the playwrights deftly handle themes that resonate with the contemporary youth experience, staging issues such as disenchantment, addiction, pregnancy, the quest for freedom and the pervasive weight of societal expectations. By addressing these pressing concerns, their plays contribute to a richer understanding of the manifold dimensions of youth problems. Consequently, through the lens of characters grappling with the complexities of modern life, the audience is invited to confront and picture on the broader social considerations embedded in these narratives. Indeed, the power of such works lies not only in their ability to entertain but also in their capacity to supply potent mirrors expressing the refusals, aspirations and conflicts innate in the lives of young individuals. Moreover, it is essential to feature that contemporary British theatre also deals with themes like parentification and dependency on young caregivers. This additional layer in the plays brings forth the often-overlooked relations within families, where young individuals find themselves shouldering responsibilities beyond their age. In doing so, the plays extend their gaze via individual struggles to address societal structures that influence the youth, thereby offering a comprehensive and stimulating examination of the modern human experience.

The term "parentification", introduced by Boszormenyi-Nagy and Spark in 1973, defines a dysfunctional family structure characterized by the reversal

DOI: 10.4324/9781003470434-3

of typical parent and child roles (Castro et al., 2004, p. 206). This phenomenon entails a young child or teenager assuming parental responsibilities,
including caring for siblings or even their own parents (Boszormenyi-Nagy
& Spark, 1973; Chen & Panebianco, 2020, p. 1078; Hooper, 2007, p. 217;
Stein et al., 1999, p. 193). As Chase (1999) notes, this drive compels the
young caregiver to mature hastily, often to the detriment of their own needs
and childhood experiences (p. 5). In this sense, parentification manifests in
various situations, such as parental absence, mental or physical incapacita-
tion, or when a parent is overwhelmed by life's obstacles. On the contrary,
dependency, as defined by Navaro (1993), refers to relying on others for
emotional support, decision-making or basic needs (p. 88). This creates an
imbalanced power relationship, with one person excessively relying on
another, potentially impeding personal growth and independence (Cridland
et al., 2016). The understanding of these concepts brings genuine insights
into the complicated bonds within family relationships, allowing for an
examination of the psychological and emotional consequences experienced
by those involved. Thus, examining these aspects highlights the interplay
between parentification and dependency, shedding light on the complex
problems individuals encounter within family units.

Numerous contemporary British stage plays depict the themes of parentification and/or dependency, clarifying the complicated psychological circumstances and emotional implications encountered by the characters.
Notable works such as *The Effect, The Ferryman* and *That Face* cleverly
demonstrate the complexities of individuals shouldering adult responsibilities
prematurely or becoming entangled in unhealthy dependencies. These plays,
through explicit character development and thoughtful storytelling, ensure an
intelligent observation of the emotions and costs inherent in such relationships. In these narratives, young characters find themselves thrust into roles
that transcend their age, grappling with the weight of adult responsibilities.
For that reason, the analysis of these themes extends beyond surface-level
portrayals, depicting the complexities and emotional features existing in the
interrelations of parentification and dependency. By doing so, these plays not
only offer a realistic portrayal of the troubles seen by the characters but also
direct audiences to critically consider societal norms and expectations surrounding family bonds. Moreover, the works encourage empathy for the
struggles of adolescents overcoming these hard relationships. By peeling back
the layers of human experience, they foster a deeper understanding of the
psychological toll and emotional intricacies involved. In turn, the audience is
led to question and reconsider conventional notions of family roles, evoking a
critical examination of societal expectations. Thus, these modern British stage
plays deliver sharp reflections on the complexities of human relationships,
leaving a lasting outcome on the viewer's perception of familial intimacies in
the contemporary world.

For instance, Lucy Prebble's acclaimed play, *The Effect,* masterfully captures the love story of Tristan and Connie, characterized as "young, innocent, beautiful" (Zuger, 2016). Premiered in 2012, the play revolves around their involvement in a clinical trial to assess a novel antidepressant (Venn, 2021, p. 48). As the narrative develops, their initially professional connection gradually falls into a complex personal relationship, creating a blurred landscape between dependency and intimacy (Prebble, 2016). The playwright's exacting portrayal artfully manages the confusing emotions and ties within Tristan and Connie's relationship, guiding viewers to contemplate the keen reaction of external factors on personal connections. That being the case, *The Effect* goes beyond a surface-level depiction, demonstrating the complex layers of human relationships shaped by clinical settings. Thus, Prebble's storytelling encourages audiences to critically consider the interplay between external influences and the intimate bonds individuals form, providing an engaging inquiry of the complexities natural in love, connection and the broader implications of dependency in the context of modern relationships.

Another significant contribution to the study of family relations and dependency comes from Jez Butterworth's (2017) history play (Lonergan, 2020, p. 472), *The Ferryman*. This compelling work plays out against the tumultuous backdrop of the Irish Troubles in the early 1980s, offering a powerful narrative set in a rural farmhouse. The focal point is the Carney family, with particular emphasis on the eldest son, Quinn, who unexpectedly assumes the role of caregiver for both elderly and young relatives under the same roof (Butterworth, 2017). However, at the heart of the play is Quinn's struggle to balance his caregiving responsibilities with a yearning for personal freedom. Accordingly, Butterworth's exceptional writing probes the emotional turmoil that arises from this detailed web of responsibility, providing a comprehensive examination of the messy connections within the Carney family. By expertly depicting the complexities of dependency within a historical context, *The Ferryman* leads audiences to evaluate the enduring effect of familial roles and obligations, even in the midst of external conflicts and societal upheaval.

Furthermore, Polly Stenham's *That Face* stands out as a notable analysis of the "failings of middle-class family life" (Peck & Coyle, 2017, p. 312), reflecting the themes of dependency and parentification. This eight-scene play has earned "huge acclaim" (Gillinson, 2023) for its compelling storytelling and intriguing narrative. Notably, *That Face* secured many awards (Grace & Bayley, 2015, p. 141) which underscore the play's influence and recognition within the theatrical landscape. The success of *That Face* not only solidified Stenham's position as a prominent figure in contemporary British theatre but was a further demonstration of her talent. Through this work, Stenham demonstrates her exceptional ability to capture the complexity of human emotions and the detailed interconnections within family relationships. The play's observation of dependency and parentification deftly adds layers to the narrative, compelling audiences to uncover the intricacies of familial bonds and the broader implications of societal expectations. Consequently, Stenham's achievement with *That Face* further contributes to the rich tapestry of contemporary British theatre, confirming her as an influential voice with an deep understanding of the human experience.

Youth Problems in *That Face*

Polly Stenham's debut play, *That Face*, not only "created a sensation" (Brantley, 2010) during its first performance in 2007 but also garnered significant attention in the theatre world (Hoggard, 2008; Lukowski, 2023; Spencer, 2007). The British playwright, just 19 years old at the time (Barber, 2009), showcased her remarkable maturity and creativity, captivating audiences with an inspiring narrative and sharp character development. The play's impact extended beyond general acclaim, with established playwrights such as Harold Pinter and Tom Stoppard attending early performances, further solidifying its reputation as a work of remarkable significance in contemporary theatre (Peghinelli, 2012, p. 21). For sure, Stenham's skill in capturing the essence of complex human experiences resonated strongly, drawing attention not just because of her age but due to her skill in crafting a compelling narrative. Accordingly, *That Face* emerges not only as a noteworthy debut for Stenham but also as a testament to her ability to address the intricacies of the human condition with a level of insight that transcends age, earning its place as a standout work in contemporary theatre.

Set in contemporary London, Stenham's dark and tragicomic play deals with a "dysfunctional" family torn apart by the mother's struggles with drug and alcohol addiction and the absence of the father (Lane, 2010, p. 194). The deliberate omission of the exact year in the script allows for universality and adaptability, enabling diverse interpretations across different productions. Essentially, *That Face* progresses as a "melodrama" (Brantley, 2010) portraying a divorced family grappling with the repercussions of fractured relationships between parents and their children in the 21st century. The play brings to the forefront the risks associated with divorce, lack of parental love, and disinterest, clarifying how these factors may adversely affect the behaviour and education of young individuals. Additionally, Stenham demonstrates the unsettling prospect of children, amidst parental neglect or absence, resorting to violence. In the play, Stenham's depiction of parentification and parent dependency on a child provides a heartfelt perspective on the real-life experiences of young individuals becoming victims of disinterested, mentally ill and alcoholic parents. As a result, through her characters, the audience witnesses the difficulties these individuals face, consistently oscillating between the role of caregiver and co-dependent, and forced to deal with the complexities of shaping their identity in an environment that demands that they mature quickly.

That Face revolves around mother Martha, son Henry, daughter Mia and Hugh, Martha's ex-husband who now resides in Hong Kong. The play begins with Mia, described as an "unhappy teenage girl" (Benedict, 2007), who is confronting the possibility of expulsion from school due to her bullying her dorm-mate. Later, Stenham presents the reasons behind Mia's behaviour and demonstrates their impact on her relationships. The play also touches upon various sexual themes, including references to "incestuous" desires between Martha and Henry (Billington, 2008). Choi (2015) even identifies the play as a "modern Oedipus", pointing to the complex mother–son relationship. However, as the play progresses, it becomes apparent that there is no actual incestuous relationship between Henry and Martha. Henry himself describes his mother's actions as "perverse" (Stenham, 2007, p. 19), which suggests a rejection of any inappropriate desires. In addition, Henry experiences his first sexual encounter with Izzy (p. 49), further separating him from any notion of an incestuous relationship.

In *That Face*, Mia and Henry, portrayed as young characters, tackle their deeply felt tragic circumstances. Each must grapple with the tough con-sequences of their parents' decisions, which has an intense effect on their overall well-being. Determining who occupies a more tragic position becomes a complex task, given that both siblings contend with unique struggles and emotional turmoil. Mia faces the harsh reality of rejection by her mother, and bears the emotional fallout of this abandonment. Meanwhile, Henry should-ers the burden of living with a bipolar mother as he wrestles with the instability and unpredictability that characterizes their shared existence. On another front, both Henry and Mia must struggle with the absence of a father figure and the emotional detachment they experience. Within the complex tapestry of familial intricacies depicted in the play, the distinctive issues con-fronted by Mia and Henry are woven together to form a narrative that emphasizes the diverse kinships of the dysfunctional family.

The Lost Child Mia's Abuse

As mentioned before, in *That Face*, Mia, a 15-year-old boarding school stu-dent, engages in abusive behaviour towards her new dorm-mate Alice. This disturbing initiation ceremony (Sierz, 2011, p. 181) involves Mia giving Alice an excessive amount of drugs stolen from her mother Martha. For Gardiner (2019), this chilling start serves as a catalyst for the play's plot, setting off a chain of events (p. 196). As the narrative progresses, it becomes evident that Mia fits the profile of a lost child, as described by Vernig (2011, p. 536). The lost child, according to Vernig, is one whose needs are overlooked by the family, especially when dealing with an alcohol-dependent parent. In such families other members tend to pay little attention to the lost child, who may develop a world separate from the family, exhibiting withdrawn behaviour. This isolation is often reinforced by family members engrossed in their own roles, leaving the lost child to cope with their world independently (Vernig, 2011, p. 537). In Mia's case, her troubled actions may be traced back to her parents' divorce five years ago, a significant life event subtly hinted at in the play. Although the reasons for the divorce in *That Face* are not explicitly stated, the timing of the event during Martha's illness suggests a profound impact on daughter Mia's behaviour and emotional well-being. Besides, the initial "terrifying hazing incident" (Hall, 2010, p. 1) might provide a connection between Mia's problematic manner and the emotional neglect she experiences within her family. Consequently, the play delivers the idea that children from uncaring or dysfunctional families may be more prone to engaging in violent or harmful actions. Therefore, Mia's character is an investigation of the loneliness and sadness often associated with the lost child, potentially affecting her ability to form close peer relationships, a problem that may persist into adulthood.

It is imperative to acknowledge that the "increasingly depraved" first scene depicted in Stenham's work is a fictional portrayal that raises problematic themes for discussion and analysis (Hickling, 2010). As noted by Anderson (2014), the separation and divorce of parents can have serious consequences for children, families and society as a whole (p. 379). While it is crucial to recognize that not all children or teenagers from divorced families will display violent actions, Anderson emphasizes that numerous factors contribute to a child's attitudes in the aftermath of such family changes. Mok et al. (2018) further state the negative result of divorce on children's attitude and mental health, potentially elevating the risk of developing violent tendencies. In the context of Stenham's play, the lost child Mia's near-deadly act of violence is portrayed as a consequence of parental neglect, illustrating her as a deeply rejected daughter within a divorced family. The fictional narrative thus emphasizes the significance of the parent–child relationship and the potential consequences of emotional neglect within the family bond. In response to these insights, Stenham's work implies a recommendation for parents undergoing divorce: that they provide emotional support and guidance to their children during and after the process. By addressing the emotional needs of their children, parents may mitigate several risks associated with the aftermath of divorce, as suggested in *That Face*. Within this framework, the play operates as a powerful reminder of the potential influence of parental actions on a child's emotional and psychological development, urging parents to be attentive to their children's needs during times of familial upheaval.

Unlike Mia, Izzy, the 16-year-old girl in *That Face*, shows hesitation during the ceremony, revealing a conflicted sense of morality. In an attempt to balance the severity of the situation, Izzy tries to cut a hole in the hat to ensure Alice can breathe. Subsequently, Mia directs Alice to engage in various tasks, including sticking her tongue out, wiggling it around, and rolling it, further focusing on the power relations at play within this distressing initiation ceremony:

MIA: Stick your tongue out.
   (Alice complies)
   Wiggle it around.
   (Alice complies)
   Roll it.
   (Alice complies)

(Stenham, 2007, p. 9).

As noted, the playwright intentionally starts a conversation about bullying, with Mia's aggressive and abusive conduct toward Alice serving as a stark illustration of power links and the quest for control. Mia's need to dominate and degrade Alice appears rooted in her own feelings of powerlessness and frustration, directly linked to the parental neglect she has experienced. This suggests that Mia's aggressive act may be a subconscious attempt to regain a semblance of control in her life by exerting power over others, particularly evident in her mistreatment of Alice. The distressing portrayal of Mia's abusive actions, including the unauthorized administration of Valium, a tranquilizer, to Alice, helps to elaborate one of the long-lived consequences of dysfunctional family dynamics. Izzy's reaction to this revelation further adds layers to the narrative, with her expressions of shock and disbelief of the stark contrast in her approach compared to Mia's. In labelling Mia a "druggie" (Stenham, 2007, p. 14), Izzy not only calls attention to Mia's worrying actions but also suggests a potential disparity in upbringing between the two characters. The playwright strategically uses the scenario involving the administration of Valium to unveil the complexities within Mia's family environment. Izzy's incredulous questioning of Mia's actions, especially considering Alice's unconscious state, presents her disbelief and anger towards Mia's blatant disregard for Alice's well-being. This central moment in the narrative illuminates the stark contrast between the characters' moral compasses, showcasing Izzy's more compassionate stance. However, as the scenes progress, it becomes evident that Mia has access to her mother's drugs (Stenham, 2007, p. 33), presenting the deeper stages of dysfunction within the family. Mia's casual sharing of details about the dosage of Valium raises concerns about her understanding of the danger and potential harm she exposed Alice to – underlining the gravity of the family's issues and the complex interplay of power, control and neglect within the household:

IZZY: Pills? How many pills?
MIA: In milligrams, I guess, forty. Maybe fifty. It was five tablets at ten each,
   so —

(Stenham, 2007, p. 14).

Mia's revelation about administering a potentially dangerous amount of Valium to Alice is a deeply disturbing act of abuse. The specificity of the dosage, articulated with a casual air that displays Mia's detachment from the gravity of her actions, intensifies the alarming nature of the situation. This act goes beyond mere negligence; it signifies Mia's inclination to violence and manipulation, suggesting a worrying lack of consideration for the well-being of others. Mia's attempt to justify her excessive dosage by dismissing Alice as a "big girl" (Stenham, 2007, p. 14) is particularly troubling. This rationalization not only showcases Mia's distorted reasoning but also exposes her lack of empathy and an alarming rejection of responsibility for her potentially harmful behaviour. Indeed, Mia's actions display the intertwining elements of physical harm, emotional manipulation and a complete lack of responsibility — a toxic combination that stresses the severity of the dysfunctional family connections portrayed in *That Face*. The playwright cleverly uses this moment to demonstrate Mia's character, exposing the deeply rooted issues and the extensive result of abuse within the narrative.

In full contrast, Izzy's reaction exhibits a sense of responsibility and genuine concern. As Izzy labels the drug dosage as "poison", Mia dismissively describes it as "mild" (Stenham, 2007, p. 15). This divergence in their perceptions not only emphasizes the severity of Mia's actions but also indicates the difference in their approaches to the potential consequences. Besides, Izzy's awareness of the possible outcomes of Mia's actions extends beyond immediate concerns, encompassing the potential involvement of their parents and the subsequent effects they may face. This disparity in action suggests the significant influence of their respective family backgrounds, particularly the quality of parental love they have experienced. Izzy emerges as a girl who is not only cherished but also affectionately called "darling" by her parents (p. 54). On the contrary, Mia is relegated to derogatory terms like the "little shit" by her mother (pp. 25, 59). These labels further emphasize the sharp difference in the emotional environments shaping the personalities and conflict-resolution approaches of the two dorm-mates.

It is crucial to note, however, that Mia's penchant for violence should not be excused. Even as the play unveils the underlying reasons for her behavior, the narrative does not seek to justify her actions. Instead, it presents a consideration of the confused interplay between personality and home environment, and their influential role in shaping individuals' attitudes and decision-making processes. This invites an understanding of the complex connections between personal disposition and external influences, contributing to a more comprehensive evaluation of the characters within the context of *That Face*.

Parental Neglect and Absence

As previously discussed, *That Face* vividly portrays the repercussions of parental neglect and absence, depicting the adverse effects on the family's children. Stenham strategically illustrates that Mia's abusive actions towards Alice stem from the dysfunctionality of her family. When Alice is discovered unconscious at school, immediate hospitalization becomes necessary to address the reactions of the administered drugs. Concurrently, Mia faces the impending consequence of expulsion due to her abusive behaviour. In reaching out to Mia's mother, the school encounters an unsettling response from Martha. The bizarre phone call reveals Martha's incapacity to comprehend the gravity of the situation, showcasing her unpredictable action and underscoring the extent of the "dysfunction of the domestic situation" (Gardiner, 2019, p. 196). In this matter, Martha's detached response to this crisis emphasizes her increasing alienation from her maternal role, exacerbating the emotional distance from Mia. Later, the school, recognizing the abnormality of Mia's family situation, questions Mia about her living arrangements and guardianship during holidays (Stenham, 2007, p. 33). Mia discloses that she primarily resides at friends' houses or her father's bachelor flat in the Docklands (p. 33), citing limited space at her mother's flat (p. 26). This revelation directs the boarding school to realize the extraordinary nature of Mia's family intimacies. Moreover, the school begins to understand that Mia's abusive tendencies might be deeply rooted in her family's underlying issues, thereby shifting the focus from blaming her to the troubled family. Recognizing the urgent need for intervention, the school contacts Mia's father, who works as a broker in Hong Kong, marking a critical moment in the play.

In the second scene of *That Face*, Mia arrives home after an arduous train journey, laden with the weight of recent events. The primary catalyst for her return is presumably linked to her expulsion from school, a consequence of her involvement in the drugging incident concerning Alice. The tension mounts as Mia steps into the London flat shared by her mother Martha and her brother Henry. They are surprised by Mia's sudden arrival and are clearly perplexed as they question the unusual circumstance of her being there on a Monday – a time when she would normally be following her boarding school routine. The air thickens with intrigue, setting the stage for the familial complexities and confrontations that will be resolved in the subsequent scenes of the play:

MARTHA: Why? Why's she here? Why?
HENRY: I don't know.
MARTHA: Little shit.
HENRY: Please don't. It's too early for this.
MARTHA: She can't stay here.
HENRY: Stop it. I'm going to buzz her in.

(Stenham, 2007, p. 25)

As noticed, the dialogue between Martha and Henry works as a mirror to the strained relationship prevalent within this family bond. Martha, seemingly brimming with frustration and perhaps harbouring resentment, queries the motive behind Mia's return, showing a reluctance to tolerate the daughter's presence. In contrast, Henry responds with an air of uncertainty, signalling his lack of awareness regarding Mia's current predicament. Acting as a mediator amidst this tense situation, Henry implores his mother not to exacerbate the situation, recognizing that it is too early in the day for a confrontation of this magnitude. His plea suggests an understanding of the unwinding events and a desire to prevent further escalation. In this regard, the dialogue between Martha and Henry acts the part of an effective lens through which to perceive Mia's status as a rejected and neglected child within the confines of her own family. This stark portrayal aligns with research findings by Rohner (2004, p. 830), and Ludwig and Rostain (2009, p. 113), explaining the serious outcomes of neglect on children that encompass a spectrum of severe consequences. In reference to this, Mia's evident lack of acceptance and love within her family environment appears to have taken a toll on her emotional well-being, thereby contributing to her violent behaviour at school.

Adding to the complexity of the situation, Mia reveals that her father, Hugh, is on his way to London (Stenham, 2007, p. 27). This disclosure brings about inquiries into the role Hugh is poised to play in the complicated family relations and how his arrival will shape the relationships and conflicts within the household. Furthermore, Martha, described as a chronic alcoholic (De Angelis, 2010, p. 558), remains oblivious to the phone call from the boarding school and continues to be unaware of her daughter's actions there:

MIA: School called. Last night. They spoke to you.
MARTHA: I don't remember.

(Stenham, 2007, p. 27)

As previously noted, Hugh, a broker residing in Hong Kong, is not only geographically distant from his children's lives but also exhibits emotional detachment. This emotional disconnect aligns with the findings of Chen et al. (2023), who mention that parental absence has detrimental effects on children's development, educational achievements and overall well-being. Their research underlines the crucial role of parental involvement and support in nurturing positive outcomes for children. When Hugh eventually arrives in London, Mia's evident anger towards her father becomes apparent, rooted in feelings of abandonment by him:

MIA: You could have stopped all of this. But you left. And she was sick when you left. But you left us anyway.

(Stenham, 2007, p. 90)

Obviously, Hugh's divorce from Martha occurred during a stage of her bipolar disease (Healy, 2010), also referred to as "manic-depressive" (Jones,

2022, p. 66) and classified as a "severe mental illness" (Venkataraman & Ackerson, 2008, p. 390). This decision had a lasting effect on their familial relations and the well-being of their two children, Mia and Henry, who were 10 and 13 years old at the time. As expected, Hugh's departure had left Martha in a vulnerable position, negatively affecting the children's welfare. His subsequent marriage to a woman described as a "geisha" (Stenham, 2007, p. 84) and the birth of their daughter display the fragmented nature of his family life and the choices he made. The decision to abandon Mia and Henry during a complicated period in Martha's life depicts underlying problems within their family dynamics. Hugh's choice to leave the children with their bipolar mother, Martha, presents a complex situation for Mia and Henry as they encounter life without their father's presence. Essentially, living with a bipolar mother adds complexity to their upbringing, given that bipolar disorder involves dramatic shifts in mood and attitudes (Latifian et al., 2023, p. 1). As a result, the instability and unpredictability associated with this condition has strained the family connections and affected the emotional well-being and stability of the children.

The absence of Hugh exacerbates the matters faced by the children, leaving them without a male role model and the support typically ensured by an involved father. Consequently, in the context of the play, Mia and Henry grapple not only with the worries of a bipolar mother but also contend with the absence of a paternal figure, which further alters the children's schooling and education. Furthermore, the act of Hugh providing school fees in *That Face* exhibits his emotional detachment from Henry and Mia. He believes that providing financial support alone fulfils his duties as a father, and he fails to provide the emotional help and physical presence essential for his children. This lack of emotional connection reinforces his limited understanding and relationship with his children, as monetary contributions cannot substitute for the emotional support they need. As the play develops, Henry reveals that he dropped out of school about a year and a half ago (Stenham, 2007, p. 85). His disdain for his father becomes evident as he reflects on Hugh's failure to notice that his son has dropped out of school.

HENRY: Thought you might have noticed when the fees stopped plopping out of your account every three months. Clearly not.

(Stenham, 2007, p. 85).

Henry's comment unveils a sorrowful sense of dissatisfaction and disappointment. Hugh's lack of awareness is a painful illustration of his emotional detachment, encapsulated in Henry's bitter revelation that he thought his father would have noticed the abrupt cessation of funds deposited into their account every three months. Hugh's failure to address the financial gap lays bare his disregard for their well-being and emphasizes his emotional distance. Henry's cutting remark implies that the boy feels neglected and overshadowed by his father, intensifying the emotional void between them. Henry's expressions not only articulate his yearning for a genuine parental connection but also depict his father's obliviousness and reluctance to be more attuned and emotionally present in their lives. Within this context, Stenham appears to convey the idea that while financial support is crucial for parenting, it alone cannot ensure a child's well-being and happiness. Thus, attention, quality time, emotional support and nurturing relationships are more vital components for a child's holistic development (Shaw et al., 2004).

Later in the play, the dialogue between Mia and Hugh at a restaurant stands out significantly and vividly portrays Hugh's apparent disinterest in his children's lives. Mia, seeking her father's attention, asks if she can smoke outside during dinner at the restaurant, despite not being a smoker. Her intention is to provoke a reaction from Hugh, to make him notice her. When Hugh asks her how long she has been a smoker Mia retorts with "Since when did you care?" (Stenham, 2007, p. 74). Similarly, in the final scene of *That Face*, Mia once again articulates her sorrow to her father, expressing the pain of neglect and his lack of interest in her and her brother Henry:

MIA: When you stopped hearing from us. When you stopped getting Henry's
    school reports. Why didn't you call? Why didn't you check?
HUGH: I thought you were OK.

(Stenham, 2007, pp. 89–90)

The exchange between Mia and Hugh once again illustrates Hugh's disinterest in his children's lives. The revelation that he had not heard from them for over a year, coupled with his nonchalant response, "I thought you were OK", depicts an extreme lack of engagement and concern on his part. Taking this into account, Hugh's failure to inquire about his children's well-being, school reports, or any updates for such an extended period, points to a significant emotional disconnect and emphasizes his neglectful approach to parenting. This interaction highlights a sharp aspect of the play that exposes the detrimental consequences of absent and indifferent parenting on the lives of Mia and Henry.

As the play progresses it becomes evident that Hugh carries a heavy sense of shame and regret for his past actions. This is vividly portrayed by his face turning red (Stenham, 2007, p. 86), a tangible representation of his embarrassment and self-reproach for abandoning his children with a mentally ill Martha in a dysfunctional family. According to Soukup (1995), dysfunction is prevalent in families dealing with mental illness (p. 11). Consequently, the shame Hugh experiences spotlights his acknowledgment of his own failings and the detrimental effect his decisions have had on his children. Hugh's choice to come and address his daughter's schooling issue becomes a turning point in the play, signifying the depth to which parental neglect can disrupt a child's life, compelling the absentee parent to take responsibility when the situation reaches a breaking point. His physical presence emphasizes the gravity of the situation and his belated but earnest willingness to intervene.

In a desperate attempt to fix the situation, Hugh resorts to bribery by providing the boarding school with digital cameras (Stenham, 2007, p. 70). This action can be interpreted as an effort to buy Mia's way back into the school, which Hugh perceives as vital for her future (p. 70). However, this act of bribery functions as a symbol of Hugh's attempt to conceal dysfunction within the family. Rather than fostering a healthy and loving environment, he chooses to rely on material gifts to maintain appearances, instead of identifying the root cause of the problem. The use of bribery by Mia's father also displays a larger issue within the play, exposing power strategies and corruption within institutions. The boarding school overlooks Mia's abusive behaviour in exchange for material gain, raising questions about the ethics and integrity of those in positions of authority. Additionally, Hugh attempts to send Martha to a clinic for treatment (p. 67). The play ends with Martha willingly leaving the flat alone, leaving Mia, Henry and Hugh unsure whether she is actually heading for the clinic (p. 97). The ambiguous conclusion leaves the audience uncertain about the future and the whereabouts of Mia and Henry.

Henry's Parentification, Martha's Dependency

In Stenham's *That Face*, as stated earlier, the themes of parentification and dependency are prominently portrayed. Godsall et al. (2004) posit that parentification is particularly prevalent in families where there is alcohol misuse by a parent, which aligns with Martha's alcoholism in the context of the play (p. 790). The character of Henry, now 18 years old, has assumed the role of caregiver and experiences parentification as he has taken on responsibilities beyond his age, for five years. In point of fact, Henry has become the primary source of support and care for his mentally ill and alcoholic mother Martha, who is dependent on him. Within this scope, Adler and Raphael (1983) note that children of alcoholics frequently discover themselves in the position of having to care for a parent (p. 6). Moreover, Soukup (1995) explains that when a parent is mentally ill, it is common for the child to assume the role of a responsible parent (p. 12). This is precisely the situation depicted in the play, where Henry takes on the caregiving duties for his struggling mother. On the other hand, Dodds (2014) describes dependency as a form of vulnerability that necessitates relying on the care and support of others to fulfil one's needs and promote autonomy (p. 183). This dependency is clearly illustrated in the relationship between Henry and Martha. Engster (2019) further explains that individuals often experience dependence when they are unable to care for themselves, which resonates with Martha's situation and her reliance on Henry's caregiving (p. 103). Henry's role as a co-dependent individual is also evident. Co-dependency, as described by Amaro

(2012), refers to being a partner in dependency, where the co-dependent sacrifices their own well-being in an attempt to save the dependent (p. 523). In this case, Henry sacrifices his education and personal freedom to take care of his mother. According to Evgin and Sümen (2022), co-dependency is common among individuals who have close relationships with those who have emotional/mental disorders or chronic illnesses (p. 1357). It is also observed in professions that focus on caregiving, and in children of parents with alcoholism or behavioural issues. In relation to this, Henry's co-dependent role aligns with these observations, demonstrating the complex ties depicted in the play.

Scene Two of *That Face* unveils an intricate dynamic between Martha and her son Henry. At first glance it appears that Martha is dependent on Henry and that there is an unsettling suggestion of incestuous acts. However, upon closer examination, it becomes clear that Martha's actions are not driven by inappropriate desires but rather the aftermath of excessive alcohol consumption the previous night, leading to her erratic behaviour (Stenham, 2007, p. 19). However, within a short time the scene showcases Martha's dependency on Henry, as well as Henry's role as a caregiver and the parentification he experiences in their relationship. The ripped pictures on the wall (p. 20), resulting from Martha's breakdown, signify her struggles with her mental health. Her apology and plea for forgiveness to Henry indicate her reliance on him for emotional support and stability. Moreover, Martha's reference to Henry as a soldier boy, drawing parallels to a Russian soldier (p. 18), implies her perception of him as a protector. In this sense, the term *soldier* connotes Henry's role as the caregiver and the extent of his responsibilities in looking after his mother. Martha's reliance on Henry for emotional and physical support is further exemplified when she experiences hyperventilation. In this vulnerable moment, Henry expertly and dispassionately aids Martha by fixing a paper bag to her mouth and guiding her in deep, slow breaths (p. 21). This scene presents Henry's parentification, where he assumes the responsibility of a parent, taking care of Martha's physical and emotional needs.

As the play progresses, Henry advises Martha about not having coffee early in the morning, which demonstrates his understanding of her needs and his willingness to offer support and guidance. This showcases Henry's parental role as he takes on the responsibility of looking out for Martha's well-being (Stenham, 2007, p. 21). Furthermore, when Martha requests a towel, Henry immediately fulfils her request by getting it for her. This act represents his attentiveness to her needs and his willingness to assist her with even small tasks (p. 33). Therefore, Martha's reliance on Henry for such basic necessities showcases her dependency on him for daily functioning. Meanwhile, the arrival of Mia introduces a conflict where she wants Henry to go with her to their father's bachelor flat in the Docklands. However, Henry feels unable to leave as he must carry out his caregiving duties to his mother (p. 34). This decision exposes the depth of Henry's parentification, as he prioritizes looking after Martha's well-being. In a moment of urgency and his inability to resist Mia's insistence, Henry quickly scribbles a note for Martha and leaves it on the bed. Unfortunately, Mia takes advantage of this and pockets the note (p. 36). This turn of events further emphasizes the degree of dependence Martha has on Henry, as her daughter manipulates the situation to potentially disrupt their attachment. Notably, this night is the first time Martha has spent an extended period on her own. When Henry does not come home, she becomes furious and reacts by cutting up all his clothes (p. 48), underscoring the intensity of her emotions and dependence on him for comfort and stability.

In Scene Five, Mia expresses her hope that their father Hugh will have a strategy to deal with the family's difficulties (Stenham, 2007, p. 57). Meanwhile Henry, who has been the primary caregiver for Martha for five years, believes that Hugh's strategy will involve dealing with their mother. This demonstrates Henry's deep dependency on Martha, as he states "She has been my life" (p. 58). Apparently, his life revolves around taking care of his mother and he feels a strong need to protect her from being locked up by Hugh, fearing that it would be on Hugh's terms (p. 59). This showcases the connection between parentification and dependency, where Henry's role as Martha's caregiver has turned into a dependency on her. In Scene Six, when Martha has created a mess in the flat, Henry takes responsibility for tidying up the room before Hugh arrives. His actions mirror his parentification as he assumes the role of caretaker and takes on household chores (p. 62). Additionally, Henry's gesture of bringing flowers as an apology for not staying the night at her home is a display of his need to make amends and seek validation and forgiveness from Martha. His concern for her well-being is evident when he suggests that she needs food, further emphasizing his parental role (p. 65).

Besides, Henry's discovery that Martha has eaten cat food in his absence reveals the extent of her dependency on him for guidance and care. Recognizing the potential consequences of Hugh taking control, Henry suggests that Martha go with him to a clinic to seek help. He fears that if Hugh were to take charge, Martha might be "sectioned", or involuntarily admitted to a mental health institution, which would limit Henry's ability to visit her (Stenham, 2007, p. 68). Consequently, these scenes illustrate how parentification and dependency are intertwined in Henry and Martha's relationship. In this context, the play emphasizes the complex situations that can arise when parentification leads to dependency and the consequences they have for family relationships.

In the final scene of *That Face*, the themes of parentification and dependency are further highlighted in the interactions between Henry, Martha and Hugh. Throughout the night, Henry has been drinking with his mentally ill mother, desperately attempting to convince her to go to the clinic (Stenham,

2007, p. 76). His urgent efforts to dress Martha more sensibly and prepare her for leaving demonstrate his continued role as her caregiver, and display the parentification he has experienced (p. 76). In his attempts to put a cardigan and shoes on Martha, Henry's actions embody his parental responsibilities as he tries to take care of her physical well-being (pp. 76, 77). However, Martha's playful shrugging off of the cardigan and kicking him away signify her resistance to Henry's attempts, demonstrating their complex link of dependency (pp. 76, 77). As Hugh enters the flat and asks to speak with Martha alone, Henry intervenes, expressing his concern by stating, "I don't think she wants to be alone with you" (p. 80). This protective instinct reveals Henry's deep connection and dependency on his mother, after years of parentification (p. 80).

By the way, Martha's dependence on Henry is apparent when she asks him to make her coffee, addressing him with terms of endearment like "baby" and "darling" (Stenham, 2007, p. 80). This reliance on Henry for simple everyday tasks illustrates her continued dependency on him for support and care. Hugh, on the other hand, asserts his authority and plans to take Martha to the Cromwell Clinic, arranging for her treatment and taking financial responsibility (p. 82). However, Henry resists, declaring, "I'm not leaving her with him" (p. 87), cementing his strong dependency on his mother and a sense of protectiveness that has emerged from his parentification (p. 87). Henry's statement, "Thought I'd do anything to fix her" (p. 93) emphasizes his deep commitment to caring for Martha and his sense of responsibility that has existed for the past five years. This sentiment further reinforces the consequences of parentification, as Henry has taken on the duty of fixing his mother's mental state. Hugh acknowledges Henry's efforts, acknowledging him as a good child but one born to inadequate parents (p. 94). This recognition underlines the complexity and the lasting influence it has had on Henry's role as a caregiver. As Martha decides to leave the flat, Henry pleads with her to stay with him, revealing his strong emotional dependency on his mother (p. 95). However, Martha ultimately leaves, signifying the culmination of their strained relationship and the play's conclusion.

Conclusion

Polly Stenham's *That Face* emerges as a touching exploration of parentification and dependency, explaining the involved threads of dysfunction within familial relationships. The characters of Henry and Martha represent a microcosm, depicting the complex interplay of caregiving responsibilities, emotional entanglements and the lasting consequences of parental neglect. Mia's abusive actions against her dorm-mate, Alice, demonstrate a stark manifestation within her life. The narrative brings attention to Mia's status as a neglected and lost child, illuminating how the absence of parental guidance can lead to destructive behaviour. The revelation that Mia must seek refuge at friends' homes during school holidays due to Martha's reluctance to care for her daughter depicts the palpable lack of space and emotional connection within the family unit. Henry's five-year-long commitment to caring for Martha further deepens our understanding of parentification and its far-reaching effects. His sacrifice, marked by an interrupted formal education, emphasizes the severe implications of assuming a parental role at a young age. The damaging consequences of Martha's actions when left alone paint a potent picture of dependency, revealing the vulnerabilities that arise in the absence of adequate care. Hugh's distant existence, both physically and emotionally, exemplifies a functional form of parental neglect. His detached approach, manifested in sporadic financial contributions and the embarrassment he feels for leaving his children with a mentally ill Martha, speaks to the lasting effect of absent parenting. Essentially, Stenham's *That Face* functions as a compelling narrative that goes beyond the margins of a dysfunctional family, inviting audience and readers to contemplate the broader societal implications of parentification and dependency. In this regard, the play calls for a detailed understanding of familial roles, the consequences of neglect and the combined emotional landscapes that shape individual trajectories.

References

Adler, R. & Raphael, B. (1983). Children of alcoholics. *Australian & New Zealand Journal of Psychiatry*, 17(1), 3–8. http://doi.org/10.3109/00048678309159980.

Amaro, L. M. (2012). Diagnosing Dr. House: Codependency, agency, and third wave contradiction. *Western Journal of Communication*, 76(5), 520–535. http://doi.org/10.1080/10570314.2012.679983.

Anderson, J. (2014). The impact of family structure on the health of children: Effects of divorce. *The Linacre Quarterly*, 81(4), 378–387. http://doi.org/10.1179/0024363914Z.00000000087.

Barber, L. (2009, 22 Mar). The interview: Polly Stenham. *The Observer*. https://www.theguardian.com/stage/2009/mar/22/polly-stenham-interview.

Benedict, D. (2007, 25 Apr). That Face. *Variety*. https://variety.com/2007/legit/reviews/that-face-2-1200559913/.

Billington, M. (2008, 12 May). That Face. *The Guardian*. https://www.theguardian.com/stage/2008/may/12/theatre1.

Boszormenyi-Nagy, I. & Spark, G. M. (1973). *Invisible loyalties: Reciprocity in intergenerational family therapy*. Harper & Row.

Brantley, B. (2010, 18 May). Do you have a mother? Then you have someone to blame. *The New York Times*. https://www.nytimes.com/2010/05/19/theater/reviews/19that.html.

Butterworth, J. (2017). *The ferryman*. Nick Hern Books.

Castro, D. M., Jones, R. A. & Mirsalimi, H. (2004). Parentification and the impostor phenomenon: An empirical investigation. *The American Journal of Family Therapy*, 32(3), 205–216. http://doi.org/10.1080/01926180490425676.

Chase, N. (1999). An overview of theory, research, and societal issues. In N. Chase (Ed.), *Burdened children* (pp. 3–33). Guilford Press.

Chen, C. Y-C., & Panebianco, A. (2020) Physical and psychological conditions of parental chronic illness, parentification and adolescent psychological adjustment. *Psychology & Health*, 35(9), 1075–1094. http://doi.org/10.1080/08870446.2019. 1699091.

Chen, L., Wulczyn, F. & Huhr, S. (2023). Parental absence, early reading, and human capital formation for rural children in China. *Journal of Community Psychology*, 51, 662–675. http://doi.org/10.1002/jcop.22786.

Choi, S. (2015). From rite of passage to rite of sacrifice: Modern Oedipus and dysfunctional family in Polly Stenham's That Face. 영미문화 (*EACS*), 15(2), 285–312. (KOAJ-Korea Open Access Journals). http://doi.org/10.15839/eacs.15.2.201508.285.

Cridland, E. K., Caputi, P., Walker, B. M., Jones, S. C. & Magee, C. A. (2016). A personal constructivist approach for investigating the patterns of dependency of adolescents with autism spectrum disorder: Case study of two families. *Journal of Constructivist Psychology*, 29(1), 30–50. http://doi.org/10.1080/10720537.2015.1005323.

De Angelis, A. (2010). Troubling gender on stage and with the critics. *Theatre Journal*, 62(4), 557–559. http://doi.org/10.1353/tj.2010.a413928.

Dodds, S. (2014). Dependence, care, and vulnerability. In C. Mackenzie, W. Rogers & S. Dodds (Eds.), *Vulnerability: New essays in ethics and feminist philosophy* (pp. 181–203). Oxford University Press.

Engster, D. (2019). Care ethics, dependency, and vulnerability, *Ethics and Social Welfare*, 13(2), 100–114. http://doi.org/10.1080/17496535.2018.1533029.

Evgin, D. & Sümen, A. (2022). Childhood abuse, neglect, codependency, and affecting factors in nursing and child development students. *Perspectives in Psychiatric Care*, 58(4), 1357–1371. http://doi.org/10.1111/ppc.12938.

Gardiner, P. (2019). *Teaching playwriting: Creativity in practice*. Bloomsbury.

Gillinson, M. (2023, 15 Sep). That Face review: Stunning revival will tear right through you. *The Guardian*. https://www.theguardian.com/stage/2023/sep/15/that-fa ce-review-orange-tree-theatre-london

Godsall, R. E., Jurkovic, G. J, Emshoff, J., Anderson, L. & Stanwyck, D. (2004) Why some kids do well in bad situations: Relation of parental alcohol misuse and parentification to children's self-concept. *Substance Use & Misuse*, 39(5), 789–809. http://doi.org/10.1081/JA-120034016.

Grace, F. & Bayley, C. (2015). *Playwriting: A writers' and artists' companion*. Bloomsbury.

Hall, K. L. (2010). *That Face: A costume design*. ProQuest Dissertations Publishing.

Healy, P. (2010, 25 May). The eternal return of mummy dearest. *The New York Times*. https://www.nytimes.com/2010/05/30/theater/30stenham.html.

Hickling, A. (2010, 7 Jul). That Face. *The Guardian*. https://www.theguardian.com/sta ge/2010/jul/07/that-face-review.

Hoggard, L. (2008, 6 May). That face to watch. *Evening Standard*. https://www.standa rd.co.uk/culture/theatre/that-face-to-watch-6694529.html.

Hooper, L. M. (2007). The application of attachment theory and family systems theory to the phenomena of parentification. *The Family Journal*, 15(3), 217–223. http://doi.org/10.1177/1066480707301290.

Jones, K. (2022). Gothic maternal bodies on the contemporary British stage. In M. Conti & K. J. Wetmore (Eds.), *Theatre and the macabre* (pp. 63–78). University of Wales Press.

Lane, D. (2010). *Contemporary British drama*. Edinburgh University Press.

Latifian, M., Abdi, K., Raheb, G., Islam, S. M. S. & Alikhani, R. (2023). Stigma in people living with bipolar disorder and their families: A systematic review. *International Journal of Bipolar Disorders*, 11(1), 1–20. http://doi.org/10.1186/ s40345-023-00290-y.

Lonergan, P. (2020). "Now for our Irish wars": Jez Butterworth's The Ferryman and the Irish dramatic canon. *Contemporary Theatre Review*, 30(4), 456–473. http://doi.org/10486801.2020.1821197.

Ludwig, S. & Rostain, A. (2009). Family function and dysfunction. In W. Carey *et al.* (Eds.), *Developmental-behavioral pediatrics*, 4th edn (pp. 103–118). Elsevier.

Lukowski, A. (2023, 15 Sep). That Face. *Time Out*. https://www.timeout.com/london/theatre/that-face-1-review.

Mok, P. L. H., Astrup, A., Carr, M. J., Antonsen, S., Webb, R. T. & Pedersen, C. B. (2018). Experience of child–parent separation and later risk of violent criminality. *American Journal of Preventive Medicine*, 55(2), 178–186. http://doi.org/10.1016/j.amepre.2018.04.008.

Navaro, L. (1993). Bağlılık ve bağımlılık, kadının bağlılığı nasıl bağımlılığa dönüşür? *Kadın Araştırmaları Dergisi*, 1(1), 88–99.

Peck, J. & Coyle, M. (2017). *A brief history of English literature*. Palgrave Macmillan.

Peghinelli, A. (2012). Polly Stenham and Mark Ravenhill: Astonishing debuts and court scandals. *Status Quaestionis*, 2, 19–32. http://doi.org/10.13133/2239-1983/10062.

Prebble, L. (2016). *The effect*. Bloomsbury Methuen Drama.

Rohner, R. P. (2004). The parental "Acceptance-rejection syndrome": Universal correlates of perceived rejection. *American Psychologist*, 59(8), 830–840. http://doi.org/: 10.1037/0003- 066X.59.8.830.

Shaw, B. A., Krause, N., Chatters, L. M., Connell, C. M. & Ingersoll-Dayton, B. (2004). Emotional support from parents early in life, aging, and health. *Psychology and Aging*, 19(1), 4–12. http://doi.org/10.1037/0882-7974.19.1.4.

Sierz, A. (2011). *Rewriting the nation: British theatre today*. Bloomsbury.

Soukup, J. E. (1995). *Understanding and living with people who are mentally ill: Techniques to deal with mental illness in the family*. Charles C. Thomas.

Spencer, C. (2007, 26 Apr). One of the most thrilling debuts for decades. *The Telegraph*. https://www.telegraph.co.uk/culture/theatre/drama/3664728/One-of-the-most thrilling-debuts-for-decades.html.

Stein, J. A., Riedel, M. & Rotheram-Borus, M. J. (1999). Parentification and its impact on adolescent children of parents with AIDS. *Family Process*, 38(2), 193–208. http://doi.org/10.1111/j.1545-5300.1999.00193.x.

Stenham, P. (2007). *That face*. Faber and Faber.

Venkataraman, M. & Ackerson, B. J. (2008). Parenting among mothers with bipolar disorder: Strengths, challenges, and service needs. *Journal of Family Social Work*, 11(4), 389–408. http://doi.org/10.1080/10522150802441825.

Venn, J. (2021). *Madness in contemporary British theatre*. Palgrave Macmillan.

Vernig, P. M. (2011) Family roles in homes with alcohol-dependent parents: An evidence-based review. *Substance Use & Misuse*, 46(4), 535–542, http://doi.org/10.3109/10826084.2010.501676.

Zuger, A. (2016). The effect. *JAMA*, 316(14), 1434–1435. http://doi.org/10.1001/jama.2016.14526.

3

"PACKING BOXES" BY/FOR THE YOUNG

Precarity and Cruel Optimism in *Wish List*

Susana Nicolás Román

Precarity and Cruel Optimism

Precarity as an encompassing term needs to be re-signified by emphasizing sensitivities of inequality and specific conditions that might be diluted in the universal generative capacity of the term. The condition of precarity indexes a vulnerability that emerges earlier when people face the precarious conditions in which they live. Judith Butler's distinction between ontological and situational vulnerability, i.e., between the vulnerability that is a universal condition shared by all forms of life (precariousness) and the vulnerabilities that are embedded in specific structures of power (precarity), interestingly connects the two concepts by stating that "precarity exposes our sociality, the fragile and necessary dimensions of our interdependency" (Butler, 2012, p. 148).

Precarity permeates neoliberal ideologies, asking us to rethink about the urgency of constituting new forms of social agreements. In this way, social infrastructures are not merely organizational; they constitute the bases of the human condition that are vital to ensuring impartial access to resources, thus readjusting our understanding and structuration of social relations. The present savage capitalism along with the effects of globalization and market pressures have accelerated the emergence of precarious times. Precarity is in fact everywhere, but its consequences are most harshly experienced in the lives of the vulnerable that need social infrastructures and care measures that prioritise society's well-being over cost-benefit approaches. The main principle of our neoliberal times predicates the choice between taxing jobs or freedom. That is the condition of the neoliberal precariat; groups of people subjected to precarious work conditions, devoid of normative structures and strictly linked to fluctuating economies.

DOI: 10.4324/9781003470434-4

Yet, many of these jobs are without any guarantee of a secure future in the workplace. Slow violence, uncertainty, the promise of happiness and cruel optimism seem adequate correlated terms in this type of professional environment. The precarious nature of jobs is such that one is exposed to different manifestations of epistemological violence in the workplace. State measures intensify the vulnerability and dependency on the system, especially for those who belong to minorities or are simply less privileged.

Isabell Lorey (2015) approaches precarity and precarization as instruments of hegemonic domination that might reconfigure new ways of maintaining human lives based on shared precariousness and that might emphasize reshaping alliances of resistance. Butler and Lorey's examination of precarity considers the interconnection between the political and the affective encounters by introducing the "affective politics of the performative", i.e., "We only act when we are moved to act, and we are moved by something that affects us from the outside, from elsewhere, from the lives of others, imposing a surfeit that we act from and upon" (Butler, 2012, p. 136). This dynamic reaction might be promisingly activated from the stage by recognizing a shared state of acknowledgment and assuming the urgency to act.

Butler (2012) insists upon the connection between lives on the ground of social bonds since "whatever sense 'our' life has is derived precisely from this sociality, this being already, and from the start, dependent on a world of others, constituted in and by a social world" (pp. 140–141). In this way, the responsibility for the precariats is also bounded to the privileged in a site of adjacency and reciprocal state of cohabitation. This world interdependency poses both ethical and political problems due to the difficult struggle for social and political forms "that are committed to fostering a sustainable interdependency on egalitarian terms" (Butler, 2012, p. 149).

The notion of progress now remains inherently linked to providing benefits and being productive. For example, Amazon's promotional message regarding hiring new workers claims that it pays "$15 an hour and provide[s] benefits from day one" (Miller, 2023, p. 126). As Om Dwivedi (2023) explicitly relates: "The work atmosphere is punitive and debilitating as workers are coerced to finish work in strict deadlines, which is monitored by algorithms that calculate breaks availed by employees, even counting the minutes one spends in the bathroom" (p. 34). The breadth of focus is primarily disheartening for young people. Consequently, we will find a clear relationship between these conditions of living and British theatre as the materialization of the profound commitment of some playwrights to the urgency of the times.

My second theoretical approach delves into the lenses of Laurent Berlant's *cruel optimism*. In the introduction to her book, she initially defines a relation of cruel optimism when "something you desire is actually an obstacle to your flourishing" (Berlant, 2011, p. 3). The idea of cruelty comes up when the object impedes the aim that initiated the attachment, making it impossible. On the contrary, the affective structure of an optimistic connection involves a sustaining fantasy expecting the object this time. The argument itself tracks the emergence of precarious public sphere, dissolutions of optimistic scenarios and how adjustments to life seem like an accomplishment.

Thus, the subsequent events that force people to adapt are better defined as *crisis ordinariness*. Berlant's reading of *crisis* as an ongoing process which disrupts normality is useful for the analysis of this chapter. As she points outs: "Crisis is not exceptional to history or consciousness but a process embedded in the ordinary that unfolds in stories about navigating what's overwhelming" (Berlant, 2011, p. 10). Berlant critically looks at how people live now, generating exemplary cases of adjustment to the loss of fantasy. She sets the elaboration of these adjustments in a historical moment that is transnational, a moment of globalization, neoliberalism and cultural systems.

Attachment is a structure of relationality. An optimistic attachment might be felt in any number of ways but Berlant explores more the conditions under which certain attachments remain powerful as they function against the development of particular beings. Berlant bases her theoretical framework on different concepts: affective present (the present is perceived, first, affectively); impasse (a time of indecision from which someone or some situation cannot advance); situation (a state of interruption that forces itself on consciousness in the present). This situation, resonating with Badiou's *event* (1999) or Bond's *theatre event* (1998), articulates my nexus between precarity and optimism in the analysed play, *Wish List*. The world is portrayed as fragile and responses to different scenes beyond fantasy might foster categorical attitudes and the rejection of differences (perhaps for not suffering or for reinforcing positions). Nowadays, the ordinary is seen as an *impasse* shaped by crisis in which people struggle to adjust to new pressures and ways of living.

Distancing herself from the work on emotions of Sara Ahmed in her famous book *The Promise of Happiness* (2010), Berlant defends the position that her book is oriented to a more formalist project. Ahmed's proposal resonates more closely with the definition of hope made by Anna Potamianou in *Hope: A Shield in the Economy of Borderline States* (1997) and Jose Esteban Muñoz in *Cruising Utopia* (2009), though less future-oriented. Berlant (2011) looks at the complexity of being bound to life, thus, "optimism is a scene of negotiated sustenance that makes life bearable as it presents itself ambivalently" (p. 14). The book conclusively attempts to produce a materialist context for affect theory based on the mixture of the ordinary with the fantasy. Other authors are mentioned to support this point (Deleuze, Massumi, Zizek and Brennan) to argue that "affective atmospheres are shared" (Berlant, 2011, p. 15), thus, affective responses might signify shared present. As Green (1999) asserts: "affect is a metapsychological category spanning what's internal and external to subjectivity" (as cited in Berlant, 2011, p. 16).

Yet, the power of the affect goes beyond the individual to provide a theory-in-practice of the contours of the world and its functioning.

Precarity Theatre and Theatre for the Young

In *Ecologies of Precarity in Twenty-First Theatre*, Marissia Fragkou (2009) acknowledges the dynamic resurgence of politics in British theatre since the 1990s, representing precarity as an addressed zeitgeist. She approaches precarity as a theatrical trope, which carries the potential to challenge spectators to understand identity politics and responsibility for the lives of Others. Her study asserts the relevance of contemporary plays to examine precarity and its nexus with political, social and emotional intersections. The focus on precarity is bound to the concept of identity both individual and collective, and provides the possibility to discuss how the human condition is embedded in material conditions that sustain life. Likewise, Mireia Aragay and Martin Middeke in *Of Precariousness* (2017) also discussed the fact that contemporary British theatre epitomizes its present prospects to the full by reflecting upon the category and the episteme of precariousness and by turning spectators into active participants in the process of negotiating ethical agency. This project refers to concepts such as *The Other* by Emmanuel Levinas (1969), The *Inoperative Community* of Jean-Luc Nancy (1991) and *Hospitality* by Jacques Derrida and Anne Dufourmantelle (2000) among other interesting philosophical terms.

After the premiere of playwright Chris Dunkley's *The Precariat* in 2013, the predisposition to connect precarity and performance explicitly was evident. This play was deeply influenced by the arousal of this social phenomenon which even included a short preface written by Guy Standing himself, the well-known market economist. Yet, the connection between these sociopolitical situations and contemporary theatre is not new in the British context. The political drama of the 1960s or the *in-yer-face theatre*, more recently in the 1990s, demonstrates the particular emphasis on the association of politics and plays in Great Britain. Contemporary theatre has for decades been differentiating itself from the ancient Aristotelean form, especially in its postdramatic form. In his study *Postdramatic Theatre*, Hans-Thies Lehmann (2006) understands that theatre may render "visible the broken thread between personal experience and perception" by deliberately adhering to the relevant concerns of the contemporary time (p. 185). The British stage is now much more centred on highly intertextual plays in which cultural memory and collective identity are narrated in an ambiguous aesthetic framework that explores vulnerability and precarity.

Young people are particularly targeted in this theatrical panorama. There is a clear specificity on the environments and the subject matter to make young people the focus and where they are given maximum responsibility and points of reflection to reach for. Theatre – as an oral, action-based, relationship-focused form – has the potential to conscientiously provoke thinking. Like oral knowledge sharing, theatrical performance demands presence and relationship: it connects witnessing audience members to the performers. As Fitzimmons argues (2020), through aesthetization and the opportunity to witness, theatre for young audiences offers a particularly helpful way to open up conversations about difficult knowledge with young people, because performance can make moments present that are sometimes distant. The field of Theatre for Young Audiences (TYA) has become extremely prolific in recent years. Researchers point out that the focus does not turn on morality or patronizing youth but much more on enhancing critical and independent-thinking skills. As Matthew Reason (2010) cautions: "It seems both condescending and dictatorial to perceive (TYA) as being primarily about the communication of moral lessons. Instead … theatre provides models of ways in which the world can be understood" (p. 107).

In what follows, I argue how the audience becomes personally involved in the precariat's social suffering while this process is also shown as deeply personal through specific perspectives of precariat characters the audience comes to sympathize with. By virtue of its freedom to imagine the perspective and voice of the other, for example, marginalized individuals and groups of society, theatre can function as a strong source of insight into precarious living. Perhaps the specific form of literature that is drama can convey that function more passionately because of its nexus with political literature after Brecht, and because it has such a direct bond with the precarity of those performing on stage and can directly invite the audience to (re)act to what is performed on stage.

Wish List: "Your Life Is a Box"

In the past few years, the cultural industries have begun to respond to the *age of austerity*. At its most controversial has been *poverty porn* television, the much criticized array of popular television programmes like *Benefits Street* (Channel 4) or *Britain's Benefit Tenants* (Channel 4). In films we find examples such as Ken Loach's *I Daniel Blake* (2016) and Katherine Round's documentary *The Divide* (2016). But it is surely in the world of theatre that some of the most intense critiques of neoliberal austerity have emerged, with plays confronting the growing housing crisis (*Love*), in-work poverty (*Beyond Caring*) and local public spending cuts (*Hope*). The precariat populates the contemporary British stage, featured in prominent venues like the Royal Court Theatre and the National Theatre among others. Many new and significant British plays have imagined the contours of an identity of this new social group aiming to reflect upon the living conditions experienced by those forced to inhabit an environment of precarity.

Katherine Soper (2017) represents one of the most promising voices in this British panorama. Awarded with numerous prizes such as the Bruntwood Prize for Playwriting, The Stage Debut Award for Best New Play, *Wish List* caused Katherine to be nominated as Most Promising Playwright at the Evening Standard Awards. The play devastatingly presents zero-hour contracts and benefit cuts in an Orwellian and Kafkaesque atmosphere. Since her mother died, Tamsin must combine long hours of packing in an online warehouse with caring for her brother Dean, 17 years old, housebound, and obsessed with compulsive rituals of his own (tapping out a rhythm and repeatedly rearranging his hair). When Dean is declared fit for work, state benefits disappear. Then, Tamsin is forced to survive in constant management impositions about figures and the lack of control over her own life. Her task is to package products for postage at an unrealistic rate: 400 an hour as a new recruit, one every ten seconds. The rise of social media and the online shopping revolution are also contended in the story as a rebooting axis contributing to dehumanizing job conditions. On the other side of the cast, the audience follows Luke, Tamsin's friend at the workplace and their superior, a nameless character, representing different sides to this machine of precarity and exploitation that has no regard for individual difficulties, motivations or needs.

In the portrayal of a non-existent or weak social contract, the value of society is overstretched by the force of the market. Amazon's universe becomes highly symbolic and explicit. No wonder that

> inside the warehouse, the domain controlled by Amazon, the worker's body becomes the company's equipment. Every breath and movement are monitored, scored and rated, reducing the physical self to machinery managed by a company brain as opposed to one's own.
>
> *(Miller, 2023, p. 126)*

The alienation and exploitation elucidated in *Wish List* criticizes the regime of neoliberal austerity, and what emerges is a critical feeling for the United Kingdom as a class-divided nation and an urgent need to struggle against the embedded discriminatory gaze of the neoliberal imagination.

In this job, Soper emphatically dramatizes the atmosphere of the precariat defined by Guy Standing. As fictional text, *Wish List* is clearly part of what Simon During (2015) has described as "the contemporary literature of precarity", which he finds to be "a literature of inconclusive illuminations" used to imagine powerful connections between the characters and the real world (p. 37). In Soper's production, the audience is immersed in the experience of precarity and vulnerability through emotional appeals to identify with these Others without normalizing the process. On the one hand, Tamsin's particular dynamics produce a consciousness of relative deprivation and a combination of anxiety, anomie (despair of escape from their precarious status) and alienation (having to do what they do not wish to do while being unable to do what they would like to do and are capable of doing). The optimistic attachment of cruel optimism is explicitly depicted in the precariat life of Tamsin who navigates between the promise of challenging advancement and harsh neoliberal reality. At the other side, the character of the Lead illustrates the globalization of the system by categorically stating job conditions as universal:

> There are people at the top of this … They don't see it from this – angle, they don't see it from here, because they just get numbers in red and they work out how to put them in the black. And it will be the same anywhere else you go.
>
> *(Soper, 2017, p. 75)*

The Lead's assertion – "None of this is personal" (p. 75) – concludes this conversation in which Tamsin is left hopeless and with no choice but to follow the rules of the system. This examination of precarity implicitly embodies vulnerability but the transforming notion of the concept as a strategic position from which to resist structural oppression seems blurred in the play. Here, the depiction of precariat subjects questions whether the individual response offers any realistic alternative to the operational elements of the system. Mostly, *Wish List* rails against reductionism focused on a one-size-fits-all system; a society that reduces people to data. Tamsin's skills and capabilities are only judged by her efficiency: "Do you consider that you possess any psychological barriers to your productivity?" (Soper, 2017, p. 73). In this scenario, the female character is forced to acknowledge a "congenital vulnerability as constitutive condition" (Cavarero, 2011, p. 200) – a redefinition of vulnerable subjects not only in relation to tangible social and economic situations or as individual experiences, but also in the context of cultural discourses connected to femininity and disability. In this way, vulnerability frames the conjunction between poverty, gender and disabilities (through the character of Dean) as part of the complex picture of the interpretation of the term. Thus, the play epitomizes the present prospects of affective and vulnerable intersections to the full, by reflecting upon the category and the episteme of precariousness and by ultimately turning spectators into active participants in the process of negotiating ethical agency and responsibility for the Others.

The phenomenon of situational vulnerability is primarily discussed through Dean's sense of dispossession related to his condition of being disabled. Indeed, the behavioural conditionality of Tamsin's precarious contract resonates with Dean's relations with the welfare system. In the UK, conditionality has increasingly been extended to unemployed and disabled benefit claimants (Baumberg, 2017) but despite his obsessive-compulsive disorder (OCD) the functional capacity assessment does not recognise Dean's disability (Allen, 2017, p. 194). In Scene Two, the testimony of Dean about the conversation with the supervisor of the Employment and Support Allowance illustrates the random assessment of the system: "They cut you off thinking you had nothing wrong with you, that's the thing. Like, I would look at this report and go 'Ok, clearly, they're fine'" (Soper, 2017, p. 32). Dean's character clearly embodies a dependent stratum of society that engenders social and economic support, which are all integral to the state's moral duty. The paramount sense of insecurity and instability is narrated throughout the play by its direct criticism of the inefficacy of the system and cost-cutting programmes.

Tamsin's life is navigated in a constant stressful situation that forces her to work while simultaneously assuming the risk of leaving her brother alone at home: "Are we gonna have a good day?" (Soper, 2017, p. 7). By portraying the lives of these characters, the play dramatizes the isolation and violence of the neoliberal self, the invisible thread of the slow violence in an austere system that limits the survival of the less privileged. Soper fully personalizes the individual responses to the core of the capitalist system with its benefits and its shadows. In fact, Tamsin is depicted as an inescapable part of the system when receiving an online package with excitement, whereas in another fragment, she reprimands Dean for buying hair gel compulsively on the internet. Thus, overall, *Wish List* evokes the need for a new ontology consisting of responsibility and care by acknowledging shared vulnerability and mutual dependence of the system and the individuals. As Allen (2017) points out, the play confronts our complicity in the very system that "has produced and normalised the burgeoning forms of *poor work* in which Tamsin, and inevitably Dean, have no option but to engage" (p. 195). In this scenario, interactions become simple and inconsequential with few opportunities for intimate conversations. The staging manages to echo this feeling of simplicity that engages the audience in a particularly secluded and suffocating atmosphere. The actors cleverly navigate a small space designed to represent the different locations of the play that is mainly focused on the workplace and Tamsin's house.

Following Berlant's concept of affect, the plot unfolds the mixture of the ordinary with the fantasy by illustrating the devastating effect of benefit conditionality on both the disabled and those who care for them. Tamsin must face the precarious conditions of her job while caring for Dean and suffering the bureaucracy of the benefit system. As she reads to Dean the letter informing him that he has been deemed "fit for work" and his benefits have been cut, Tamsin desperately tries to convey optimism and resilience, reassuring her brother about a happy future. The resilient attitude is perceived in this excerpt:

TAMSIN: We're gonna make it without them. Okay? Fuck them. Fuck them and their fucking review and reconsideration and all that bollocks. I don't fucking care, we can do this ourselves, we can — I can work, and this — this isn't fucking *fair*.

(Soper, 2017, p. 79)

The sense of dehumanization is partially redeemed by the behavioural depiction of the characters. As Tamsin grows close to her co-worker Luke, a 16-year-old confident youth, she gradually reveals herself beyond her fragility: the intelligence that rarely surfaces, the interests and ambitions she keeps to herself or a soft sense of humour. Their drink-date singing of Meat Loaf's, *I Would Do Anything For Love*, frantically exposes tenderness and humanity as hopeful elements amidst the dramatic devastation of the consumer society. Empowered by this relationship, Tamsin eventually appeals for resistance and opposition to the system by claiming individual responsibility and shared brotherhood. In this particular moment of the play, Soper glimpses momentary hope and casts the audience as witness by calling for them to reflect upon the subjectivities towards the Other of what Berlant explores in her dichotomy of *promised happiness* and *cruel optimism*. The playful intimacy between Tamsin and Luke highlights magical interactions of humanity deconstructing places and conversations where everything is trying to eliminate tenderness and care. That oscillation between pain and sudden beauty is what captures the emotional intensity of the audience addressing a challenging reflection on contemporary neoliberalism and its effects on young people's lives.

Nevertheless, Scene Eight unfolds the visibility of cruel optimism effects that shatter the possibilities of resistance. Dean, in a moment of distraction, burns both of his palms while cooking. This act ultimately embodies the impossibility of the characters to fit in the system, by confronting the audience with the incoherence of the Employment and Support Allowance bureaucracy by assessing functional abilities for work. The attempt of Tamsin and Dean to belong to the community ends up in a portrayal of harsh, stigmatizing reality. On the other side of the balance, Luke's options continue as he abandons the job and starts a new life at college. Here, Soper might suggest education as the alternative to precariat jobs, yet Tamsin's responsibilities with her dependent brother shape their futures in *boxes*. Formally, Berlant's concept of *cruel optimism* can be identified here. The promises of happiness (cf. globalization, commercialism and welfare state) are deconstructed in Tamsin's reality. The narrative of *Wish List* gives us unpromising closures depicting the present and skips idealism as well. This constellation of always-vulnerable figures, traversing both the fiction and the performance event, highlights our ontological reaction to being destabilised and dispossessed in affective, social or material ways.

Conclusions

Butler avers that capitalism lets

> people die. And there are a group of people who know that they can be
> left to die, they can be sacrificed. And that means that they go through
> life feeling like they are at least in the perspective of society ungrievable.
>
> *(Seeliger and Villa Braslavsky, 2022)*

As ethical beings, the perspective of accepting the value of some lives over others is completely impossible. Reciprocity lies in the basics of ethics where "the life that *is* not our own, is also our life" (Butler, 2012, p. 140). Yet, the communal and social responsibility is nowadays contested by precarious life conditions and the impositions of the neoliberal welfare stare. Nonetheless, it must be remembered that as humans we are all vulnerable and that is precisely why we need social infrastructures and care measures that prioritise society's well-being over cost-benefit analysis. This chapter has turned to the concepts of precarity and cruel optimism in *Wish List* to illustrate the demanding ethical obligations to all Others who cohabit the earth with us. Theatre assumes a responsibility for both its audiences and its tropes, as well as for theatre itself through an "aesthetic of response-ability" (Lehmann, 2006, p. 185).

Soper's play successfully dramatizes a tragedy of dependency, frustration and immobility while it directly criticizes the UK's dehumanizing jobs and austerity measures by displaying the dignity and strength of its characters. The cathartic effect of the drama offers the readership/audience a temporary immersion in the lives of the characters that is transformed into a reflective practice on representations of precarity and cruel optimism in connection. Yet, the strategies of individual resilience do not seem to offer a realistic opportunity to overcome Tamsin and Dean's harsh reality by directly addressing the responsibility of the system and the labour market.

Boxed in by her family duties and stuck in the online business, the protagonist clearly embodies the life of the precariat and the unseen victims of capitalist economies and organizations. Although the box constitutes the play's most memorable symbol, precarity is ubiquitous in the structure of the play by acknowledging the normalization of some labour practices in order to fully preserve the system of production. The biased and unfavourable regulations control and dictate the lives of the masses while providing incentivised measures for a select few. This uncertain scenario is shaping the beginning of the precarious age, one that is particularly harmful and discriminatory for young people. For Tamsin and thousands of others, there is no social system of support; there is no chance of actively resisting or having their dreams fulfilled in a world of cruel optimism.

References

Ahmed, S. (2010). *The promise of happiness*. Duke University Press.

Allen, K. (2017). Wish List. Review. *Journal of Poverty and Social Justice*, 25(2), 193–196.

Aragay, M. & Middeke, M. (Eds.) (2017). *Of precariousness: Vulnerabilities, responsibilities, communities in 21st-century British drama and theatre*. De Gruyter.

Badiou, A. (1999). *Manifesto for philosophy*. State University of New York Press.

Baumberg, B. (2017). Benefits conditionality for disabled people: Stylised facts from a review of international evidence and practice. *Journal of Poverty and Social Justice*, 25(2), 107–128.

Berlant, L. (2011). *Cruel optimism*. Duke University Press.

Bond, E. (1998). *Commentary on the war plays. Plays: 6* (pp. 246–363). Methuen.

Butler, J. (2009). Performativity, precarity and sexual politics. *AIBR. Revista de Antropología Iberoamericana*, 4(3), i–xiii.

Butler, J. (2012). Precarious life, vulnerability, and the ethics of cohabitation. *Journal of Speculative Philosophy*, 26(2), 134–151.

Cavarero, A. (2011). Inclining the subject: Ethics, alterity and natality. In Jane Elliott & Derek Attridge (Eds.), *Theory after "theory"* (194–204). Routledge.

Derrida, J. & Dufourmantelle, A. (2000). *Of hospitality*. Stanford University Press.

During, S. (2015). Choosing precarity. *Journal of South Asian Studies*, 8(1), 19–38.

Dwivedi, O. (2023). Precarity and resilience in Kavery Nambisan's The Story That Must Not Be Told. *Asiatic*, 17(2), 31–42.

Fitzsimmons, F. & Heather, M. (2020). We are all treaty people: Indigenous–settler relations, story and young audiences. *Theatre Research International*, 45(1), 37–54.

Fragkou, M. (2009). *Ecologies of precarity in the twenty first century: Politics, affect, responsibility*. Methuen.

Green, A. (1999). *The fabric of affect in the psychoanalytic discourse*. Routledge.

Lehmann, H. T. (2006). *Postdramatic theatre*. Routledge.

Levinas, E. (1969). *Totality and infinity: An essay on exteriority*. Duquesne University Press.

Lorey, I. (2015). *State of insecurity: Government of the precarious*. Verso.

Miller, M. (2023). Mutual aid as spiritual sustenance. *Daedalus*, 152(1), 125–130.

Nancy, J. L. (1991). The inoperative community. In Peter Childs (Ed.), *Theory and history of literature* (pp. 1–42). University of Minnesota Press.

Reason, M. (2010). *The young audience: Exploring and enhancing children's experiences of theatre*. Trentham Books.

Seeliger, M. & Villa Braslavsky, P. I. (2022). Reflections on the contemporary public sphere: An interview with Judith Butler. *Theory, Culture & Society*, 39(4), 67–74. https://doi.org/10.1177/02632764211066260.

Soper, K. (2017). *Wish list*. Nick Hern Books.

4

"IT'S JUST THE PERSUADING BIT"

Children, Performance and Climate Action

Rachael Newberry

Introduction

Children have been a key focus of climate-related discussion for some time, seen as both a symbol of hope and regeneration, and a potent warning of how climate breakdown and ecological destruction is already impacting the future of humanity. Indeed, the image of 15-year-old Greta Thunberg in a bright yellow raincoat and long plaits sitting in front of the Swedish parliament on strike from school in 2018, brought greater attention to the climate crisis than any climate scientist or politician has yet to do. As Ariane de Waal (2021) argues: "Attempts to press home the urgency of the climate crisis often rely on the figure of the child [...] the child serves as a privileged signifier of the planet's vulnerability" (pp. 43–44). Furthermore, the child is often deemed to stand at the intersection between nature and culture, a pure connection or "important political site submerged within the term *natural*" (Lakind & Adsit–Morris, 2018, p. 33). Thus, the child serves as an impossible ideal which encompasses fear, redemption, hope and possibility.

Given the contradictory, complex and yet enduring position children occupy in many aspects of climate discourse, it is of particular note that the figure of the child is often physically absent from the theatrical stage itself. Plays which take climate chaos as their main topic of exploration often do so from the perspective of an adult-centred world. Although the titular characters of Lucy Kirkwood's climate-based play *The Children* (2016) are explicitly referenced, there are no actual children present, and even those mentioned are no longer children themselves. Similarly, Duncan Macmillan's *Lungs* (2011), essentially a play about the ethics of having children, has no children in it, whilst the child protagonist, Rachel, in Tanya Ronder's *F*ck the Polar Bears* (2015) utters only a couple of words throughout the entire

DOI: 10.4324/9781003470434-5

play. The fact that she is often dressed as a fluffy polar bear further alienates her, turning her into an emotive, cute and vulnerable symbol of the effects of environmental destruction. There are many other dramatic examples, from the climate-themed body of work by Caryl Churchill through to that of Katie Mitchell, a well-known eco-dramaturg with a strong commitment to environmentally focussed work.

Environmental theatre has thus far trodden an unfamiliar path, attempting to reimagine classic texts through the lens of eco-theatre, as well as struggling to come up with new and interesting ways to represent and examine the theme. Many early adopters of ecologically driven original theatre tended to take a didactic approach, proffering statistics and personal solutions that would often evoke feelings of guilt or helplessness, rather than optimism. Ronder's play is a case in point. As Icelandic au pair Blundhilde repeatedly reminds us: "Coffee grains go in the green bin" (Ronder, 2015, p. 32). Similarly, playwright Macmillan and climate scientist Chris Rapley's collaborative monologue, *2071: The World We'll Leave Our Grandchildren*, performed at the Royal Court in 2014 and directed by Katie Mitchell, is less of a drama and more of a 75-minute lecture delivered by Chris Rapley, Professor of Climate Science at University College, London. The play only really has the potential to move audiences when Rapley mentions his granddaughter, the subject of the subtitle. He explains, "There will be carbon atoms that were generated by this event that will still be in the air by 2071, in the air that my granddaughter will breathe. That's our legacy" (Macmillan & Rapley, 2016). As Dominic Maxwell's review of the piece notes, this emotive interruption from data and statistics "gets you in the gut as well as in the head" although again, children are alluded to rather than featuring as characters in their own right (Maxwell, 2014).

Theatrical decisions to exclude, or at least fail to include children from theatre that explores themes of climate destruction may, of course, be prudent responses to the oft cited adage, *never work with animals or children*. Indeed, as Broderick Chow states, "Working with young people to produce program innovation is as rewarding as it is challenging, but it is not a gig for cowards" (Arrighi & Emeljanow, 2014, p. 74). Whether it is bravery or stupidity that motivates some artists to work with children, it would be fair to say that engagement with the climate crisis, and environmental theatre more generally, is often *about* rather than *with* or *for* children.

We might, then, need to look to alternative performative art forms to witness the inclusion of children, not only in discussions about the climate crisis, but also in the final performance. In the rest of this chapter, I look in detail at the way in which artists and performers have sought to incorporate the ideas, thoughts and wishes of children into their own ecologically themed art works. More specifically, I consider the climate-focused work of three British artistic creators – the London-based visual artist Cornelia Parker's video installation *All at Sixes and Sevens*; The National Theatre Wales commission, *Kidstown*, by artists Nigel Barrett and Louise Mari; and the Newcastle-based touring theatre company Cap-a-Pie's collaboration with children, entitled *Climate Catastrophe!* These three case studies, in different ways, offer possibilities, and some challenges, for theatre and performance artists to listen to, collaborate with, and showcase, children's voices in the work they make about the future of the planet.

All at Sixes and Sevens

Cornelia Parker's interest and engagement with environmental concerns have been well documented. In a recent interview she explains how she felt after attending a workshop for scientists and artists two decades ago. "I came away pretty shell-shocked," she says. "I had a four-year-old daughter … What kind of a future was she going to have?" (Spence, 2023). Like Rapley, who looks to the future his own grandchild is likely to inherit, and in keeping with the tenets of environmental discourse more generally, Parker places the child at the centre of her own experiences of eco-anxiety. Yet her concern for her own young daughter at that time extrapolates out to embrace the thoughts and words of children more generally later in Parker's career. No stranger to collaboration, in 2017, Parker worked with primary-aged children in London to create a series of drawings in which the children wrote headlines from various UK and US newspapers onto blackboards. Parker says of the project,

> I wanted to do something with primary school children because they have this incorruptibility … It's quite poignant, because these children are going to live with the consequences of these news headlines. They can't control any of it, they're just innocent bystanders.
>
> *(tate.org.uk)*

Parker's observation that children are incorruptible speaks out in stark opposition to the corruptibility of the fossil fuel industry, and, by extension, the theatre industry itself. Indeed, The National Theatre only ended its relationship with Shell in 2019, having taken sponsorship from the energy company for their annual Youth Theatre Festival from 1995 to 2007 (oh, the irony!). The incorruptibility of children allows them to inadvertently expose corruption through the lens of naivety or innocence, rather than for political or personal gain. Being positioned at the juncture between innocence and experience, children are ideally placed to illuminate these double standards.

Parker revisits her collaborative partnership with these "innocent bystanders" in 2023 for her video installation *The Future (Sixes and Sevens)*, part of the Southbank Centre's *Dear Earth* summer exhibition. The piece, almost nine minutes long, again featuring a group of primary-aged children (all at/of sixes and sevens), is given a room of its own in a crowded exhibition space, and broadcast across two large screens, testament to Parker's significance as an artist. As Rachel Spence (2023) notes:

> Dancing a tightrope between anxiety and hope, it blows a hole through arguments that *climate art* is an oxymoron. Although that genre is often afflicted by faux-scientific didacticism, Parker's film does what such work should do, operating both as call to action and organic, imaginative experience.
>
> *(Spence, 2023)*

The children on screen respond to an unseen and unheard interviewer, presumably Parker herself, about their own hopes for the future. As visitors to the gallery, we are invited to fill in the linguistic gaps left by the silent interviewer, becoming active participants in the piece as the children share their responses to various assumed provocations. Parker's decision to collaborate with children gives them a chance to speak to a (mostly adult) audience in a world that often fails to listen. Like the planet itself, children are often voiceless, powerless and generally blameless. But unlike the more-than-human world, children can be given the opportunity to speak through language. Indeed, for me, the most poignant moment in Parker's film comes when a small boy wearing a bright green *Stingrays are Relatives* T-shirt, enthusiastically explains: "I think if people just stop. Stopping's actually pretty easy, it's just the persuading bit that's hard".[1] The simplicity with which the child vocalizes his solution to how we might tackle over-consumption, capitalism, and greed in the face of unstoppable climate chaos is sobering. "Just stop!"[2] he says. In many ways, of course, he is right. Stopping *is* relatively easy. The difficulty *does* come in the persuading. Perhaps, Parker seems to suggest, in her inclusion of this video, that it is in the persuading that children might have the most impact.

This particular child's solution to environmental breakdown seems *natural*, there is an innocence in the simplicity with which he verbalizes his response. Yet at the same time, he is positing complex ideas about accountability, capitalism, and individual versus corporate responsibility. What is it, we may ask, that he wants us to stop doing? And how might we be persuaded to do so? How might – through the medium of theatre and performance in the UK – children go about persuading adults to reimagine an alternative world that puts climate action at its core? One of the ways this might be achieved is through the medium of play. As Rob Hopkins (2019), founder of the Transition Towns movement asks:

> What if [...] play were at the heart of the everyday – even for adults? What if we were to see more and more people bringing play and imagination into politics? What if our daily lives included more opportunities and spaces where play was possible? Would it decrease our anxiety?

Would it build empathy? Would it establish connections? And would it help us to be more imaginative and positive about the future and its possibilities?

(p. 28)

Kidstown

This question of play, and how it might generate hope for the future is explored in a collaborative project between National Theatre Wales (under the direction of Lorne Campbell), and performance artists Nigel Barrett and Louise Mari. National Theatre Wales is committed to working with Theatre Green Book in all its productions and *Kidstown* is no exception. Barrett and Mari visited three locations throughout South Wales in the summer of 2023, welcoming children between the ages of 6 and 11, and offering them "a space to imagine the world they want to live in and shape a better future for all of us" (Barrett & Mari, 2023, para. 4). The space (a walled area in a green field) is "a treasure island of stuff. All recycled" (buzzmag.co.uk) – in which children are invited to make sense of their surroundings in ways they may not have previously considered. Barrett and Mari (2023) explain:

> We wanted to make something for children that thinks about theatre and storytelling in a different way. Something that children could create without us dictating the parameters of what the outcome might be. So we've made a live performance, a story, an installation, a game called Kidstown – where children can do and make whatever they want, have fun and play with other children, without any rules […] As theatre makers we are handing over the arena to the children, then our job will be to listen and ask questions while their imaginations get to work.
>
> *(para. 15–17)*

Whilst the children's concerns and anxieties about environmental chaos might not initially be obvious through imaginative free play, the responses gathered by "journalists" Barrett and Mari during the project, reveal an anxiety, or pre-occupation with the natural world the children may only be able to articulate through the medium of play. When asked by Barrett, "What is happening in the volcano at top of town?"[3] one child gravely replies, "It's erupted".[4] Another child displays concern for the overuse of resources, explaining, "They are doing too much tape, and it was a little bit at the start, and now they're getting too mad".[5] Of course, it is easy for adults, myself included, to project our own eco-anxieties onto these children, however, children's imaginations are not independent of the contemporary world in which they live and learn, and any observations they make about their natural environment within the safety and freedom of *Kidstown* can be extrapolated out into wider society. As Gilli Bush Bailey asserts, children are far from "being in a state of autonomous separation, free from insidious interpolation and deformation by the social" (Arrighi & Emeljanow, 2014, p. 116).

While Kidstown offers children the opportunity to perform in a space without rules, it also allows them to act as audience members (or critics) of one another in the process of creating. The comment about "too much tape" can be seen as a critique of consumerism as much as it is about the way children learn to police their contemporaries, instilling boundaries upon an event that begins from a position of agency and permission. Like the boy in Parker's installation who demands we *just stop*, the children here engender a sense of accountability amongst its audience, even if that audience is restricted to those who are also (child) participants.

Unlike Cornelia Parker's video installation, there is no "finished product" to be shown or displayed in *Kidstown*. Once the day comes to a close, the kids leave and the site is packed up. The event is over in the same way that a traditional theatrical performance can be said to be so. So how might *Kidstown* seek to generate a legacy that counters the one that Rapley imagines for his grandaughter in 2071? One way this can be achieved is, of course, experiential. The memory of *Kidstown* lives on in the minds of the children who attend, many of whom live in socially deprived areas with little access to art and culture outside of the school day. Another way in which the project has continued to create a lasting impact is through its collaboration with local schools who have used the ethos of the project to generate ongoing debate and project work, thus living up to the objectives of National Theatre Wales, which include: "Being a truly national theatre: relevant, accessible and embedded in communities" (National Theatre Wales, 2018, p. 1).

And finally, Barrett and Mari have envisaged a future for the project through the collection of "data" from each event to be crafted into a script, (recycled, if you like) and incorporated into a more traditional staged performance piece entitled *Requiem for the Children*. In their report for the 2022/23 financial year, National Theatre Wales (2023) state:

> The voices captured during these two years will inspire and feature in the 2024/2025 show Requiem for the Children, a bilingual musical explosion themed on the crises our children will face if we do not act now. Drawing new content from every location it visits, this will be an internationally touring collaborative show.
>
> *(p. 6)*

Unfortunately, at the time of writing, due to Arts Council funding cuts, this element of the project is still on hold. We might read this hiatus in the development of the project in the same way we have traditionally been taught to consider children more generally, as being in a *state of becoming*. While outside the control of the team (and also disappointing for the artists), there is something poetic in the idea that both the project, and children more generally, are seen as *unfinished*. As Jules Simon puts it, "children-as-students are newcomers who are not born into the world as finished products that merely need to be sorted out in a Platonic version of testing and categorizing but are, rather, in a state of becoming" (Simon, 2010, p. 7).

However, this common-sense notion that children are on a journey towards becoming has been challenged by Darren O'Donnell, artistic director of the Canadian-based theatre company Mammalian Diving Reflex, whose tag line is, "Ideal entertainment for the end of the world" (mammalian.ca). O'Donnell argues:

> it is possible to conceive of young people not as headed towards a perfected state, but as who they are right now, a view that prioritizes the young person's being at that moment over that of the adult they may eventually become.
>
> *(Arrighi & Emeljanow, 2014, pp. 15–16)*

O'Donnell continues:

> Being smart in the way kids often are is not about mere knowledge or analytical accuracy applied to experience, producing generalizable insights. Instead, it is about being smart by virtue of valuing the truth in the moment, by responding honestly and immediately: smart kids are at the level of *being* (rather than becoming) as disenfranchised as that being might be.
>
> *(Arrighi & Emeljanow, 2014, p. 25)*

If we turn back to Parker's stingray T-shirt child, or *Kidstown*'s volcano erupting child, we can see this definition of smart in action. These children are able to articulate a particular type of intelligent curiosity *at that moment* that embraces collaboration, negotiation and play at the time of its creation. Hopkins' (2019) enquiry into the politics of play is worth noting here. By asking: "What if we were to see more and more people bringing play and imagination into politics?" (p. 28), Hopkins is suggesting a radical reworking of political discourse that has been taken up by the artists I explore in my final case study.

Climate Change Catastrophe!

The merging of play and politics is part of the remit of the Newcastle-based community theatre company Cap-a-Pie who, in collaboration with school children across the region at Key Stage 2, as well as scientists and engineers from Newcastle University, created *Climate Change Catastrophe!*, a film shown at the United Nations Climate Change Conference (COP26) in 2021. A global study in 2021 found that

Climate anxiety and dissatisfaction with government responses are widespread in children and young people in countries across the world and impact their daily functioning. A perceived failure by governments to respond to the climate crisis is associated with increased distress.

(Hickman et al., 2021, p. 863)

Thus, it is imperative that children are included in discourses around climate change and governmental response. It is therefore useful to consider a range of artistic responses led predominantly by children that harness such anxiety and redirect it in more fruitful ways.

On their website, the director of Cap-a-Pie, Brad McCormick, states, "Everything you see in the show, pretty much, has been inspired by, or written, or co-devised, by the young people" (cap-a-pie.co.uk). Producer Katy Vanden argues:

The university researchers and engineers [...] learnt that children have the freedom of imagination to think up climate solutions that have not yet been considered by adults working on the issue, and by forming a direct and creative link between these two groups the theatre team provided a positive lens to look towards the future with a constructive outlook.

*(*Climate Change Catastrophe!*, 2021)*

The element of *being smart* that Vanden highlights here, whereby children offer solutions to the crisis, are shared in the trailer for the project. The children's ideas are voiced by adult actors Hannah Goudie-Hunter and Liam Scarth, who speak the children's words as though they are children themselves. Scarth shares the following solution with viewers: "My idea to cool the entire city down is that aliens come every day with tanks of ice-cold water" (cap-a-pie.co.uk). It seems a pity to me that the directors chose such an obviously unrealistic and unachievable example from the input of almost 400 KS2 children they worked with to use in the trailer. Their creative decisions may well have been based on humour value and there is a difficult balance to make between humour and the very real effects that a warming planet is having upon its inhabitants, both human and more-than-human. On the other hand, while it is evident that aliens will not arrive with ice cold water to save us from a climate catastrophe, the anxiety expressed in this statement bears considering. There is a very real fear here that humans will *not* be able to find workable solutions to climate breakdown. There is also a recognition that *something* needs to be done to cool parts of the planet down. The children (and probably adults too) simply do not have the tools to realistically suggest what this might be.

Furthermore, the word *catastrophe* in the title of Cap-a-Pie's performance piece suggests something more sinister than the finished product offers, diminishing the catastrophic results of climate change that have been predicted. It is hard not to see this disparity between the possibility of catastrophe and the playful ways in which they are presented by Goudie-Hunter and Scarth as coming from the place of white Western privilege, a place where the reality of climate change still feels somewhat distant and unimaginable. Indeed, the UK is not yet under threat of rising sea levels in the same way that places like Bangladesh, Indonesia, China and India are. So, while playfulness can, and should, be a part of our engagement with planetary climate change, it bears remembering that the UK is geographically relatively well placed to avoid "climate change catastrophe" in quite the same way that more vulnerable areas are already experiencing.

Finally, unlike Cornelia Parker's collaborative project for *Dear Earth*, children do not appear in the finished performance of *Climate Change Catastrophe!* at all. In fact, the tag line, "Made by kids, for grown-ups" (Climate Change Catastrophe!, 2021) is particularly misleading, given the piece appears to be aimed at a very young demographic, possibly even pre-schoolers. The very positive collaborative aspects of the project, in which school children work with not only a theatre company, but also climate scientists and engineers, is lost in the final piece, which, for me, was the least successful part of the project. Since almost 400 children, from a range of schools, were invited to contribute, I question why they were not given the opportunity to appear in the final film. Perhaps Cap-a-Pie were adhering to Hannah Arendt's belief that, as Joseph Betz puts it, children "need privacy to grow and develop well. They should be kept away from the glare of floodlights, stage lights, camera lights" (Betz, 1992, p. 379). Whether Arendt has a point or not, children are unlikely to be kept away from any lights at all in a world that, to some extent, exposes everyone. And as climate anxiety amongst children is unlikely to diminish, it seems useful to consider a range of artistic responses to climate chaos which embraces play, playfulness, politics and performance, and includes children throughout the entire process, right up until the finished moment.

While the scope of the climate crisis may be overwhelming, theatre and performance can help us examine the decisions and values that have led to the current moment, and also motivate shifts in perception and practices to help mitigate the catastrophic effects of climate change in the future. In the UK, we still do not have an effective example of a traditional stage performance/play that welcomes children as characters with voices that matter. While writers and artists are working with children to make new work that foregrounds climate action, in many cases this work is not reaching the mainstream. Parker's *All at Sixes and Sevens* is probably the most effective example of reaching a wider audience, but even this is generally amongst those who are already sympathetic to, and knowledgeable about, climate change.

Children as Co–collaborators

I shall now consider two recent examples of collaborative work that puts children at the very centre of the process. The first is O'Donnell's Mammalian Diving Reflex, as mentioned earlier. Since 2012 the company have brought their project, *Night Walks with Teenagers*, to the UK on many occasions. The second is Tim Etchell's *That Night Follows Day*, performed at the Southbank Centre in 2018.

Night Walks with Teenagers "focuses on the power of walking together" (mammalian.ca) and was created with local youth who planned, designed and led public walks through cities such as Leeds, Newcastle and Bristol. In her review of the project, Lyn Gardner comments: "Mammalian Diving Reflex give agency to children and young people, and, in the process, help us reassess our relationship with them … All of which leads to the possibility that we might only be playing at being adults" (Gardner, 2015, para. 1–3). Gardner's comment pre-empts the questions posited by Hopkins (2019) earlier in my enquiry: "What if play were at the heart of the everyday – even for adults?" O'Donnell has harnessed this question, calling for a new social contract in which children act as co-collaborators in the artistic process. He offers a radical rethink of the relationship between generations, stating, "Children and young people should be folded much more into the decision-making processes that drive our society, the level of their participation read as a barometer of a given institution's commitment to human rights" (O'Donnell, 2018, p. 12). While Mammalian Diving Reflex do not specifically foreground climate related themes in their work, this statement bears consideration in the climate-focused work that is being made with children in the UK.

One theatre-maker who has taken up the mantle in this respect is Forced Entertainment's Tim Etchells, whose collaborative piece *That Night Follows Day* puts children's voices at the very centre of the performance. Made for an adult audience, Etchells explains on his website,

> *That Night Follows Day* speaks to the ways that adults project onto children, and to the ways that adults and children alike are both constrained and made by language as they try to describe their experiences and imagine their own futures.
>
> *(Etchells, n.d., para. 3)*

Etchells asks, "What are the rules that the adult world lays down? What are the expectations that it establishes? What kinds of things are young people told? What kind of restrictions do they operate under?" (Etchells, n.d.).

These pertinent questions add another dimension to the topic of children, theatre and climate change. What, indeed, are young people told about climate change, and how do they process this information? It is a complicated enough topic for adults to grapple with, embracing the fields of science, pro-test, sociology, colonialism and capitalism, to name just a few. The added Derridean impossibilities that language presents, are, for Etchells, further complicated by the imposition of an adult-centred language upon children, and the projection of an eco-anxiety that children might not feel. What both O'Donnell and Etchells seem to be exploring, in their radical work, are ways of engaging with children and young people at their own pace, and with equal input. Taking their cue from Walter Benjamin's claim that "the theater will unleash in children the most powerful energies of the future" (Benjamin, 2015, p. 202), both theatre makers harness these energies and allow them to flourish. Indeed, as one of the young contributors in *That Night Follows Day* explains: "All the power is in the hands of the young people".

Conclusion

Theatre has come a long way in its engagement with climate-related issues since, in 2009, the theatre critic Robert Butler suggested that "Perhaps theatre wasn't cut out to do green issues. Plays are about human relationships. Plays are about families" (Butler, 2009, para. 3). It doesn't need spelling out that green issues *are* about human relationships and families, so perhaps we have moved further than we think in addressing the theme of climate change in the theatre. However, there are still no traditional plays for adults in the UK that centre the concerns of children in respect of the climate. The three case stu-dies I have presented – site-specific work, educational collaboration, and visual art – may, then, be the medium through which this lacuna is addressed. There is no doubt an urgency in centring children in debates, projects and collaborative theatre-making about climate change given "the lives of today's children will increasingly be marked by climate change disruption before they reach middle age. Evidently, climate change will exceedingly be the defining issue of their time" (Trott, 2019, p. 43). As O'Donnell and Etchells both show us, to have any chance of success, creative projects involving children must allow them the opportunity to create work that they have been empowered to make. Rather than viewing children as the Romantics did as *unfinished*, or as Hannah Arendt (1954) argues, "not finished, but in a state of becoming" (p. 182), we might reimagine them as fully realized "beings at that moment" who are empowered to participate, collaborate and offer effective solutions to the threats facing us.

To end, asked about her views on how climate action can become embed-ded in society, co-leader of the Green Party in England and Wales, Carla Denyer argues:

> there is a huge role for artists, writers … everyone with a creative bent, because so many stories … that are set in the future, are apocalyptic, they envisage a future where humanity has really messed things up, or

they are set in a future where climate change doesn't really exist … I think we need more stories about where climate change does exist, and we solved it, and here's what our new society is like … humanity is a storytelling species and we need people to help us imagine that future so we can get to it.

(Denyer, 2024)

The climate crisis has been called a crisis of imagination. We cannot say the same about children. If children have the imagination to believe aliens might deliver ice cold water to cool down a city, or that a volcano is erupting in a small town in South Wales, they have the imagination to tell stories that are playful, climate-centred, and hopeful. It is for the adults to listen, and also recognize that, as Gardner says, we might only be playing at being adults in the first place.

As Alexandra Lakind and Chessa Adsit-Morris posit:

We subscribe to an energizing urgency, envisioning a pedagogy that obliges everybody to venture off the beaten path to meet the unexpected. In other words, this post-Anthropocene pedagogy is not about what we do with/to children. Rather, it hinges on (re)conceptualizing childhood and the associated norms we uphold or dismantle. We need alternative imaginaries for the near term … when humanity will be in the midst of dealing with the effects of climate change and the struggle against capitalism, instead of the post-apocalyptic "doom-and-gloom" stories that don't include imaginaries for grappling with these crises.

(Lakind & Adsit-Morris, 2018, p. 38)

At this current moment in time, we are bound to a future that we cannot predict. Children have been cited as a "resource to rescue us from the 'future we [adults] threaten' by functioning as "the connection to nature we [adults] have corrupted" (Sheldon, 2016, p. 39). I don't believe it is the job of children to rescue us from the future. However, perhaps if the creative industries were to harness the qualities that children possess – playfulness, imagination, incorruptibility – they might be able to take our hands and lead us to the future. In the face of the global crisis, there is no other choice. We must find ever more imaginative ways to engage the creative industries in addressing climate chaos. It might not be possible to conjure aliens with ice cubes, but if we listen, work with, and harness the qualities that children possess in the moment, the persuading might not be so hard after all.

Notes

1 Unpublished reflection notes.
2 Unpublished reflection notes.

3 Unpublished notes.
4 Unpublished reflection notes.
5 Unpublished reflection notes.

References

Arendt, H. (1954). The crisis in education. In H. Arendt, *Between past and future* (pp. 170–193). Penguin Books.

Arrighi, G. & Emeljanow, V. (2014). *Entertaining children: The participation of youth in the entertainment industry*. Palgrave Macmillan.

Barrett, N. & Mari, L. (2023, 4 July). *Kidstown*: Centring Welsh children's voices, imaginations and futures. National Theatre of Wales. https://www.nationaltheatrewales.org/press/kidstown.

Benjamin, W. (2015). Program for a proletarian children's theatre. In M. W. Jennings, H. Eiland & G. Smith. *Walter Benjamin: Selected writings, volume 2 part 1: 1927–1930* (pp. 201–206). Belknap Press of Harvard University Press.

Betz, J. (1992). An introduction to the thought of Hannah Arendt. *Transactions of the Charles S. Peirce Society*, 28(3), 379–422.

Butler, R. (2009, 22 May). Green shoots of climate-change theatre. *The Guardian*. https://www.theguardian.com/stage/theatreblog/2009/may/22/climate-change-theatre.

Chow, B. & O'Donnell, D. (2014). Young mammals: The politics and aesthetics of long-term collaboration with children in Mammalian Diving Reflex's The Torontonians. In G. Arrighi & V. Emeljanow, *Entertaining children: The participation of youth in the entertainment industry*. Palgrave Macmillan.

Climate change catastrophe! (2021). A new show about climate change, made by kids, for grown-ups. Cap-a-Pie Theatre Company. https://www.cap-a-pie.co.uk/shows/climate-change-catastrophe/.

Denyer, C. (2024). "Online questions" programme by Alex Forsyth. *BBC Sounds*. https://www.bbc.co.uk/sounds/play/m001yj7g.

De Waal, A. (2021). More future? Straight ecologies in British climate change theatre. *Journal of Contemporary Drama in English*, 1(9), 43–59.

Etchells, T. (n.d.). That night follows day. Timetchells. https://timetchells.com/projects/that-night-follows-day/.

Gardner, L. (2015, 16 Feb). In between time festival review. *The Guardian*. https://www.theguardian.com/stage/2015/feb/16/in-between-time-festival-review-bristol.

Hickman, C., Marks, E., Pihkala, P., Clayton, S., Lewandowski, R. E., Mayall, E. E., Wray, B., Mellor, C. & van Susteren, L. (2021). Climate anxiety in children and young people and their beliefs about government responses to climate change: a global survey. *Lancet Planet Health*, 5(12), 863–873.

Hopkins, R. (2019). *From what is – to what if: Unleashing the power of the imagination to create the future we want*. Chelsea Green Publishing.

Kirkwood, L. (2016). *The Children*. NBH Plays.

Lakind, A. & Adsit–Morris, C. (2018). Future child: Pedagogy and the post-anthropocene. *Journal of Childhood Studies*, 43(1), 30–43.

Macmillan, D. (2011). *Lungs*. Oberon Modern Plays.

Macmillan, D. & Rapley, C. (2016). *2071. The world we'll leave our grandchildren*. John Murray.

Maxwell, D. (2014, 8 Nov). *2071* at the Royal Court Jerwood Theatre. *The Times.* http s://www.thetimes.com/article/2071-at-the-royal-court-jerwood-theatre-2mgk5gchncv.

National Theatre Wales. (2018). *Report of the trustees and consolidated financial statements.* Watts Gregory LLP.

National Theatre Wales. (2023). *Report of the trustees and consolidated financial statements.* MHA LLP.

O'Donnell, D. (2018). *Haircuts by children and other evidence for a new social contract.* Coach House Books.

Parker, C. (2023). *All at sixes and sevens.* Three artworks. Dear Earth Exhibition, South Bank Centre. https://www.tate.org.uk/art/artists/cornelia-parker-cbe-ra-2358/ three-artworks-cornelia-parker-has-created-with-unusual-collaborators.

Ronder, T. (2015). *F*ck the polar bears.* Nick Hern Books.

Senior, A. (2016). Beginners on stage: Arendt, natality and the appearance of children in contemporary performance. *Theatre Research International*, 41(1), 70–84. https:// www.cambridge.org/core/journals/theatre-research-international/article/abs/beginner s-on-stage-arendt-natality-and-the-appearance-of-children-in-contemporary-p erformance/A01E2D20BDAD39F096A8AC4D6AA6928A.

Sheldon, R. (2016). *The child to come: Life atter human catastrophe.* University of Minnesota Press.

Simon, J. (2010). *What about the children? Benjamin and Arendt: On education, work, and the political.* Information Age Publishing. https://works.bepress.com/julesimon/9/.

Spence, R. (2023, 29 Jun). Cornelia Parker on art and the environment. *Financial Times.* https://www.ft.com/content/d8860266-39bf-4d34-bbe5-c9e314878968.

Trott, C. D. (2019). Reshaping our world: Collaborating with children for community-based climate change action, *Action Research*, 17(1), 42–62. https://www.buzzmag.co. uk/ntw-kidstown-nigel-barrett-louise-mari-unique-theatrical-experience/ https://mamma lian.ca/https://timetchells.com/ www.tate.org.uk.

5

THE CANCELLATION OF *THE FAMILY SEX SHOW*

James Peachey-Baker

In 1968 the Lord Chamberlain's authority to censor theatre productions ended. As Hellard, Nicholson and Handley (2004) note, "This system required that the Lord Chamberlain license every public theater [sic] production: from local pantomimes to grandiose performances in the West End" (p. 210). Prior to their staging, performance scripts were required to be submitted for scrutiny by the Lord Chamberlain's examiners who would, thereafter, assess their propriety for public consumption. Due to the office of Lord Chamberlain operating under the sanction of royal oversight, "he was under no obligation to explain his staff's decisions" (p. 210). Conclusions made to restrict works being mounted were often left uncontested by playwrights who "had no opportunity to appeal against his decisions" (p. 210). Specific principles, rules and documented codes of desired practice were never formalized under the Lord Chamberlain's jurisdiction and, as a result, proved nebulous and difficult for theatre makers to successfully navigate.

Since the abolition of the Lord Chamberlain's Office, British theatre makers and venues have been free to practise beyond the purview of formalized state sanctions and censorship; however, this isn't to suggest that artists have been entirely able to operate beyond cultural, societal, institutional pressures to curtail, moderate and subdue their given artistic content in response to moral, political, ethical or religion-based concerns (or indeed, a combination of these respective phenomena). Catherine O'Leary (2015) identifies how contemporary censorship is likely to derive from a multitude of decentralized sources and that a fusion of simultaneous pressures often results in the eventual censorship of content (p. 7). Some of these decentralized sources that lead to a specific case of performance censorship are discussed below within an interview transcript with Josie Dale-Jones of ThisEgg Theatre Company.

DOI: 10.4324/9781003470434-6

The interview addresses Dale-Jones' performance, *The Family Sex Show* (2019–2022); a performance commissioned by TheEgg, Theatre Royal Bath, in England. The performance was developed as part of the venue's Incubator Programme which was funded by the Leverhulme Trust and designed to develop ideas that "create exciting productions for young audiences" (Theatre Royal Bath, 2022). The performance was also supported by notable other venues and partner organizations including Shoreditch Town Hall, National Theatre Studios and Arts Council England.

The remit of the proposed project included an hour-long stage performance, a podcast and freely available online information including workshop activities for families that dealt with notions pertaining to sexuality, gender, boundaries and pleasure. The scope of the work was intended for children and families aged 5+ (*The Family Sex Show*, 2023). The performance was undertaken in consultation with the School of Sexuality Education, a charity located in the UK whose remit includes providing in-school workshops on consent, sexual health, porn and positive relationships (School of Sexuality Education, 2023).

Writing about the project in *The Guardian*, Dale-Jones (2022) described some of the principal aspirations of the work. She stated, "Its aim is to reimagine the way we think and talk about relationships and sex" and continues, "[the project] exists in the hope that it can be a part of breaking down some of the systems of oppression alive today" (para. 2). The content of the stage piece was described by Dale-Jones (2022) as, "a fun and playful performance made up of songs, dances and personal stories. It is about bodies and how society views them" (para. 2).

Even before the work was made available for public viewing the project received notable criticism in relation to its thematic and content. The work contained a sequence that garnered significant controversy wherein "everyone on stage takes their clothes off to the level they feel comfortable to. For some people, that's taking off all of their clothes and being completely naked" (*The Family Sex Show*, 2023). The act of undressing was described by Dale-Jones as an attempt "to present bodies as just that – bodies" (Dale-Jones, 2022, para. 6). Other examples of the furore levelled against the project surrounded the content of the show's accompanying website, which according to CitizenGo[1] (2023) featured "definitions of 'BDSM', 'frottage', 'hand job' and 'squirting'" (para. 3).

In April of 2022 a fervent online campaign was launched on CitizenGo in response to the marketing, publicity and online resources of *The Family Sex Show*. The campaign demanded that, "theatres immediately scrap the production!" (CitizenGo, 2022, para. 3). By the 19th of April 2022 the campaign had gathered significant momentum and media support. Enough so that ThisEgg posted a thread via Twitter (currently known as X) announcing that the proposed Spring 2022 tour of *The Family Sex Show* had been cancelled and that "violent and illegal threats and abuse" (ThisEgg, 2022) had been directed at "the company and venues by a small group of people with extremist views" (2022). At the time of writing, 41,474 people had signed the online petition hosted by CitizenGo. In an article about *The Family Sex Show* published by *Vice*, Sophia Smith Galer (2022) describes CitizenGo as "a controversial Spain-based advocacy group with links to the extreme Christian right in the US and Eastern Europe, whose intentions are to roll back legislation on abortion and LGBT rights" (para. 2).

Twitter responses to the announcement of the cancellation of the performance were polarized. Champions of the work sent messages of solidarity and well wishes; rueing the loss of a performance that might have "introduced young people to a safer sexual future in their teens" (Walford, 2022).

Whilst detractors questioned the safeguarding measures of the work as an exercise in "How to Sexualize kids for ADULTS" (AdultHumanFemale, 2022), Chantal Mouffe (2007) presents the notion that within public space, consensus can never emerge. Instead, she describes public space as a dimension for *dissensus* where contested ideologies, ideals, values and judgements collide. *The Family Sex Show* catalysed public dissensus; specifically in relation to the subject matter of child protectionism, LGBTQIA+ representation and safeguarding. Furthermore, Mouffe suggests that public space might be best understood through an agonistic model of democratic politics where disparate hegemonic positions compete with little hope for reconciliation or resolution. In relation to *The Family Sex Show*, Twitter became a powerful tool in platforming and amplifying dissensus.

What follows is an interview with Artistic Director of ThisEgg and Director of *The Family Sex Show*, Josie Dale-Jones.

JAMES: Can you tell me, in your own words and from your own viewpoint, the story of what happened with *The Family Sex Show*; from the commissioning stages through to the final production and podcast?

JOSIE: Yes. So, I wanted to make a show about relationships and sex education for young people. I run my own theatre company and the project was very small. This project was going to be three people in a room, making a show. Very quickly we realized it needed to be bigger; in terms of who was going to be involved in the making, the voices in the room and who was going to be on the stage. I was supported financially to develop the idea, do the in-depth research and scale it up in terms of the creative team. And as part of that, it was really important that I had people who really know about relationships and sex education as part of the team, so I made connections with different experts, charities and organizations who specialize in this. We had these experts as consultants and devised with lots of different collaborators over five years because it was such a massive topic and we wanted to do it properly and sensitively. And also, because fundraising in the subsidised theatre sector is generally quite difficult; especially when you've got a team that big; it's harder. So, it just took time and time was absolutely what it needed. When we were ready and after long conversations with venues about holding the production, I booked a tour. When we eventually had the money to make that tour happen, COVID happened. I wondered how the cultural landscape might shift during the pandemic and how a show might need to change shape to support that. I wondered if UK audiences might be more open for a show like this after COVID. I wondered if the space for conversation we wanted to make way for would still *need* to be created. During lockdown, people had time to really do some thinking about themselves and about some of the issues we covered in *The Family Sex Show*; consent, boundaries, gender, sexuality, etcetera. In the meantime, *Sex Education* had come out on Netflix and everyone was watching that. That was a very different offer to the show, but I was really pleased that lots of the same topics were being addressed and in the mainstream. We'd really purposefully not wanted to do film or TV or anything on screen, but *Sex Education* was a massive part of a cultural shift in talking about relationships and sex education with young people as well as adults. But what had also obviously happened over that period was how we use online platforms. Pre-tour, we'd done some training days at *The Family Sex Show*'s receiving venues to outline what responses we thought we might have to the show. And what adverse press we might get, how to answer frequently asked questions and the wellness of the front of house teams. I am not sure any of this made a difference. It is hard to prepare for something like what happened. Basically, we went back into rehearsals and then, although the tour had been announced for quite a while, somehow somewhere someone saw something they didn't like. It was the first week of rehearsals and I checked Twitter before I went into the rehearsal room and I saw a tweet that had tagged the *Daily Mail* about the show. I sent it to the people managing our press to say that it was there and half an hour later it had been picked up over and over; being shared and retweeted on a mass scale. We started having crisis meetings. We were taking all of the performers' and creative team's names off of the website and everything, because we were all already being targeted individually. And then it was that weekend that all of the press got hold of the story and published whatever they could find and sort of, whatever they wanted. We carried on rehearsing because the cast and venue were still content going ahead with it and because, making theatre is our job and this was our current work. The profile of the show continued to grow online and in the press. This caused lots of phone calls and emails to venues and their staff. There were multiple threats to people; the creative team and venues. The police and local authorities were made aware. They took the situation seriously and were understanding of our position. They offered security around the performances on tour, for example. By this point members of the public were saying that they were going to protest, but people are allowed to protest. It was more about how we managed that and made the performances feel like a safe enough place for families to visit and experience the show. Then a petition started to get the show shut down. And tens of thousands of people signed that. Wild. This was a small-scale touring show in the UK that maybe 3,000 people might have eventually seen. At this point, just before our final week of rehearsals, the venues decided not to go ahead with the planned tour dates. The show was cancelled. In short, the fallout of this was financial as well as reputational. I am still, two years on, asked to assess the reputational damage of working with me in this country.

JAMES: It's so useful to hear your narration of what happened. When and what the key points were. I wasn't aware of the catalysation of someone tagging the *Daily Mail*. It seemed like *The Family Sex Show* was a bit of a departure in terms of theme and content to some of your previous work. Is that a fair deduction?

JOSIE: I mean, yes and no. I always make stuff that has got a political edge to it or that is linked to a social injustice of some sort. Another show I had made, *dressed*, was rooted in an experience of sexual assault. *The Family Sex Show* was asking questions like "where does the power imbalance and the different forms of manipulation and abuse start?" We don't openly talk about this in our society. It can start in the playground. We wanted to make something for young people that might be part of offering a more consensual version of relationships.

JAMES: I wonder whether in the fundraising stage, *The Family Sex Show* was more difficult to procure support for because of its content and themes? Or was it comparable to a lot of the other projects you've done before?

JOSIE: Initially I got the funding first round every time with Arts Council England. After COVID that became more difficult.

JAMES: As I understand it, the receiving venues for the project were in discussion with one another and wanted a unified approach as to whether to cancel the show. Were they the ones who ultimately made the decision to cancel the work?

JOSIE: As in who made the call?

JAMES: Yeah.

JOSIE: Venues.

JAMES: Right.

JOSIE: Yeah. It was really disappointing. Not just that they'd cancelled the show, but the signal that they were sending out by cancelling was loud and it was clear. By cancelling the show, they were cancelling what the show stood for, which really was equality and a celebration of difference. If you say that you're an inclusive venue, that you want to be anti-racist, that you want to be queer inclusive, that you want to invite disabled artists in, then you need to stand behind those convictions. That's not to underestimate the pressure that the venues and their staff were under. We're human and we need to look after the people around us. At the same time, these kinds of shows can be acts of resistance and they can be a form of activism.

JAMES: Yeah. I was reading someone's Ph.D. on censorship and children's theatre,[2] which I think had it been written later on, your piece would very much be at the forefront of. In it, the author was writing about a conference that she attended where there was also someone from the Belarus Free Theatre[3] talking about how, in failing to fund risky work, or allowing it a platform, the net result is that artists feel unable to address difficult subject matter. And by doing so, resistance or pushback to discourses that prohibit people from being themselves and developing an inclusive community are undermined. Essentially artmaking becomes more sanitized and generic. I'm interested in the rhetoric around the decision to cancel the performance. Presumably venues aren't explicitly saying that the work is, in some way, going too far and that the content has upset too many people to justify staging it. But that the safety risk to venue staff is too great. Which, of course, must be a consideration. Whether it's *the* consideration predominantly driving the decision, is perhaps more nebulous.

JOSIE: Ah, there's always that ambiguity around it. Yeah.

JAMES: Nevertheless, it does send out a particular message, doesn't it?

JOSIE: I think that there was a fear of losing audience over the show, which I can understand, especially post-COVID. There was so much worry about re-establishing audience and about even more financial loss. But it's also interesting because as far as I know, *The Family Sex Show* wasn't selling any worse than other shows. And most of the backlash was not coming from people in England, so it was not going to actively impact any audience relationships.

JAMES: Short of your own previous work, were there any existing works from other companies that inspired the making of this show?

JOSIE: I've always been interested in children's theatre in this country and the form of children's theatre next to "adult" theatre. Stylistically, *The Family Sex Show* was not a traditional show or what we would usually expect to see programmed for kids in the UK. It's much more European in form.

JAMES: There's a book called *Not in Front of the Children* (2007) that talks about propriety and censorship in relation to children. And in that, the author identifies this close connection between the innate conservative cultural values of the UK and America. But it also suggests that, as a nation we're close enough to Europe to know that other more progressively liberal things are happening in relation to the treatment of children. And although it does feel like the UK is part of that liberal culture to some degree, it also seems completely divorced from it in others. It's interesting you mentioned a European theatre-making sensibility because, to me, that differentiation between adult and child doesn't seem to be quite so entrenched on the continent, perhaps as it does here. I just wanted to ask about the role of social media and the online campaign that had the show shut down. Which proved so significant in the journey of the show. The online commentary around the work was incredibly divisive and polarizing. Was that a surprise to you, or something that you'd envisaged prior to announcing the show?

JOSIE: I thought that there would be people that didn't like the idea of the show. I didn't think that it would escalate this quickly; before we had done a single performance. We were ready to enter a dialogue with people who had questions about the show, but less ready for people who didn't want a conversation, less ready for trolls I guess. The online commentary felt really one sided. And as soon as someone tried to offer a different opinion, they got personally harassed. "Supporters" of the show would end up sending me a private message saying, "I'm so sorry, but I had to come off socials because I stuck up for you but they won't leave me alone so I have deleted my comment and am coming off socials". On top of that, none of the bigger organizations who were involved in supporting us – the venues and the funders – ever put out a statement to say that what was being said online wasn't true. So, by cancelling the show and publicly removing funding, it looked like we were exactly what people online were painting us to be. No one ever publicly backed us. Which is why it's been hard to work since.

JAMES: Yeah of course. I'm so sorry.

JOSIE: I mean, it's all just wild.

JAMES: Yeah, it's horrible. And the material from social media in response to the work is uncomfortable to read. Even if you have an absolute detachment from the project. I wonder why you think theatre is an interesting or valuable context within which to address what might be perceived as taboo issues with young people, as opposed to other mediums?

JOSIE: I think there's something about a real-life human being, talking to another real-life human being. When audiences see something online, or on their screens, or listen to something, the artist doesn't necessarily have much control over the context. Over how people consume those things. As a consumer, you can easily start an episode of something halfway through. There's something about theatre where the audience have made a commitment, ideally at least, to come from the beginning and stay until the end. To go through a whole journey together rather than dip in and out. And I think theatre and maybe cinema, are the only times that we get to do that. And I think for me that's a really important part of it. Theatre is just bringing people together. And I don't think that I necessarily have any answers, but I absolutely want to have open conversations about taboo subjects. And of course, it's totally possible to listen to a podcast on your own and then have a conversation with a mate about it. But it's different from having experienced it together. Knowing that someone else has seen it and you can have a conversation about it, and there's not much else that does that.

JAMES: I remember from touring Bootworks' show about bereavement,[4] there was a particularity about the space carved out after the experience where families would often hang around and meet the characters in the show and talk about bereavements they might have had. There's something about theatre being dialogic, isn't there? For me, there's something specific about the reciprocity of theatre that isn't offered by other mediums. And, in terms of the cancellation of the show, you've really got to go out of your way to be outraged by a theatre show because to be offended by it, you've got to buy a ticket, you've got to drive your family to the theatre, you've got to be there at a set time and space. You've got to block it out in your calendar. Your show has not snuck up on anyone in their living rooms whilst flicking through the channels.

JOSIE: Yeah, yeah it's really active. You really have to decide to go.

JAMES: As small-scale touring theatre artists, I think there's a propensity to question from time to time, whether your work has made much impact. If you really wanted to change the world and change people's perceptions, you'd do a Netflix series, right? But your piece has really catalysed a conversation: 47,000 signatures from around the world campaigning to stop the show. That's real reach.

JOSIE: The press around the show has reached 1.8 billion people. And the strength of the reaction does suggest that the arts does have value and we are intimidated by its potential power. Which you know, if we want to be positive, we'll take that from it.

JAMES: So, what were the elements of the show that proved most controversial?

JOSIE: We never really set an age guidance. We just said that it was suitable for five years old plus. It's a family show. You can come along as a family. And what we meant by that was that there's nothing in the show that a five-year-old is not allowed to see. And we decided that in close consultation with all sorts of organizations. So, it's okay if a five-year-old comes. It doesn't mean we made it *for* five-year-olds, but that's obviously the idea that people latched on to; that this is a show for five-year-olds. That was one thing. And the other was that we said that there was nakedness in the show. Which there was in one moment of the show, there was a moment where some performers were topless. We were transparent about that on the content note for the show, along with the themes including gender and sexuality. From this though, somehow, most of the conversation was then around turning children gay and the company of performers being paedophiles. The language around it was dated. Really old-school homophobia, transphobia, often also racist and misogynist.

JAMES: So, some of the outrage felt like it was a mask for something else? Almost like an attack on cultural otherness?

JOSIE: I think it was. Yeah.

JOSIE: I got an email just the other day, probably 500 words or so, comparing me to Jimmy Savile. To which I thought to myself, "Oh, lovely. It's still happening". It's been 18 months now. The email asked me to "please stop the show". The show was never on!

JAMES: I think one of the things that COVID did was give people time and space to think and consider their position in the world and more fervently express their outrage at cultural events. I'm thinking about the George Floyd killing, for instance. Black men are being wrongfully murdered in America by police year on year, right? And yet here's a particular instance that garnered wider public outrage. I'm interested in how these individual moments help catalyse commentary on a wider social issue. At that time, it felt like people had greater time and capacity to be outraged because they weren't at work. They could really invest in the cause of it.

JOSIE: Yeah. Have you read *So You've Been Publicly Shamed*, by Jon Ronson?

JAMES: No.

JOSIE: I really recommend it. It's really interesting in terms of the role of social media. At one point there's a comparison to social media storms being the equivalent of a public hanging. Where social media has taken over from that and people are getting justice from basically putting someone on the stake, but online.

JAMES: People revel in it, don't they? I really dislike cancel culture. And it seems to be a strategy adopted by both the right and left. For me, to be liberal minded means that you're invested in discourse and dialogue and argumentation. But at this point in time, it seems that if you don't like something, often the tendency is to just try to shut it down. You cancel it; and that doesn't seem useful in furthering any kind of cultural debate.

JOSIE: Yeah. And there are absolutely people that I wish didn't shout their opinions so loudly with their ears covered. But I would rather that everyone's able to have an opinion and share it. I was on a panel at the National Theatre in relation to their staging of *The Crucible*. I think I was framed as the witch that had been hunted or whatever. Great. And I was asked whether if J. K. Rowling was going to give a lecture at a university, I would try and stop it from happening? And my response was, "No". Our politics are absolutely and completely different, but I wouldn't stop her lecture from happening. I would just hope that people had enough critical thought to be able to listen to what she had to say and decide upon their own opinion. That is also the other thing: do we have an education system in which we're taught to think for ourselves? That's part of the problem, right?

JAMES: There were also concerns raised that were directed at the online activity resources in relation to the show. Which seemed to be addressing sexual practices that I don't know how I feel about discussing with children. Because when I say I'm an advocate of talking to kids about sex, I'm probably thinking of fairly normative forms of sex. Pegging, for instance, was one term that was explained on the performance's website. How did you conclude which sexual practices kids should know about?

JOSIE: We had a glossary on the website. The website acted as a repository for information about the show *and* the podcast. We were not doing anything about BDSM or pegging in the show. I don't think kids need to know about that. But it's OK if they hear or see the words. The decision that we ended up coming to when considering whether we keep these words on our website was that if the website is a resource for people to use to find out what things mean, then typing in "pegging" to Google is going to be worse than them coming on to our website and looking at the definition of what pegging is. And that sort of ended up being our decision-making process – that this might be a safer way to understand something than the world wide web.

JAMES: The controversial screenshot from your company's website that kept on being reposted on social media contained information about animals and masturbation. The screenshot contained the suggestion that families, "use the internet to find some examples of other animals that masturbate" and to "draw the animals you found". Not knowing what I might find, I googled "animals and masturbation" to see what kind of "questionable" materials it might return. However, ultimately, it just provided lots of interesting information about dolphins. It strikes me that the public's projected comprehension of what the show *might* be and what this Google search *might* return has created a hysteria that operates beyond the reality of the material circumstance. If you really leaned into this, you could market yourself as the latest coercive, dangerous, radical theatre maker. Not that you necessarily want to; but in some contexts that might play well.

JOSIE: I guess I could go to Europe and sell myself as this radical, banished artist. It's all about the branding.

JAMES: If you were to do the project again, is there anything that you would have done differently? Would you have reconsidered any content in the show?

JOSIE: It's a question I get a lot. And here's the conclusion. In terms of the actual show, I would not change anything. I would not like to change the way that we describe the show or the information that we gave to audiences ahead of booking the show. I don't want to take away the content note or the age guidance. I would change the title. I don't know what to.

Mostly I would want to be open and transparent and honest with audiences and I would want them to consent to bringing their children and knowing what they were coming to watch. But I think on one level – and I'm not saying that this is the way that I want to go – but on one level, this whole experience has just taught me to just put on a show and don't tell anyone what's going to happen. A lot of people have just said, "Oh, you were just too honest". And I'm like, "Well, then I'm happy that this is who I am". But also, what a messy world this is then.

JAMES: When we toured *The Many Doors of Frank Feelbad* (Bootworks' show about dying for children), on the flyer accompanying the work, the first line was "Frank's lost his mum". Which I felt was pretty clear in inferring the content of the show. But one parent asked that we be more specific about the content of the piece, so we changed the copy to describe the work as, "a show about bereavement for families". Once we had bowed to that request and changed the marketing, it really negatively impacted ticket sales thereafter because it sounded like it was going to be this harrowing experience at the theatre. So, it's just really difficult to get right. *The Lion King*'s about dying and Disney doesn't state at the beginning of the film that Mufasa's going to die. You want people to see your work without being deterred. It's a very difficult balance. It strikes me that in offering content information to audiences ahead of the performance that you were trying to do all the things that a conscientious, responsible theatre maker would do and it's cost you. But then for future productions, where does that leave the sector? The danger of all this is that we've now got a foreseeable future of safe, middle-of-the-road theatre-making for children in the UK. And venues become more risk averse. For the latest show that we're[5] making with nine-year-olds (*NINE*, 2019) there's a moment in the work where we ask the young people involved, "What do you know about this that adults don't think you know about?" The kids in the past have talked about sex, rape, the situation in Israel and Palestine, Father Christmas not being real, ketamine. It's revelatory to a lot of parents and adults what the children know. But I think a lot of parents prefer the ignorance of not knowing. And although the show has always been well-received, I wonder whether parents would sign their children up to perform in the work if they knew in advance what their kids might disclose.

JOSIE: I don't have kids and I'm not super young, but I'm also not old. I also know that kids now have got such a different childhood to what we had and we will never be able to understand the things that they know that we didn't. They have access to so much, they have these electronic devices readily to hand. It's just different and we'll never be able to protect them from whatever we think they need protecting from. It's not in our control, but we can help them to navigate their way through.

JAMES: There's a report that gets released every year in the US[6] and it's for ageing academics to try and bridge the gap between their generation and the generation of freshman students that they're going to be teaching. It contains information about what's happened over the last eighteen years and how culture has changed. And I remember one year it said that for this generation, the Twin Towers has always been rubble. And that made me think, "wow" I remember that as a cognitive memory, but they have only ever experienced that as a part of history. One year it said that pornography, for this generation, had never been something hidden under the bed. I'm not so old there wasn't the internet during my formative years but pornography, to me, was often a naked image being slowly loaded at 56Kbps. So, the wildest sexual fantasy was always, to some degree, being driven by my own capacity to imagine. It wasn't the case of having the whole internet at your immediate disposal. Where you can see absolutely anything you might want to see. Or stumble across things you might not already be conscious of. Whereas I think now, kids are growing up in a context where they can see every form of sex imaginable. And therefore, navigating what sex is for them is so difficult. Negotiating that must be overwhelming.

JOSIE: It's really, really hard. Yeah.

JAMES: But that's why your piece would have been so valuable. Is there anything else that you want this interview to cover that feels important to you, in conveying your perspective on things?

JOSIE: I don't know. There are all sorts. I think I'm just mostly still just sat here, with a big question mark over my head. I'm like, "What is going on? What do we all want really?" There are multiple different angles – and they all intersect. But I think we've covered all the big ones like cancel culture, censorship, children's theatre in the UK, how we think about children in England, freedom of expression, all those things.

JAMES: Great.

JOSIE: It's sort of funny that the critics got the opposite of what they wanted. They made this play a thing.

JAMES: I'm desperately trying to find the term for an event or a moment that typifies a culture war. In the same way the George Floyd killing is emblematic of a much wider cultural concern. That it's not the only thing that's happening, but it's a form of catalyst that mobilizes a discourse.

JOSIE: That's what I was trying to say the whole time, when it was all happening, I was talking to other theatre makers and saying "regardless of what you've read or what you think, something fishy is going on here and this won't be the last time it happens. Can we have a conversation about what this means for all of us together?" Because I don't think that this is just about the show. I think this is about something that is happening more widely. And nobody's paying attention to it.

(End of interview)

What has been discussed above is a specific example of where a segment of the public, a funding body, programming venues, project partners and performance makers all intersect in contributing to the cancellation of a theatre performance. The transcript also highlights the power of online social media, in this instance X, in helping mobilize discourses encouraging censorship of live theatrical works. Jon Ronson (2015) identifies X as a medium that operates largely beyond the influence of "the criminal justice system or the media" (p. 179) in which "we [the public] make our own decisions about who deserves obliteration" (p.179). What is clear is that, in the 21st century, social media has helped amplify public discourse around theatrical productions and complicate the previous hierarchical logics of theatre censorship; and at such a rapid pace that venues, funders and theatre-makers struggle to navigate the complexities of deciding upon a proportional response to public dissensus. Only time will reveal whether Lyn Gardner's premonition materializes when she writes that the success of the critics on X in cancelling *The Family Sex Show*, "will only encourage them to set their sights on other shows whose content and intent they wish to misconstrue" (Gardner, 2022).

Online critics of *The Family Sex Show* suggested that the piece normalized, "the nudity of unknown adults in front of children" (Dr Em, 2022, para. 1) claiming that, "By bringing children to this show, parents are highlighting that they have weak boundaries to predators and that they are not aware of the risks" (Dr Em, 2022, para. 7). And furthermore that, "There is no difference between taking children to *The Family Sex Show* and taking them to a seedy peep show or strip club!" (CitizenGo, 2022, para. 3). Whilst proponents of the work might contend that children "need access to information and ideas precisely because they are in the process of becoming functioning members of society and cannot really do so if they are kept in ideological blinders until they are 18" (Heins, 2007, p. 12). The evidently polarized dissensus surrounding the thematic and content of *The Family Sex Show* created what Darren O'Donnell (2006) describes as a "social discomfort" (p. 31) which he advocates as a quality that is, "often necessary if we have any interest in increasing our social intelligence" (p. 31). He continues in identifying antagonism in artmaking as a requisite quality for increasing our social understanding around a given subject matter. However, in this case, the work at the source of this social discomfort and antagonism was prematurely ended. The potential for further discourse was abruptly cut short and therefore our capacity to better understand the complexities of the content addressed within the performance become lost.

One result of this censorship has been the removal of choice from parents and children who might otherwise wish to engage with the work. Perhaps this constitutes a severe penalty given the robust content warnings that accompanied the proposed performance. As Ott (2008) recognizes, "Theatre is a communal activity and children do not attend alone but accompanied by a parent, teacher or guardian" (p. 7). As such, theatre, through its shared experience, may be one of the more useful mediums within which adults can address controversial, complex or taboo subject matter alongside young people. What is more, the cancellation of the work may well have set a dangerous precedent to audiences and artists. As Gardner (2022) points out in her article about *The Family Sex Show* for *The Stage*, the cancellation of the work "raises questions for artists about what they can make and for whom and how they can make it safely and present it in ways that will keep artists, venue staff and audiences safe." She continues,

> You may think that cancelling one show is not so significant. But it is, particularly in a climate in which both the government and certain sections of the population are increasingly hostile to the arts and to the liberal values it espouses.
>
> *(Gardner, 2022)*

The decision to cancel *The Family Sex Show* speaks to certain attitudes, prevalent within the UK, levelled at children. "Anglophone culture has been engrossed by the innocent or sexually endangered child and its socially pathologized counterpart, the erotic or sexually knowing child" (Renold et al., 2015, p. 3). Both depictions of the child offered here convey the fictional binary often at play when describing British children. Children are commonly positioned as, "symbolic figures as opposed to material actors" (p. 3). It is my contention that performances for, and with, children are particularly likely to court controversy and emotionally driven responses from the public due to this propensity to comprehend children as symbolic totems for innocence. As Helen Freshwater (2013) attests, "cultural anxieties around the child remain strong enough to prevent intellectual engagement" (p. 181). Failure to cognitively perceive the child as they are, as opposed to how we might emotively wish them to be, risks visceral impulses to protect children prohibiting their access to information that may well help serve them to stay safe. David Archard (2015) posits the notion that determining childhood as a time of asexual innocence is fraught with danger because it is commonly the ideal of "purity, virginity, freshness and immaculateness which excites by the possibilities of possession and defilement" (p. 40). Denying children access to robust and detailed sex education has further safety implications. Children cannot describe unwanted sexual encounters to trusted adults if they don't have the vocabulary and comprehension necessary to describe what happened. As such, a child's limited access to information about sex helps protect the abuser. It's a phenomenon which will persist for as long as "Children and sex are seen as antithetical" (Jackson & Scott, 2004, p. 235).

Dale-Jones' appearance as the emblematic witch placed on trial at the National Theatre's post-show discussion of Arthur Miller's *The Crucible* might seem apt, given the circumstances under which the original text was written. Just as Miller faced the weight of imposed censorship as part of the "Red Hunt" led by Senator Joseph R. McCarthy under the auspices of the House Committee on Un-American Activities, X has functioned as its own contemporary crucible within which public opinion has galvanized around what is perceived as being a righteous cause. The cancellation of *The Family Sex Show* has been the unfortunate by-product of what Peter Bradshaw (2015) summarizes as X's "instant-Salem culture of shame". The cancellation of *The Family Sex Show* might prove to be a watershed moment for British theatre censorship. It will be interesting to see how programming choices, funding decisions and artistic trajectories continue to be shaped by the notoriety of this work and the public's diverse response to it.

Notes

1 CitizenGO describes itself as, "a community of active citizens who work together, using online petitions and action alerts as a resource, to defend and promote life, family and freedom" (CitizenGo, 2023).
2 Sallis, T. (2019). "A front line analysis of controversy and censorship in contemporary British theatre". Doctoral dissertation, University of Winchester. Elsevier.
3 Natalia Kaliada, Director of the Belarus Free Theatre.
4 *The Many Doors of Frank Feelbad/Being Frank* (2015).
5 Bootworks Theatre.
6 Previously called the Beloit College Mindset List (1998–2018). Latterly renamed The Marist Mindset List.

References

AdultHumanFemale. (@Women_Stand_Up]. (2022). How to sexualize kids for ADULTS? Tweet. Twitter. https://x.com/women_stand_up/status/1516439622720622595?s=46&t=LaXIE1Q2RDSVEFAW96FmFw.

Archard, D. (2015). *Children, rights and childhood.* Routledge.

Bradshaw, P. (2015). Here come the Oscars: Still a cruel joke in a cruel town. https://www.theguardian.com/commentisfree/2015/feb/18/oscars-awards-night-winner-tv.

CitizenGo. (2022). Scrap The Family Sex Show. https://citizengo.org/en-gb/fm/207302-scrap-family-sex-show.

Dale-Jones, J. (2022, 10 May). Cancel culture? My play was shut down by rightwing activists before it even opened. *The Guardian.* https://www.theguardian.com/commentisfree/2022/may/10/cancel-culture-rightwing-activists-family-sex-show.

DrEm. (2022). Why are we allowing "The Family Sex Show"? *The Critic.* https://thecritic.co.uk/why-are-we-allowing-the-family-sex-show/.

Freshwater, H. (2013) Children and the limits of representation in the work of Tim Crouch. *Contemporary British Theatre: Breaking New Ground,* 1, 167–188.

Gale, S. S. (2022, 28 April). How a global hard-right Christian group helped cancel a sex education play. *Vice News.* https://www.vice.com/en/article/dypbew/family-sex-show-citizengo.

Gardner, L. (2022, 25 April). Theatre should be concerned by the cancellation of The Family Sex Show. *The Stage.* https://www.thestage.co.uk/opinion/theatre-should-be-concerned-by-the-cancellation-of-the-family-sex-show.

Heins, M. (2007). *Not in front of the children; Indecency, censorship and the innocence of youth.* Rutgers University Press.

Hellard, D. S., Nicholson, S. & Handley, M. (2004). *The Lord Chamberlain regrets … A history of British theatre censorship.* British Library.

Jackson, S. & Scott, S., (2004). Sexual antinomies in late modernity, *Sexualities,* 7(2), 233–248.

Mouffe, C. (2007). Artistic activism and agonistic spaces. *Art and Research: A Journal of Ideas, Contexts and Methods,* 1(2), 1–5. https://chisineu.files.wordpress.com/2012/07/biblioteca_mouffe_artistic-activism.pdf.

O'Donnell, D. (2006). *Social acupuncture: A guide to suicide, performance and Utopia.* Coach House Books.

O'Donnell, D. (2018). *Haircuts by children and other evidence for a new social contract.* Coach House Books.

O'Leary, C. (2015). Introduction: Censorship and creative freedom. In C. O'Leary, D. Santos Sanchez & M. Thompson (Eds.), *Global insights on theatre censorship* (pp. 1–30). Routledge.

Ott, M. (2008). *Child actor ethics: Children in plays with adult themes.* Lambert Academic Publishing. Renold, E., Ringrose, J. & Egan, R. D. (2015). *Children, sexuality and sexualisation.* Palgrave Macmillan.

Ronson, J. (2015). *So you've been publicly shamed.* Picador.

School of Sexuality Education. (2023). School of sexuality education; Supporting schools to provide relationships & sex education. The School of Sexuality Education Website. https://schoolofsexed.org/.

Smith Gailer, S. (2022). How a global hard-right Christian group helped cancel a sex education play. *Vice News.* https://www.vice.com/en/article/dypbew/family-sex-show-citizengo.

Theatre Royal Bath. (2022). Incubator programme. https://www.theatreroyal.org.uk/support/current-projects/#:~:text=The%20Incubator%20is%20an%20ideas,plays%20for%20children%20and%20families.

The Family Sex Show. (2023). The Family Sex Show – I have so many questions. Website. https://thefamilysexshow.com/faq.

ThisEgg. (@ThisEgg_) (2022, 19 April). The Family Sex Show: Cancelled before it opened - where do we go from here? Tweet thread. Twitter. https://x.com/thisegg_/status/1516336468784029698?s=46&t=LaXIE1Q2RDSVEFAW96FmFw.

Walford, R. (@BeckyWalford). (2022, 19 April). I'm so sorry this happened. Being informed only makes us all safer. This was carefully structured with safeguarding experts … . Tweet. Twitter. https://x.com/beckywalford/status/1516480876552486915?s=46&t=LaXIE1Q2RDSVEFAW96FmFw.

PART 2

Adaptation and Appropriation

6

A TALE OF TEMPTATION AND REDEMPTION

Staging Christina Rossetti's *Goblin Market* for a Young Audience

Ester Díaz Morillo

Introduction

The Victorian poet Christina Rossetti first published her well-known poem *Goblin Market* in 1862. Narrating the story of sisters Laura and Lizzie and how they confront the temptation of the goblin merchants selling their fruits, this poem has received much scholarly attention and many interpretations, and it has also been adapted for the stage several times. Not intended as an allegory according to Rossetti, the uncertainty of the poem has prompted it to be read allegorically by many scholars. In that sense, *Goblin Market* has been studied from many different perspectives, from feminism to a Christian standpoint. One point where all interpretations tend to coincide, however, is the sexual and homoerotic undertones of Rossetti's poem. It is precisely this ambiguity and sensuousness in *Goblin Market* that lures artists to offer their own interpretations.

This chapter will explore how Kath Burlinson and Conor Mitchell adapted Rossetti's poem for a young British cast and a young audience in 2003 for the Youth Music Theatre UK company, paying special attention to how they dealt with the inherent sensuousness and potential sexual content of Rossetti's verses. This chamber opera, performed by young artistes aged 11–17, was composed for six female soloists, a large chorus and orchestra, with all the main roles played by girls, and was aimed at teenagers over 12. The production focuses on the sisters' youth, as Rossetti does in her poem, and chooses accordingly a young cast to do so. This is what makes this theatrical production so compelling to be thoroughly examined, as it is portrayed by and aimed at young people, while the source poem has experienced a long tradition of being targeted at a varied audience. As Lorraine Janzen Kooistra (1994) explains, Rossetti's *Goblin Market* makes a very interesting case study

DOI: 10.4324/9781003470434-8

due to its history of crossing audience boundaries, for it was first published for an adult audience, but later reinterpreted for a younger audience to the extent that *Goblin Market* has become a classic of children's literature, notwithstanding the sexual and (homo)erotic tensions in the poem which have even caused it to be featured in a *Playboy* publication (p. 249).

After briefly discussing the numerous interpretations which *Goblin Market* has been given, this chapter will explore the ambiguity and sensuousness of the poet's language so as to fully understand the difficulties and challenges of adapting this poem for a young audience in the 21st century. Following that line, for instance, when Lizzie suffers the assault of the goblins, the depiction could be regarded as an attempted rape with its violent imagery. Further, the moment which sees Lizzie returning home to Laura can be given a Christian interpretation, due to its Eucharistic resonances. It is an instance of breaking out of domestic confines and feminine propriety, and yet it is a passage full of homoerotic imagery. Moreover, both female and male teenagers play the goblins, which can be viewed as typical Gothic creatures meant to evoke terror and disgust; they represent an uncanny presence which haunts the characters, and their fruits associate them with seductive and destructive sexuality.

The next sections of the chapter will fully centre on Burlinson's and Mitchell's theatrical adaptation for the British stage. Engaging at times with previous studies on different musical adaptations of Rossetti's works by Mary Arseneau and Sharon Aronofsky Weltman, these sections will offer a comparison between the production and the source poem in order to see their similarities and divergences, but also to explore what is being adapted and what has been omitted, as well as the potential implications of these decisions. There will be a focus on which aspects of the source text this chamber opera emphasizes and on the portrayal of the sexual ambiguity so prominent in *Goblin Market*. By looking at the depiction of gender and sexuality in this adaptation for a young audience, we will be able to observe how the composers make direct connections with the present time.

Further, this is a poem which recounts a female experience of temptation, fall and redemption, where a sister acts as a female Christ figure in order to save her sibling, stressing the importance of sisterhood. Consequently, this chapter will concentrate on how this musical offers new perspectives on the poem and suggests potential dialogues between the poem and contemporary issues. Especially relevant will be the portrayal of the (homo)sexual connotations of the poem and its gender dynamics. In brief, this chapter will analyse how musicians re-present and interpret the poem according to their own contemporary concerns, using *Goblin Market* as a mirror of modern issues. This musical adaptation, in fact, focuses on the female experience and the path to maturity, and it does not shy away from presenting sexual threats, the temptations of adolescence, and the darkness in Rossetti's poem, providing new ways of examining *Goblin Market* and breathing new life into the poem.

One Poem, Myriad Interpretations

Christina Rossetti's poem *Goblin Market* (1862) narrates the story of Laura and Lizzie, two sisters living together and who are allured by the tempting cries of goblin merchants chanting about the delicious qualities of the fruit they sell. Rossetti was quick to declare that she had not meant to write the poem as an allegory, and yet this is precisely how *Goblin Market* has been mostly read. William Michael Rossetti, the poet's brother, was among the first ones to note this when he wrote in his notes to *The Poetical Works of Christina Georgina Rossetti* (1904) that "[s]till the incidents are such as to be at any rate suggestive, and different minds may be likely to read different messages into them" (p. 459). From that moment, numerous scholars have analysed the poem from many different points of view, and the interpretations it has received keep on increasing in number and variety. It is possible to find multiple feminist readings, but also several scholarly texts from the Christian perspective. Though it may look straightforward, *Goblin Market* proves to be still one of the most enigmatic poems in the English language. In addition to this ambiguity, many have also noted the sexual connotations and even homoerotic undertones which can be traced in these verses. Paradoxically, this highly contrasts with the fact that the poem has been considered a children's classic, most probably because of the fantasy and fairy-tale elements behind which hide the potential sexual nuances, and which largely contributed to the illustrations made from the early 20th century on, such as those by Arthur Rackham.

Among the most important and frequent perspectives from which the poem has been interpreted is the feminist. Scholars in this line have regarded *Goblin Market* most especially as a tale of female resistance and sisterhood. As noted by Jan Marsh (2012), Rossetti was volunteering at Highgate Penitentiary, an institution for the reformation of "fallen women" (p. 229) when she wrote the poem. Hence, the poem could be seen as a moral allegory for those who, like Laura, had fallen from virtue. Furthermore, *Goblin Market* can be read from a Christian standpoint, for Rossetti was a devout Christian who also wrote many religious poems. Mary Arseneau (1993) has written about the Eucharistic language and imagery employed by Rossetti, particularly when Lizzie, as a female Christ-figure, sacrifices her own body for her sister's sake and then offers it to Laura for her to drink and eat, which finally leads to Laura's full restoration (pp. 89–90). These two are the most interesting perspectives for the purposes of this chapter, yet *Goblin Market* has been read from myriad angles, including Marxist criticism, new historicism, Freudianism, queer theory, ecocriticism, ecofeminism, among others. In brief, that ambiguous quality which permeates the poem enables us to read it from different perspectives and find new levels of meaning behind its saturating imagery. What is more, Rossetti's poem proves to be not only ambiguous as regards its potential interpretation, but it is also sexually ambiguous and lavish with a sensuousness that above all concerns the close relationship between the sisters.

Ambiguity, Sensuousness and the Gothic in *Goblin Market*

As briefly mentioned above, sensuous descriptions abound in Rossetti's poem. "Sweet to tongue" (Rossetti, 1904, 1. 30), "luscious" (1. 61) or "sweeter than honey from the rock" (1. 129) are some of the attributes Rossetti employs when depicting the goblin fruit, and the same adjectives could be attributed to *Goblin Market* as a poem, for the author pays extra attention to all sensory experiences throughout her descriptions and language. Unsurprisingly, Rossetti is the Pre-Raphaelite poet most adapted to music (Arseneau, 2020, p. 165). Furthermore, the poem frequently features an erotic imagery which does not escape the reader. For instance, there are several references to juice and juices, as well as to dripping, and Rossetti constantly resorts to suggestive verbs such suck, squeeze and bite. As a matter of fact, the verb *suck* appears seven times throughout the poem and interestingly recurs above all in the passage which narrates the moment in which Laura succumbs and eats the goblin fruit, where the word *sucked* appears five times in the course of ten lines:

> Then *sucked* their fruit globes fair or red:
> Sweeter than honey from the rock,
> Stronger than man-rejoicing wine,
> Clearer than water flowed that juice;
> She never tasted such before,
> How should it cloy with length of use?
> She *sucked* and *sucked* and *sucked* the more
> Fruits which that unknown orchard bore;
> She *sucked* until her lips were sore;
> Then flung the emptied rinds away
> *(Rossetti, 1904, ll. 128–137, my emphasis)*

Rossetti's erotic imagery, nonetheless, is also evident in her descriptions of – female – body parts such as lips, cheeks and breast, and even the close relationship between the sisters includes moments of eroticism with Lizzie delivering lines such as "Hug me, kiss me, suck my juices" (Rossetti, 1904, 1. 468) and "Eat me, drink me, love me" (1. 471). Additionally, this sensuousness can be seen when depicting the goblin fruit. As it happens, the sensual descriptions employed by Rossetti here have potential sexual connotations: cherries are described as "[p]lump unpecked" (1. 7) while peaches are "[b]loom-down cheeked" (l. 9) and pomegranates are "full and fine" (l. 21). Moreover, the fruits themselves might have sexual double-meanings: cherries have been frequently associated with virginity, melons to female breasts, while pomegranates have a long history of being connected with the forbidden fruit as well as fertility due to the myth of Persephone, and the pear can be linked to the form of the female body.

Further to that line, there are three key passages in the poem with strong sexual nuances. First, the moment when the goblin men harass Laura and finally lure her to taste their fruit in exchange for *a golden curl* could be read as a seduction on the part of the goblins. The associations with Laura's fall into temptation with her loss of sexual purity are clear, for she is asked by the goblins to trade a golden lock for the fruit, for which Laura "dropped a teat more rare than pearl" (Rossetti, 1904, l. 127), and she will later refer to the "fruit forbidden" (l. 479) when talking to Lizzie. Moreover, the goblin assault on Lizzie resembles an attempted rape, for Rossetti employs here a powerfully violent imagery to describe the goblin attack:

Lashing their tails
They trod and hustled her,
Elbowed and jostled her,
Clawed with their nails,
Barking, mewing, hissing, mocking,
Tore her gown and soiled her stocking,
Twitched her hair out by the roots,
Stamped upon her tender feet,
Held her hands and squeezed their fruits
Against her mouth to make her eat.
…
Though the goblins cuffed and caught her,
Coaxed and fought her,
Bullied and besought her,
Scratched her, pinched her black as ink,
Kicked and knocked her,
Mauled and mocked her …
    (Rossetti, 1904, ll. 398–407, ll. 424–429)

The use of verbs such as claw, kick, knock or maul lets us see the violence experienced by Lizzie in this "masculine sexual aggression" (Burlinson, 1998, p. 45). Lastly, the Eucharistic and sacramental imagery employed by Rossetti when Lizzie comes home to Laura (Rossetti, 1904, ll. 465–472) has been explored by authors such as Arseneau, but, at the same time, Rossetti's language thrives on heavy homoerotic resonances as well, representing, in Burlinson's words, "same-sex, incestuous desire and activity" (Burlinson, 1998, p. 45). In order to save Laura and restore her health, she has to suck the juices from her Lizzie's face and body. When eating the goblin fruit, Laura "sucked and sucked and sucked the more" (Rossetti, 1904, l. 134), and now she "clung about her sister/Kissed and kissed and kissed her" (ll. 485–486). In this passage, the poet draws on pregnant verbs such as kiss, suck, hug, eat, drink and love.

To finish this section, it is interesting to point out the Gothic elements in *Goblin Market,* first examined by Ellen Moers in terms of sexuality in her work *Literary Women: The Great Writers* (1976). In this poem, it is possible to find some Gothic motifs, but Rossetti's treatment is somehow different from Gothic conventions. The title of the poem already points to the dream-like qualities to be found in its atmosphere, as well as pointing to the liminality of the place, a goblin market, where boundaries between opposite realms are blurred, those realms represented by Laura and Lizzie, on the one hand, and by the goblins, on the other. As is commonly explored in Gothic fiction, this poem also narrates an act of transgression, which takes place by a blurring of boundaries.

Furthermore, Rossetti's goblins might be regarded as Gothic creatures, for they represent the uncanny Other, a presence which haunts the female characters in the poem, and whose fruits associate them with the typical Gothic monster due to the sexual connotations. As observed by Serena Trowbridge (2013), the otherness of the goblins is clearly defined in the poem from the outset. Goblins are, then, a grotesque element that are set out as seducers in the poem (p. 119). Though described as half-animal (Rossetti, 1904, ll. 71–76), their voices are seductive, "kind and full of loves" (l. 79) and the sisters do not fear them at first. Their true savage nature is only revealed when Lizzie confronts them (ll. 391–397). Yet Rossetti undermines the traditional approach of the Gothic as regards women, for she depicts transgressive women but offers them redemption. Burlinson (1998) notes that the "narrative of temptation, sacrifice, and redemption differs from conventional Christian allegory, because in *Goblin Market* women are both sinner *and* redeemer, sinned against and redeemed" (p. 45, original emphasis).

Conversely, it has been argued that a discourse of vampirism may be found in Rossetti's *Goblin Market* as well, since the poet places a great emphasis on consumption, appetite, carnality and orality (Burlinson, 1999, p. 292). Moreover, both goblins and vampires seduce virginal young women who are then condemned to live in a state of near-death. The destructive consequences of consuming the goblin fruit can be seen in Jeanie, who "pined away" (Rossetti, 1904, l. 154) and then "dwindled and grew grey" (l. 156). Laura follows a similar consumptive process after tasting the goblin fruit, becoming lifeless, until saved by her sister, a progress which is mirrored in the chamber opera.

The Process of Adapting Rossetti's Poem for a Young Audience in the 21st Century

The musical production of *Goblin Market* was first presented at the Lyric Theatre in Belfast in 2003 and two years later the same production was taken to the Edinburgh Festival Fringe at the George Square Theatre. The project was initiated by theatre director and published writer Kath Burlinson, as she saw the need for more productions with leading female roles. Burlinson was therefore attracted to Rossetti's verses as a text which recounts the experience of young women and emphasizes the negotiation and navigation of their own lives and sexuality. As a matter of fact, Burlinson was already a Rossetti scholar; she did her Ph.D. dissertation on Christina Rossetti, supervised by Dr Isobel Armstrong at the University of Southampton, and she had published a book on the poet, entitled *Christina Rossetti*, in 1998. With the aforementioned purpose in mind, she adapted *Goblin Market* and wrote the libretto, working together with Conor Mitchell, a talented young composer who provided the music for the production.

Rossetti's verses have been for the most part retained in Burlinson's libretto. Nonetheless, compared with the source poem, this play features modifications and textual additions, but always in the same spirit of the source text, for Burlinson considered it important to keep intact the "blend of sexual symbolism, moral content and social comment" (Burlinson & Mitchell, 2003, p. 1) of Rossetti's words. In that line, lyricist Burlinson took inspiration from another of Rossetti's works, most precisely from her prose work *Speaking Likenesses* (1854), a work of fiction for children in which the Victorian author reflects on the behaviour of three young girls who end up punished or rewarded because of their actions. This work allows Burlinson to add a stronger narrative structure to the production and to introduce new characters: Claire, Clara and the Aunt. Though mainly musical, the chamber opera also includes some brief moments of spoken dialogue and new lyrics not taken from Rossetti's texts.

In visual terms, the musical presents two worlds colliding, where, in line with the previously seen Gothic elements to be found in Rossetti's poem, there is a constant blurring of boundaries between the different realms represented on stage. As such, the audience sees the Victorian world of the Aunt, Claire and Clara, dressed according to this period. Yet it also features many elements of the folklore and fairy-tale universe, for the world of Lizzie and Laura is presented visually in the style of a German fairy-tale. In fact, following the line of fairy-tale illustrated editions of the poem, mostly marketed towards children throughout its history, the play shows the sisters according to the conventional fairy-tale universe: their clothing is modest and chaste, covering them to their toes, with hair neatly tied and braided. Their purity and innocence are further emphasized by their young age and rosy cheeks. Therefore, the show is presented against the background of the purity and innocence of childhood fairy-tales. In brief, following this type of illustrated edition for children, the musical production focuses as well on the sisters' youth, that is why it is performed by a young cast, with all the main roles played by girls. Another aspect which draws this production closer to the fairy-tale illustrated editions of *Goblin Market* is the emphasis during the performance on the domestic sphere, to where women are mostly relegated, represented by the constant presence of the bed on the left-hand side of the stage. This also attests to how the magical glen described by Rossetti has invaded the girls in this crossing of thresholds. Yet the play is more in line with Rackham's celebrated illustrated edition of Rossetti's poem from 1933, for there is a darker subtext awash with sexual connotations in this fairy-tale world, as shall be later explained.

Speaking of performance, the goblin ensemble, comprised both of boys and girls, is very physical. It is very useful to dwell on this fact indeed, for, borrowing Weltman's words about Polly Pen and Peggy Harmon's musical adaptation of *Goblin Market* (1985), there is a "trans-gender performativity" (Weltman, 2020, p. 162), since several girls also portray the goblins, thus performing onstage the sexual temptations these creatures play in Rossetti's narrative. In fact goblins are portrayed in the poem as seducers and therefore, as the only symbolic male characters these girls accordingly play their part in seducing Laura and in physically assaulting Lizzie. Consequently, just as Weltman (2020) claims that Pen and Harmon's 1985 *Goblin Market* re-introduces "homosexual desire" (p. 22) by having women embody male characters, it could be argued that Burlinson follows a similar line by having girls in the goblin ensemble adopting these goblinesque shapes and aggressive postures.

Though mixed, a couple of boys are presented as the leaders of the goblins. Each of them develops their own physicality, for they are not merely part of an ensemble. Every goblin character is unique but works together very closely. There is a strong emphasis during rehearsals and performance given to the animality informing them and the natural elements – water, fire, air, earth – that drive them as goblins, overshadowing the actor's own gender to put a stronger accent on their animality as goblins. The play thus partakes in the Gothic qualities to be found in Rossetti's poem, for goblins are presented to the audience as the uncanny Other, as previously mentioned. That is to say, as creatures who haunt the female characters and whose physical appearance points to their Otherness and grotesqueness, since they appear onstage as half-animal creatures, as described by Rossetti. Accordingly, the young actors dance and contort their bodies in uncanny ways onstage. Musically speaking, on the other hand, the goblin world is about seduction. Rossetti described them as sounding "full of loves" (Rossetti, 1904, l. 79). Thus, Mitchell musically portrays them as working in the world of tonality and harmony. Consequently, their voices are harmonious and alluring, and their constant chanting and repetitive goblin melody conceals their true nature until the moment in which Lizzie confronts them and they become savage and vicious.

Interestingly, the action is presented in three different spheres or worlds: the human world of the Aunt, Clara and Claire, in which the audience hears the Aunt telling the story in Rossetti's *Goblin Market*. This reframes Rossetti's narrative, for these characters are always present onstage, usually sidelined while contemplating the action taking place. In this human sphere, moreover, Burlinson establishes a parallel structure with the narrative of Rossetti's poem, for Clara is given characteristics reminiscent of Laura, as an adventurous and curious girl, while Claire is more conservative and cautious, as Lizzie in *Goblin Market*. Then, there is the fairy-tale world of Lizzie, Laura and the goblins, and the transcendental sphere of Jeanie, who is presented as a ghost and serves as a commentator and harbinger of doom, without being seen or heard by Laura and Lizzie. It is the relationship between these different realms that is the point of exploration of this adaptation, both in the musical and the textual aspect. This fundamental narrative structure around the human, fairy-tale and transcendental world consequently opens up numerous theatrical as well as musical possibilities. As such, the composer Conor Mitchell started working with the closest relationship between two notes – i.e. the semitone – so as to represent the relationship between Laura and Lizzie.

"Never Tasted Such Before": Addressing Sexual Ambiguity Onstage

Before delving into the analysis of the chamber opera, it is significant to ponder on Burlinson's words during a podcast interview, for here she highlights how the young cast interpreted and understood the text "very much in relation to where they were in their own understanding of the issues" (Burlinson, 2023). For the younger ones, the play was more literal. Yet, for those in puberty and in the arena of sexual expression, the allegorical interpretations of the poem were more pertinent, that is, those perspectives which underscore the negotiation and navigation of seduction and sexuality, a universal reality which this play sought to draw attention to.

The show begins after an instrumental prologue, marked as *moderato* and *ghostly* in the score by Mitchell, where the wind instruments stand out; these instruments will be, in fact, linked to the goblins' presence throughout the score. The first speaker is the Aunt, who has just finished reading from a book to her two young listeners the cautionary tale of Jeanie. The audience only hears her very last words, which strengthen the sense of Jeanie's doom as they emphasize how she wasted away until she died and was buried where no grass and no daisies would grow. It is interesting that Burlinson chooses to keep these lines featuring the daisies, employed by Rossetti as symbols of innocence when Lizzie says that "[w]here she lies low:/I planted daisies there a year ago" (Rossetti, 1904, ll. 159–160), for there "no grass will grow" (l.

158). These lines, thus, associate Jeanie's fall with loss of sexual innocence by implying that she was no longer a pure and innocent maiden. Consequently, the version does not shy away from including the sexual innuendo implied by these lines about Jeanie, setting off the tone and content of the rest of the show. The Aunt, thus, imposes a Victorian morality on these girls, admonishing them to be obedient instead of "wilful and curious, and bold" (Burlinson & Mitchell, 2003, p. 3), faults to which Jeanie herself admits later.

At this point, Jeanie appears onstage as a ghost, invisible to the Aunt, Clara and Claire, but visible and audible for the audience. She performs *Jeanie's Song*, where the girl gives her version of the story: how she ventured in the glen despite the admonitions and met the goblin men. She sings about tasting "things ... never tried before" and taking "their gifts" to finally find that "the thing [she] wanted most, [she] wanted more" (Burlinson & Mitchell, 2003). The song very explicitly leads hearers to ponder about sexual temptation as Jeanie sings lines such as "I tasted things that touched my very core" and "I took their fruit between my lips" (Burlinson & Mitchell, 2003). After taking their fruits, she pined in the moonlight, wailing, screaming and crying, for she could not hear the goblin cry any more, growing sore in head, body and soul. Although the adaptation targeted a young audience, there is a strong emphasis on sexuality and the consumption afflicting the female body which does not escape older audiences.

As a contrast to the sad story of Jeanie, the Aunt begins narrating the story of Lizzie and Laura, which she invents for her young audience. She compares these sisters to Clara and Claire, describing Lizzie as "timid and cautious" and Laura as "adventurous and wild" (Burlinson & Mitchell, 2003). The emphasis is given to the importance of sisterhood, as Clara and Claire start singing each a different line of "There's no friend like a sister" when Lizzie and Laura appear for the first time on stage singing the next two lines, and later performing the last line, "peas in pods and sides of a coin" (Burlinson & Mitchell, 2003), together in unison. The story then revolves around the warning against the goblin men. While Lizzie and Laura sing that they "must not look at goblin men" and "must not taste their fruits" (Burlinson & Mitchell, 2003), the goblins enter the stage after an instrumental break and sing the first lines in Rossetti's poem about their lush and tempting goblin fruit. The lusciousness of the fruit is, in fact, preserved in the play as a key aspect of the drama, and this to such a point that even the teenagers performing the show were well aware of their eroticism (Burlinson & Díaz Morillo, 2023). At certain points the sisters keep singing "must not look" (Burlinson & Mitchell, 2003) while the goblins produce an uncanny chant in a similar rhythm but with mostly minor third intervals between the two melodic lines. The minor third is generally thought to "convey sadness" (Curtis & Bharucha, 2010, p. 335), so the melody arouses apprehension in the audience and anticipates the sisters' fate.

The tempo of the music gradually accelerates to increase the sense of tension, trepidation and threat among the audience. It is noteworthy that the next time the sisters sing together "we must not look at the goblins" (Burlinson & Mitchell, 2003) while the goblins keep up their chant, Lizzie and Laura stop singing in unison. Though they maintain the same rhythm – sometimes even in unison with the goblins – their melodic lines separate by a minor third interval until hitting a perfect fourth interval – Lizzie sings a C and Laura an F –. This perfect fourth sensorially conveys consonance between the sisters, if only briefly. At one point Lizzie imitates Laura in canon, but Laura continues singing in a higher octave. The separation between the sisters begins, thus, to musically creep in, so as to anticipate Laura's fall into temptation. By the end, the sisters and the goblins sing at the same time, but never in unison: the goblins keep harassing the girls to taste their fruits, while the sisters stand close together and admonish each other "not to peep at goblin men" (Burlinson & Mitchell, 2003).

The goblin chant becomes ever more insistent and the sense of trepidation builds in crescendo while the rhythm of their chant becomes quicker. Lizzie and Laura seem to be fully trapped, surrounded by these goblins who keep luring them with their fruit. Jeanie appears once more to echo Lizzie in her warning to Laura not to be charmed by the goblin fruits. The ceaseless and drumming chant of the goblin ensemble allows the audience to ponder on the threatening aspect of the temptation. When Lizzie finally escapes the goblins, nonetheless, Laura stays behind, completely entranced by the fruits. She now sings more tenderly, and the goblins imitate her: they abruptly stop their insistent chant to sing more melodiously and enchantingly to continue with their seduction. This melodic transition coincides with Laura singing the line from Rossetti's poem describing how the goblins sound "full of loves" (Rossetti, 1904, l. 79). There is then an instrumental break, where a single violin plays a solo part in adagio while the Aunt recites lines 81 to 86 of the poem where Rossetti employs a series of similes to portray Laura giving in to temptation. Jeanie accompanies Laura throughout this episode, to remind viewers that she was seduced as well. The goblins once more begin their drumming chant, accelerating the rhythm of the music. The instrumental melody line reaches the climax when Laura finally clips a golden curl to buy the fruit. At this point the Aunt resumes her narration of lines 129–136, interestingly keeping Rossetti's insistence on the word *suck* with all its erotic connotations, and ending her account with the line "She sucked until her lips were sore" (l. 136), followed by an instrumental break which leaves the audience reflecting on Laura's actions.

Following that moment, Lizzie reprimands Laura for staying out so late in a *moderato* rhythm until she reminds her of Jeanie's story, at which point the rhythm of the music slows down to emphasize Jeanie's terrible fate. Laura then starts to tell Lizzie about the wonderful fruit she has tasted, retaking a quicker tempo. While Laura keeps singing about the fruit, Lizzie continues reminding her of Jeanie, and the goblin ensemble joins the sisters in chanting about their fruit, saturating the audience's senses in a similar way to what Laura has just experienced by tasting the goblin fruit. The tempo of the music slows while the sisters get ready for bed. While the sisters sleep together, two goblins gently sing the verses from "Golden head by golden head" (Burlinson & Mitchell, 2003) as a duet. The show retains, thus, the voyeuristic and (homo)erotic connotations of this moment, as underscored by illustrators such as Dante Gabriel Rossetti, for the goblins peep into the sisters' sleep and force the audience to share in this moment as onlookers. Moreover, by preserving Rossetti's verses in the goblin duet, Burlinson emphasizes the homoerotic image of the double nature of the sisters as well, depicted as:

> Golden head by golden head
> Two sweet sisters tucked in bed
> Like two pigeons in one nest
> Folded in each other's wings
> Like two blossoms on one stem
> Like two flakes of fallen snow
> Like two apples on one branch ripened to a blushing glow
> Cheek to cheek and breast to breast locked together in one nest
> Cheek to cheek and breast to breast one is welcome, two is best
> *(Burlinson & Mitchell, 2003, p. 11)*.

Still in line with Dante Gabriel Rossetti's illustrations, Burlinson has decided to feature a dream sequence, where goblins creep on from under the sisters' bed and take Laura to dance with her and handle her as a puppet before returning her to bed. In this visual manner, the creator of the production aims to portray how the goblins corrupt Laura's dreams and her inward obsession with the goblin fruit. The instrumental music which accompanies this passage has a quick tempo in order to create a frantic atmosphere, accelerating until reaching *presto*, which is a very fast tempo, and then a *rallentando* to *andante*, which is moderately slow, when Laura gets back into bed and the Aunt, Clara and Claire return frontstage to continue with the story.

The chamber opera mirrors Rossetti's description of Laura's desperation and decay. This can be observed from the moment they sing "By the Brook" (Burlinson & Mitchell, 2003), which underscores the idea that Laura is doomed to waste away in her longing for fruit. The lyrics emphasize more than once the following lines:

> If you taste forbidden fruit
> You only taste it once
> Not twice, not thrice, but just one time

Don't you know that simple rhyme?
(Burlinson & Mitchell, 2003, p. 16)

These lines are first sung by Lizzie, and then repeated by the goblins and Claire. Clara, just as Laura, does not understand this, and, thus, the Aunt simply says that she should "ask [her] brothers. Some day they will tell you" (Burlinson & Mitchell, 2003). In this brief comic aside, the sexual connotations are made clear for the audience to understand: Laura has fallen and now she will pine away, for she has lost what she can only lose once – her (sexual) innocence. At this moment, Jeanie appears again and sings "If I Had a Sister" (Burlinson & Mitchell, 2003), where she expresses her desire to be able to save Laura as she sees her withering, just as it happened to her. Jeanie performs alone with passion, showing her regret as she is unable to save Laura from her own destiny. She also complains about not having had a sister to save her in time, for she is now "fallen, damned and defiled" (Burlinson & Mitchell, 2003) for all eternity. This is one of the musical highlights in the production and could even be regarded as one of the showstoppers, for it aims to appeal to the audience's emotions and share in Jeanie's unfair fate. Her doom, and Laura's impending downfall, are further intensified in the next song – "Let Me Yawn" (Burlinson & Mitchell, 2003) – where Lizzie and Laura sing together, while Jeanie sings at the same time about her own fate by drawing comparisons with Laura. One more time Jeanie says about herself that she was "wilful, curious and bold" (Burlinson & Mitchell, 2003).

The process of Laura's decay is carefully portrayed in this production. Interestingly, it is Laura herself who begins singing about her own decline in the song "Day by Day, Night by Night" (Burlinson & Mitchell, 2003). A goblin man joins in the song, followed by Jeanie, until they all end up singing together but in different voices. At this point, the sisters repeat a previous song – "Housekeeping Worthy Work" (Burlinson & Mitchell, 2003) – but Laura modifies the lyrics to further underscore her physical and moral decline, for she now finds housekeeping a "dreary work" and "a bore" (Burlinson & Mitchell, 2003) and she is unable to eat. The goblins interrupt the song and the sisters' chores by alluring Lizzie with their "Come and buy" (Burlinson & Mitchell, 2003) chant. At this, Lizzie stops and reflects on her longing to buy the goblin fruits for fear her sister might die, and yet she feels afraid of falling herself, as her lines "but fear to pay too dear" and "but fear that I may fall" (Burlinson & Mitchell, 2003) suggest. In the lyrics Lizzie sings at this point, it is remarkable that Burlinson keeps the references from Rossetti's source poem to "the joy brides hope to have" (Burlinson & Mitchell, 2003) while talking about Jeanie, making explicit for the audience once more that Jeanie's fall is linked to loss of sexual innocence.

Lizzie is here given a little solo, entitled "Brave the Storm" (Burlinson & Mitchell, 2003), which aims to emphasize her bravery in deciding to act and help her sister, instead of staying safely at home as she has been told and has been doing all her life. The song is followed by an instrumental interlude in a very fast tempo – *presto*, which continues to accelerate – in which wind and percussion instruments, as well as the piano, predominate. It culminates in a goblin chant, marked as *aggressive tempo* in the score, where the goblins keep reciting "One is fallen, one to fall/One is left to hear our call" (Burlinson & Mitchell, 2003) to add trepidation to the scene and let the audience anticipate what is about to happen to Lizzie. After that, Lizzie takes centre stage once more and sings "In Myself Believe" (Burlinson & Mitchell, 2003). This song allows her to take courage in order to brave the goblins so as to save her sister. Here she emphasizes that she needs "to buy some fruit but not to taste/ for if I do, I die" (Burlinson & Mitchell, 2003). Moreover, so as to help the audience understand what will happen later, Burlinson adds to Rossetti's narrative an explanation through these lyrics of what takes place when one does not eagerly taste the fruits, for Lizzie sings that "goblin fruit/if purified of greed/can change its evil influence" (Burlinson & Mitchell, 2003). That Lizzie is terrified of the goblins is made evident throughout the lyrics of this song:

> I want so much to run from here
> Yet will not, cannot leave
> I must stand firm, and brave the storm
> In myself believe
> In myself believe
> *(Burlinson & Mitchell, 2003, p. 23)*

Thus, there is an emphasis on the process of transformation in Lizzie, from the sensible and homely character of the beginning of the show to when she reaches the climax where she faces her worst fears out of sisterly love. Burlinson underscores her character development in the show, allowing Lizzie to mature and grow, and conveys with great strength the courage of Lizzie's actions. Still when Lizzie is singing, the goblins begin to appear and tempt her with their fruit. When Lizzie refuses to eat their fruit and insists on buying without tasting, the goblins become furious and start their attack on the girl, hissing and behaving in animalesque ways. Once more, in line with previous illustrated editions of the poem, most especially Rackham's, the goblins tear at Lizzie's body and clothes with violence. The rhythm of the music keeps accelerating as the goblins pounce on Lizzie while singing the list of their fruits in an aggressive manner and making goblin noises. For the purposes of the play, hollowed out peaches were employed onstage and these were filled with yoghurt. Therefore, the young actress playing Lizzie is truly physically mauled onstage, though naturally in very choreographically controlled movements.

Through that episode, Lizzie struggles to maintain a barrier against the goblin fruit, closing her eyes and shutting her mouth lest the goblins "should cram a mouthful in" (Rossetti, 1904, l. 432). That goblin fruit rejected by Lizzie "as foul and corrupting ends up smeared all over her face" (Burlinson, 1999, p. 307). During the final moments of the attack, the Aunt resumes her narration, reciting lines 422–434 from Rossetti's poem with only minor modifications and omissions, but also adding previous well-known lines such as "White and golden Lizzie stood,/Like a lily in a flood" (Rossetti, 1904, ll. 408–409), thus underscoring the importance of her bravery and self-sacrifice by retaining Rossetti's imagery. The goblins exit the stage, while a ravaged Lizzie, soaked in goblin fruit juice, makes her way home to Laura. The music becomes more mournful, slow and quiet, until only a single violin can be heard.

As mentioned earlier, the show does not shy away from the (homo)erotic ambiguities which permeate Rossetti's poem. Accordingly, the musical production retains the scene of the sisters' reunion after the goblins' attack on Lizzie. In a melody which begins scored as *moderato* with a "ghostly feel" (Burlinson & Mitchell, 2003), Lizzie sings to Laura to "hug and kiss [her]" (Burlinson & Mitchell, 2003). As a matter of fact, the lyrics mostly preserve the erotic and sacramental imagery employed by Rossetti in this passage. Yet there is an interesting omission, for Lizzie sings line 468 from Rossetti's poem, but skips the part where she says "suck my juices" (Rossetti, 1904, l. 468) even though the following lines "Squeezed from goblin fruits for you,/Goblin pulp and goblin dew" (ll. 469–470) are retained in the song. At that point, Laura shyly approaches her sister in amazement and asks her about her actions. The music increases in tempo as Laura besets her sister with more pressing questions. The climax is reached when both sing in unison "tell me, touch me, love me" (Burlinson & Mitchell, 2003), at which point Laura kisses Lizzie, whose face is completely smeared with goblin fruit. The Aunt begins to sing for the first time – for thus far she has been merely reciting – and in a faster tempo, telling the audience of the process of Laura's painful restoration to health. A goblin man joins in the song and both end by singing together the line from Rossetti's poem which lends the title to the song, "Like a Caged Thing Freed" (Burlinson & Mitchell, 2003).

The song ends in C minor and progresses in the following instrumental break towards C major, marking a clear contrast between the darker feeling of the previous song by the Aunt and the goblin, and the new happier sound of the instrumental melody which points to Laura's restoration. After a few moments of instrumental music, Claire and Clara sing a line together and then Jeanie takes centre stage once again, singing about Lizzie's bravery and how Laura's soul now "will reappear/purified of lust and sin,/heart transformed by love and care" (Burlinson & Mitchell, 2003). All the girls – Clara, Claire, the Aunt and Jeanie – join together singing in this song, except for Laura, and even the goblin man again joins their song to produce a chorale of beautiful harmonies. The Aunt repeats alone her previous lines and is joined later by Clara and Claire. While the three sing in unison, Jeanie and the goblin man sing together, repeating the same lines in canon as an echo to the Aunt and the girls. It is interesting to observe that Jeanie is associated with the goblin man in this melody, as both sing in unison for the most part, linking the fallen woman with the seducer. Finally, the five characters end the song, singing the line "Like a caged thing freed" (Burlinson & Mitchell, 2003) together in a perfect G major chord: the Aunt, Claire and Clara singing in G, Jeanie in B, and the goblin man tackling the higher note in D.

One of the key things Burlinson does structurally at the very end of the play is to transform to a certain extent the moral ending. In her poem, Rossetti describes Laura's full restoration and portrays her as telling "the little ones" (Rossetti, 1904, l. 548) about her fall into temptation and the importance of sisterhood. Nonetheless, Burlinson transforms this last scene, also avoiding the influence of illustrated editions. In it, the two smallest cast members appear in bed playing the children in Rossetti's poem, while Laura tells them her tale of sisterhood and female heroism. After that, the last thing that happens onstage is that one of the children is given an apple by one of the goblins and bites into it. In that way, the notions of temptation, appetite, transgression and even seduction are seen as passed on to the next generation, as something inevitable that each generation has to face. Thus, unlike Rossetti, Burlinson gives the spectator no narrative closure, for these are all universal experiences each of us must endure.

A Mirror of Contemporary Issues: Through Sisterhood into Adulthood

As said before, the musical begins with the Aunt talking to her two young listeners, Claire and Clara. Though the Aunt is presented as a narrator, she is an unreliable one, for she plays with power and manipulation, deliberately withholding information at certain points. The Aunt reinforces the Victorian idea of womanhood, and she attempts to impose rigid aspects of socialization on these two young girls. Her narration aims to offer an exemplary model of good behaviour to these young girls, instructing them about feminine restraint while they pursue their domestic chores. In that sense, for instance, there is a song entitled "Housekeeping Worthy Work" (Burlinson & Mitchell, 2003), which reinforces the importance of the female housekeeping duties, at the end of which Clara sceptically asks if Lizzie "actually like[d] doing housework" (Burlinson & Mitchell, 2003). Her Aunt's answer makes it clear that this narration is also aimed at teaching them feminine propriety. Yet, at the same time, throughout her narration, the Aunt seems to be directing the girls along a different path, towards the imagination. In physical terms, the character of the Aunt is presented as an impressive figure, around 6.4 foot in height, fully dressed in Victorian costume with a long skirt. Both physically and morally, the Aunt is thus an imposing character which represents Victorian attitudes.

Furthermore, the play engages with previous illustrated editions of Rossetti's celebrated poem, as mentioned earlier. From the moment of its publication, the poem *Goblin Market* has been continuously interpreted as a moral tale and, more precisely, as an allegory about the fallen woman and the virtuous woman in many cases. Dante Gabriel Rossetti, the poet's brother, was the first illustrator of the poem, and he himself promoted this view. *Goblin Market*, thus, ironically follows this intrerpretation at the beginning, presenting the play as a moral tale encouraging girls to be good and obedient. That is what the Aunt instructs the girls at the beginning by narrating the story of Jeanie. Yet the play overturns this narrative by emphasizing the importance of finding one's own way to maturity through navigating temptation and emerging sexuality, where the magical glen acts as a liminal space. The new end proposed by Burlinson in this chamber opera further highlights the significance of this aspect. Thus, Laura is not merely presented as the morally bad sister for transgressing the boundaries, as Lizzie herself must cross the boundaries of her own domestic sphere, of her "feminine propriety" (Burlinson & Mitchell, 2003, p. 1) and face the glen to save her fallen sister.

When undertaking the adaptation of Rossetti's poem, Burlinson decided to give the character of Jeanie a more central role, thus expanding her narrative, for she is only mentioned in passing in the source poem and yet offered some theatrical possibilities. Transforming the narrative, in *Goblin Market* spectators become acquainted with Jeanie's story through the Aunt's reading, as she tells her story as a cautionary tale in line with Rossetti's original storyline, through Lizzie's admonishment of Laura. Moreover, this female character appears and sings on stage in the form of a ghost, as mentioned before, invisible to the rest of the characters on stage. This provides a very interesting feminist revision of the narrative: while in Rossetti's verses readers encounter Jeanie and learn her story from Lizzie's lips, in this theatrical adaptation Jeanie is given a voice and she is the one to tell her own story, incarnating thus all the "fallen women" (Burlinson & Mitchell, 2003) who were not saved in time. Though invisible to the characters, she is plainly visible to the audience, who hear her sing about her so-called misbehaviour. Jeanie appears when Laura is tempted by the goblin fruit and then wastes away. The character of Jeanie, therefore, contributes cohesion to the musical, and she acquires great relevance in the plot, for she succeeds in representing those fallen women who had no sister to save them, unlike Laura. This association is reinforced every time she performs "Jeanie's Song" onstage (Burlinson & Mitchell, 2003), which underscores her sense of isolation, for there was no one to support her when she fell into temptation, and, therefore, she is forever lost and remains unredeemed.

As a contrast to Jeanie's solitude, sisters Lizzie and Laura are offered as examples of the relevance of female companionship and support. This is clearly seen, for instance, during the lullaby-styled song entitled "Early

Birds" (Burlinson & Mitchell, 2003) with lyrics mostly written by Burlinson, which reflects on and expands lines 524–529 from Rossetti's poem, where Lizzie watches over her sister's sleep, anxiously waiting for her full recovery:

> That night long Lizzie watched by her,
> Counted her pulse's flagging stir,
> Felt for her breath,
> Held water to her lips, and cooled her face
> With tears and fanning leaves
> *(Rossetti, 1904, ll. 524–529)In the produc-*
>   *tion, Lizzie sings this lullaby song solo,*
>   *promising Laura to keep watch over her*
> *sleep, adding new lyrics to Rossetti's verses,*
>   *but retaining their imagery, as the first*
>   *verses of the song show, when compared to*
>   *the previous stanza in Rossetti's poem:*

> I will watch you all night long, I will cool your face
> Feel for pulse and wait for breath,
> Hold in my embrace.
> I will fan and keep you cool while the fever rages through.
> By your side I'll wait till dawn, hoping dawn will waken you
> *(Burlinson & Mitchell, 2003, p. 27)*

This musical moment allows Lizzie to express once more her everlasting love for Laura. Thus, the production continually emphasizes the importance of sisterhood, providing the audience with scenes of sisterly love and affection, self-sacrifice and brave actions in order to protect one another. At the same time, it underscores Jeanie's lack of these qualities, and how the absence of a true sister damned her for eternity. This is what this production aims to highlight and convey to its – especially young – audience. A piano melody, followed later by the full orchestra, introduces the next scene where Laura awakens and finds herself fully restored to health. The music helps the audience to savour and fully delve into the moment of transformation in Laura's body and soul, reminiscent of Disney films such as *Beauty and the Beast* (1991), where a transformation back into human form takes place during a similar instrumental moment. After the brief instrumental interval, the Aunt sings about Laura's recovery. While Lizzie and Laura rejoice in this moment, Jeanie laments again her eternal damnation and the fact that her story cannot be reversed nor changed. In a flashforward moment, the audience sees Laura with two children of her own, following Rossetti's narrative. Laura now recites her own story and then breaks into a song when she retells the heroic way in which she was saved by her sister. Lizzie, nonetheless, under-scores how Laura helped her as well to "brave the unknown, overcome doubt" (Burlinson & Mitchell, 2003), leading her to become braver and stronger. This song leads to the end of the musical.

In that sense, it is especially relevant to examine this ending, for in it, Jeanie sings once more her song "If I Had a Sister" (Burlinson & Mitchell, 2003), at which point all the other girls who until that moment have played female goblins come onstage wearing the same type of costume as Jeanie. As Burlinson notes in her libretto, this group of women represents "the legions of fallen women no-one saved" (Burlinson & Mitchell, 2003, p. 29). Visually, they are all the same and are presented thus to the audience. The lyrics of the song further emphasize the moral lesson of the story and connect her fall to her loss of sexual innocence, for Jeanie explicitly states that:

> If I had a sister I'd be saved
> Not to lie in a *shameful, shameful* grave
> *(Burlinson & Mitchell, 2003, p. 29, my*
> *emphasis)*

Jeanie is then joined in her song by this chorus of women, singing together but in canon. The song grows in intensity and the girls sing the last note with the word *grave* in unison, Jeanie singing in a higher pitch, her voice resounding above all the rest. This song gradually transforms into "No-one Like a Sister" (Burlinson & Mitchell, 2003), which includes Lizzie, Laura, Laura's children and all the other girls already onstage. All the girls in the cast – around 35 in total, including the six female leads and the girls from the goblin ensemble – perform the song in a strong moment as a choral lament for all the fallen women in the world, underscoring the relevance of female empowerment through sisterhood, which is the main message in this production, as stated before. The production ends, thus, with a powerfully emotional choral song, where Lizzie and Laura sing together the final notes, while the rest of the female performers and the orchestra fall silent. Yet, just as the sisters finish their last note, Laura's children start chanting the goblin theme together with a single woodwind instrument as accompaniment, as wind instruments are associated with the goblins throughout the score of this production. Jeannie then begins to sing alone "I was always told, always, always told" (Burlinson & Mitchell, 2003) almost obsessively, using a semitone (E–F) interval, which is the smallest musical interval. Her continuous singing is echoed by other female performers onstage, whose rhythms overlap to create a reverberating effect on the audience. A final instrumental chord interrupts their chanting, which is sounded just as one of Laura's children bites into an apple. And, so, history repeats itself.

Conclusion

Due to its emphasis on physicality and sexuality, to a certain extent it is quite telling to reflect on Burlinson's own words (Burlinson, 2023) regarding this chamber opera before concluding this chapter. The playwright claims that, since the climate has changed remarkably from nearly 20 years ago and we are living in a post-pandemic world, many things are different and would be different in a new performance of this show, because it was a very physical theatre piece, in all respects, where the actors worked very closely together. Burlinson admitted not being sure whether her musical could be performed just as it was in the early 2000s.

In point of fact, and as has been seen, this theatre production retained the sensuality of the source poem, even though it was performed and targeted at young people. With this in mind, the libretto attempts to stay as true and as close to the source poem as possible, from the sexual connotations of the *fruit forbidden* to the sensuousness of several passages. For instance, the (homo) erotically ambiguous scene of Eucharistic resonances, which sees Lizzie coming home to Laura to restore her sister, is retained. When Lizzie finally comes home to Laura, the actor is completely covered in yoghurt, so the actor playing Laura has to literally lick that yoghurt from Lizzie's face. It is a moment of high drama and erotic hues which is visually presented to the audience. Yet, when performed live, this scene seems to emphasize the power of self-sacrifice out of love more than its eroticism. When performed on the stage, sometimes certain scenes may acquire new meaning and/or stress a particular aspect. This points to the aims of the play, for both Rossetti and Burlinson anticipate the relevance of sisterhood in the 21st century, when like-minded movements such as #MeToo will later develop.

As it happens, the female experience takes centre stage in this production, where viewers are transported to a female-dominated world. Recounting the universal experience of young women when dealing with their lives and sexuality, this is the final message of the play: to find your own way to adulthood and to always remember that "there's no one like a sister to help you on your way" (Burlinson & Mitchell, 2003, p. 30). Keeping the spirit of Rossetti's original work, Burlinson has seen the pertinence and timelessness of the issues raised by the poem, which continue to be as important today as in the 19th century, for redemption and sisterhood prove to be key to navigate and survive in this society.

Acknowledgements

This publication has been supported by a Ph.D. fellowship (FPI-UNED 2021). I am also deeply grateful to Kath Burlinson for kindly providing me with all the necessary materials for my research.

References

Arseneau, M. (1993). Incarnation and interpretation: Christina Rossetti, the Oxford Movement, and "Goblin Market". *Victorian Poetry*, 31(1), 79–93.

Arseneau, M. (2020). Musico-literary Pre-Raphaelite poetry. In H. Bozant Witcher & A. Kahrmann Huseby (Eds.), *Defining Pre-Raphaelite poetics* (pp. 143–178). Palgrave Macmillan. https://doi.org/10.1007/978-3-030-51338-2_6.

Burlinson, K. (1998). *Christina Rossetti*. Northcote House Publishers.

Burlinson, K. (1999). "All mouth and trousers": Christina Rossetti's grotesque and abjected bodies. In I. Armstrong & V. Blain (Eds.), *Women's poetry, late Romantic to late Victorian: Gender and genre, 1830–1900* (pp. 292–312). Palgrave Macmillan. https://doi.org/10.1007/978-1-349-27021-7_14.

Burlinson, K. (guest) & Díaz Morillo, E. (host). (2023, 11 Feb). Staging Christina Rossetti's "Goblin Market". Audio podcast episode. In *The Pre-Raphaelite podcast*. The Pre-Raphaelite Society. https://www.pre-raphaelitesociety.org/podcast/episode/89a18144/staging-christina-rossettis-goblin-market.

Burlinson, K. & Mitchell, C. (2003). *Goblin Market*. Josef Weinberger.

Curtis, M. E. & Bharucha, J. (2010). The minor third communicates sadness in speech, mirroring its use in music. *Emotion*, 10 (3), 335–348. https://doi.org/10.1037/a0017928.

Kooistra, L. J. (1994) Modern markets for "Goblin Market". *Victorian Poetry*, 32(3/4), 249–277.

Marsh, J. (2012). *Christina Rossetti: A literary biography*. Faber & Faber.

Moers, E. (1976). *Literary women: The great writers*. Doubleday.

Rossetti, C. G. (1904). *The poetical works of Christina Georgina Rossetti*. Annotated by W. M. Rossetti. Macmillan.

Trowbridge, S. (2013). *Christina Rossetti's gothic*. Bloomsbury.

Weltman, S. A. (2020). *Victorians on Broadway: Literature, adaptation, and the modern American musical*. University of Virginia Press.

7

"WE'RE WOMEN. NOT CHILDREN. NOT LITTLE GIRLS"

Zadie Smith's Theatrical Adaptation of Geoffrey Chaucer's *The Wife of Bath*

Pilar Botías Domínguez

Introduction

One of the characteristic features of *The Canterbury Tales* [1] is its diversity and variety. Although an unfinished work, Chaucer gifted us with a masterpiece of English literature, and not only in form (rhyme royal, rhyming couplets or prose); we also encounter variation in genre. These tales are part of a greater piece. The stories are gathered together as part of the story of a pilgrimage from the Tabard Inn in Southwark to the holy martyr St Thomas à Becket's shrine in Canterbury: "This composite work [*The Canterbury Tales*] is not simply a collection of stories paired off with their individual tellers, but a poem whose interests are divided between story-telling and a satirical analysis of human personality" (Winny in Chaucer, 1977, p. 2).

It is believed that these tales were inspired by *The Decameron* by Giovanni Boccaccio. There is evidence that Chaucer consumed a great amount of Italian literature and he may have been inspired to write something alike in the English tongue. His is an unfinished work; only 24 tales survive. *The Canterbury Tales* appears in 92 manuscripts, but these do not date from Chaucer's own time but were made by 15th-century amanuenses. [2]

One of those tales is reinterpreted by Zadie Smith in her contemporary adaptation, "The Wife of Bath's Prologue and Tale". [3] In the work by Chaucer, we encounter a female pilgrim, Alisoun, The Wife of Bath. In the General Prologue we learn many details of her persona. We know she is "somewhat deaf" [4] (Chaucer, 1977, l. 446) and she makes a living of cloth-making (l. 447). We picture her wearing "stockings ... of fine scarlet red" (l. 456) and her face coloured with the same hue looks "bold ... and fair" (l. 458). In line 459, we read "she was a worthy woman all her life", even in her afterlife where Zadie Smith brings her back once again to reinvent and to reassess womanly issues.

DOI: 10.4324/9781003470434-9

Issues which are still contended and debatable in the 21st century. As Marion Turner (2023) in her biography of the Wife of Bath asserts: "The Wife of Bath is the first ordinary woman in English literature. By that I mean the first mercantile, working, sexually active woman" (p. 2). The Wife provides a more realistic view of a woman who exposes her virtues and vices without restriction; being faithful to what she believes.[5]

In the same vein, Zadie Smith transports The Wife via her adaptation to a more contemporary setting. Smith's theatrical debut provides a 21st-century account of the London borough where she comes from, Brent. *The Wife of Willesden* comprises three different parts resembling the structure found in Chaucer's work: the Tale is preceded by The General Lock-In and the Prologue to the Tale, together with a Retraction at the end. This work was written to celebrate Brent as the 2020 "London Borough of Culture" and it was premiered in November 2021 at the Kiln Theatre, a local theatre in the borough mentioned above. It is written in verse couplets and as Smith (2021) declares on the title page: "translated from the Chaucerian into North Weezian".

Zadie Smith's *The Wife of Willesden* is innovative and challenging.[6] She transforms and adapts *The Wife* by Chaucer to the very particular circumstances we can find in the current century and in a particular part of London. Thus, the tale becomes an inclusive account of Brent and it portrays the London she knows through "experience, though noon auctoritee" (Chaucer, 1977, l. 1), to quote Alisoun herself. Smith translated the source text to North Weezy (North West London dialect) intertwined with Jamaican patois, posh English, or cockney. The text itself is dedicated to the Windrush generation[7] and thus it seeks to address a political and cultural issue. However, this chapter focuses on the universal application this text can offer. Although Smith provides her own perspective through her own experience, I believe the feminine issues are relatable to women across the world.[8]

This chapter aims primarily to tackle those instances where Alvita (Alisoun) exemplifies *sovereigntee* and gives her own opinion of female sexuality and pleasure. Consent and feminine pleasure are two contentious topics which even nowadays are taboo at times. Nonetheless, these two topics were debated in great detail in a work form the 14th century. Therefore, we can surmise there is still a need to talk openly about these issues, particularly to young people. Knowledge is power, experience provides that knowledge and *The Wife* confirms it. In this eclectic work we find violence, both physical and psychological but also empowerment and reinvention: "Her indiscretions and shortcomings stand not as types of moral weakness, but as details of a complicated personality" (Winny in Chaucer, 1977, p. 5).

Alvita as well as Alisoun are not the emissaries of morality, yet they defend what they find is fair and demand a revaluation of the male gaze: "Who peyntede the leon, tel me who?" (Chaucer, 1977, l. 692) Smith, in her adaptation, validates how contemporary this matter still is. Alvita questions the *happily ever after* dream about first love. She explores the different marriages she has had and talks openly about her husbands (a total of five men). She also points out the shock her words may cause to the public, words uttered by a woman. The ultimate purpose of this chapter is to show how a text from the 14th century has served as a source for a contemporary text for and about women. Alvita, in her mid-fifties, recounts her experience as wife and widow, but ultimately as a woman. She talks blatantly about sex, pleasure and consent. Furthermore, she discusses tolerance and the choice to decide whether to have children. Alvita will not tame her tongue; as Smith anticipates in the Introduction: "She nah easy and she talk her mind" (Smith, 2021, p. xviii).

The General Lock-In

Zadie Smith's impressive adaption reveals a mastery of its kind. She remains absolutely truthful to Chaucer's character while concocting different scenes and updating the topics to the 21st century. Consent and feminine sexual pleasure are two of the most salient ones. These are treated in a raw and unapologetic manner, not suitable for prudish minds. As Smith (2021) points out in the Introduction, both Alison and Alvita share "a startling indifference to the opinions of others and a passionate compulsion to live her own life as she pleases" (pp. xvi–xvii).

Before the Prologue, Smith contextualizes the setting in the "General Lock-in". A group of people from diverse walks of life are gathered in the Colin Campbell, a local pub on Kilburn High Road run by Polly Bailey. All are there to be part of the theme for the night, *Celebrating Local Stories*. One of those people is presented as Alvita, the Wife of Willesden, a woman who seems to be the one attracting the attention, although her entrance to the scene is not immediate. When it is time to start sharing stories the male gaze is pinpointed and its accuracy doubted.

> All telling their stories. Mostly men. Not because they had better stories but because they had no doubt that we should hear them
>
> *(Smith, 2021, p. 8)*

Even a snippet from a conversation between a couple is included, mockingly expressing their views on marriage as something related to cosmology and fate. As if the alignment of stars is the cause of matrimonial success. The author is blatantly bored with these nonsensical stories when she sees Alvita. She reckons (for we know the author is female) she has a story worth telling. The introduction of Alvita is extravagantly comic, yet remarkably close to Chaucer's text. Her husbands explain: "she's a bit deaf herself", "And skilful! Makes her own clothes, every stich" (Smith, 2021, p. 9); "Her underwear is dramatic – and red/like the soles of her knock-off 'Choos'" (p. 10). Later,

"With that gap-toothed smile she strides around town" (p. 11).[9] There is also a contemporary adaptation of her garments. For instance, her hat is referenced as a Zulu *Isicholo* (a South African hat for married women)[10] and her skirt is portrayed as a piece of clothing *showing* [11] her shape.

The last husband and youngest one, Ryan, tells the audience that Alvita has been *hitched* five times to five different men.[12] To his comment, Winston (Husband no. 3) adds a remark implying that there must have been more men before marriage: "Without counting back-in-the-day bredrin"[13] (Smith, 2021, p. 10). Alvita's alleged libertinism is deliberately questioned by two of her husbands, which resonates with the male gaze previously mentioned at the beginning of the General Lock-In. Asma, a local rebel wife, protests and defends her friend: "She's a well-travelled woman" who "allows/Herself adventures" (p. 10).

Husband no. 2, Darren, addresses Alvita's sense of freedom but also her *pilgrim* soul: "She likes to wander. Hates to be tied down" (Smith, 2021, p. 11). Thus, due to her skill in treading the world she is known as an expert on matters of the heart. This savvy is defined in both Chaucer's and Smith's texts: "Cupid's dart has pierced/Her so often, she's an expert on love" (Smith, 2021, p. 11).[14] This statement serves as a prelude to the famous lines at the beginning of the Wife of Bath's Prologue: "Experience, though noon auctoritee/Were in this world, is right ynogh for me" (Chaucer, 1977, ll. 1–2). Smith's own version of the Wife's Prologue opens with the same message. Alvita, like Alisoun, will tell you her own story, unapologetically, uncensored yet ultimately genuine.

The Wife of Willesden's Prologue

In Smith's adaptation, Alvita is presented as a "world-class raconteur" (Smith, 2021, p. 15). As previously mentioned in the Introduction, there is a melting pot of different accents. Her characters deliberately switch from North Weezy to posh English; we come across instances of Jamaican patois and of cockney. This is very different to Chaucer's Middle English, yet this is another deliberate effect of the play. By means of this eclectic mix of accents it is subconsciously inviting audiences from across London. This is a play about and for *the people*, down-to-earth, raw and genuine.

ALVITA: Let me tell you something: I do not need any permission or college degrees to speak on how marriage is *stress*. I been married five damn times since I was nineteen!

(Smith, 2021, p. 10)

Like Alisoun, Alvita states her authority, not through books but through experience.[15] They both aim to explain their own version of marriage and, especially, their sorrow and despair. In other words, what the happy endings in fairy tales do not tell the reader. Alvita's story is the complex process of becoming a wife to five different men and not losing her identity in the process. Nonetheless, both women are criticized for this very reason of being married five times. The Bible is used in both texts to back up this argument. Because Jesus went to only one wedding, in Cana of Galilee, it is deduced that one husband is enough for each woman. Both Wives cannot understand the wrong of this. They wonder if there is a right number of men or a set limit for every woman. According to Alvita: "And if there *is* a right number of men,/That's news to me" (Smith, 2021, p. 17).

Ian, Darren, Winston, Elridge and Ryan are the five husbands involved in the play. All of them are considered not total "wastemen" (Smith, 2021, p. 15). After officially presenting them, Alvita gives the reason for her selection of men. If we compare this fragment with Chaucer's text we find the same hilarious answer and erotic overtones. Whereas Alvita talks about their "*ass-ets*', different for each person" (Smith, 2021, p. 19), Alisoun goes beyond and states that she "has picked out the best,/Both of their lower purse (scrotum) and of their strongbox" (Chaucer, 1977, ll. 44a–44b). Physical and pecuniary *attributes* were considered in the choosing of her husbands.

Her sincerity escalates to the point of admitting her eagerness to find the sixth husband. She declares she is not going to "wait for (her) hymen to grow back./That's not me"[16] (Smith, 2021, p. 19). She asks for advice and asks Pastor Jegede whether if your husband dies, the wife is then absolutely free to find and marry another man. The Pastor is not comfortable answering positively to this question; he is perturbed by Alvita's lack of reticence, even of moral correctness.

The next question which arises is that of virginity and sex for pleasure. Alvita discusses with her Auntie P the issue of virginity and the teachings of St Paul. Alvita pinpoints that St Paul commanded people not to have sex for fun but only for reproductive purposes. But also, if "they cannot contain, let them marry: for it is better to marry than to burn" (1 Corinthians, 7:9). However, she declares that for her it is a piece of advice because "everyone got to make their own choice/In life" (Smith, 2021, p. 21). Plurality and tolerance are two characteristic features of how Alvita conducts her speech. She is not imposing her way of seeing the world but offering a different story to the conventional storytelling about marriage. At this point, God utters "Everyone. Asexual. NOW" (Smith, 2021, p. 21). The irony is found in the fact that sexuality is part and parcel of our nature as human beings. Even the absence of it, *asexuality*, validates its existence. This is supported by rational evidence: "how's/He (St Paul) expecting to make more pure virgins/When there's nobody to give birth to them?" (p. 22).

Regarding the topic of tolerance, specifically tolerance from women to women, there is a powerful scene where Kelly, Alvita's niece, makes her first entrance: "Alvita's very nerdy, shy, and put-upon niece, dares to raise her voice" (p. 22). She represents Alisoun's niece in the original text. This character embodies the personification of young women who are not yet confident to express their inner doubts and passions. While still talking about virginity, Kelly, overcoming her shyness, expresses:

KELLY: Maybe that's not meant for everybody? Like, Mum, maybe God makes some people true saints, yeah? But with some he's like: s'up to you … Like, I totally get Jesus was pure and he was into that but are you sure it's got to be like that for me and you?

(*Smith, 2021, p. 22*)

Kelly is not criticizing or rejecting Christian precepts but offering the possibility of other alternatives in the way we tackle virginity and sexual preference. Alvita, triumphantly, acknowledges that she must wait for the next husband. She cannot marry another one before the current one has died, or that would be bigamy: "The only thing I'm willing to admit/Is you probably have to wait till one dies/Before you move on, because bigamy-wise/That'd be an issue" (Smith, 2021, p. 23). Ian (Husband no. 1), is compared to St Paul. He is the archetype of a reactionary man who is easily perturbed by Alvita's explosively erotic behaviour; her "sinful embrace" (p. 23). This first relationship is described as mixing sanctity and a supernova; it is not about right or wrong, chaste, or sinful, it is about different perspectives regarding marriage, love and passion. Not necessarily being passionate means being sinful. However, she admits that she delights herself in being who she is; she does not need to feign for a greater good: "My thing is: you want to think you're a saint?/Fine. But don't slut-shame me because I ain't/About that" (p. 24).

The next scene contains sexual and erotic overtones. Alvita's outspokenness in questions of sexual freedom is astonishingly frank and unfiltered. Some readings might accuse Alvita of having a faulty morality, but the immediacy of her speech makes the audience think this is an honest and spur-of-the-moment commentary.[17] She commences a debate with Auntie P and Zaire, Alvita's best friend. They talk about the working function of genitals[18] and other purposes. Alvita opens up the conversation, directly addressing her aunt in the following manner:

ALVITA: … This equipment between our legs which we carry: why d'we have them in the first place? Or you reckon it's some kind of mistake?

(*Smith, 2021, p. 26*)

According to her aunt's prudish beliefs, the genitalia are only used for two main purposes. The first for the act of urinating which is a physiological process. But also, to differentiate a man from a woman. In her expostulation there is no room for sexual pleasure, not least female sexual pleasure.

Nevertheless, Alvita uses rationality once again to offer another alternative purpose of female genitalia. She reckons that if obtaining pleasure by means of the genitalia is available to women, why it is something apparently forbidden or shameful?

ALVITA: Auntie's a comedian. But she knows well from experience how these
    things go. It's crazy to me that Pastor gets mad when I talk about
    women's pleasure and the idea that if there *is* a God he can't hate on his
    own gift, which we must see is not just for making babies or … wee.

(Smith, 2021, p. 26)

Zaire, Alvita's friend, raises the question of childbirth. A woman does not
necessarily need to use her genitalia for reproductive reasons. She wonders if
it should be compulsory for a woman to follow the path of motherhood just
because this is (in theory) what they are meant for. The question of whether
to have kids or not is a contentious issue nowadays. There is still a huge
pressure on women who are not willing or do not feel the need to become
mothers.[19]

ZAIRE: But just cos you have working genitals we don't *have* to go down the
    kid road? All of us don't need babies. It's cool if your road is kids. But
    that's not all these are for.

(Smith, 2021, p. 27)[20]

Alvita proceeds in her exemplification of marriage as a bond where there is
room for sexual pleasure: "And in *my* marriage I'll use *this* for fun" (Smith,
2021, p. 28).[21] It is not a shameful act but a consensual act: "I demand pleasure./That is your debt to me. It's not pressure,/Exactly, it's about consent"[22]
(p. 28). For her, a husband owes her a debt. She knows she deserves it and
demands consensual sex where both parties can enjoy pleasure.[23]

At this point in the play as well as in the original text, there is a break in
the thread of the story. The Wife addresses the topic of power. In these lines,
Alvita proceeds to talk about the conditions of her marriage. In this proviso
she specifies what she considers a truthful union:

ALVITA: You'll agree to owe me love, good sex, and that when we marry, your
    body and soul will be mine.[24] As long as we're a thing. From that time till
    we're done, your body is my playground, it's for me, not for you.

(Smith, 2021, p. 28)

This is one of the irreverent speeches which can meet with disapproval
among male readers. In fact, Alvita's words were received with "some consternation, too, especially from some of the men" (Smith, 2021, p. 29). She
addresses the fact that in a mutually consensual relationship, the physical
bodies must be used as the *playground* or the space where both enjoy the act.

Also, this message can be expanded to the point of talking about understanding and generosity when it comes to one's own feminine pleasure.

The Wife's enterprise is to explain through her experience and to warn men not to make the same mistakes. As we will see in the analysis of the Tale, the ultimate purpose is to talk about what women really need and want. She claims she can be "wild and rough" (Smith, 2021, p. 31) at times, so she asks for an open-minded disposition to what she has to say.

Alvita proceeds with her story by giving an account of her husbands. According to her, three were good men and two were not (Smith, 2021, p. 31). The three, she tells, are the oldest. They are men who have already found their place in the world. Their maturity is praised by her, yet their sexual drive is not. She realizes that she demands more when it comes to satisfying her sexual desire.[25] This maturity contrasts with the fleeting character of younger lovers who need "a magic potion/To get their love, respect, and devotion" (p. 32).

She begins with husband Darren (no. 2). During her account of events, she addresses the topics of jealousy, marital infidelity and double standards. She has proof of her husband being unfaithful to her. However, he claims that it is his cousin who he is seeing and not a lover. She uses this example of alleged infidelity to talk about double standards. Her outings with male company trigger her husband's jealousy. She claims that he becomes judgemental and jealous *just because* she is hanging out with a male friend without proof of any misconduct: "But that's what I've found/About husbands. They chat too much breeze/About women. Got way too many theories" (Smith, 2021, p. 33).

Husband Winston (no. 3) warns the audience not to trust a "gold digger" (Smith, 2021, p. 34). They would pursue your money and not your love. Ultimately, she will get alimony and get financial support and security. Husband Ian (no. 1) talks about the fact that if a woman's income is larger than a man's, this fact would make him doubt his own masculinity: "When a man/ Earns less than his wife you'll find he can't/Respect himself" (p. 34). This way of treating men's own manliness in terms of pecuniary advantage over women is an example of toxic masculinity.[26]

No matter the case, the blame is always to be placed on the wife. Even the possession of beauty is a wife's own fault. Husband Darren's comeback addresses the impossibility of a wife being faithful if she is pretty. All these misogynistic arguments lead Alvita to come to the conclusion that it is not women's fault. Yet female superiority poses a threat to the very foundations of manliness. She claims that "everything you once loved about us/Becomes the problem. If we still attract/Attention" offering an explanation of this behaviour: "But deep down? It's all insecurity" (Smith, 2021, p. 35).[27]

Husband Elridge (no. 4) on his part talks about the loss of sexual attraction or even passion once the sacred union takes place. He also accuses women of behaving differently before marriage so as to reveal their true identity afterwards: "The thing about women is they/Act a certain way up until the day/You wed" (Smith, 2021, p. 36).[28] Furthermore, he does not take responsibility for the loss of passion, in this case, it seems it just involves one in the relationship: "New becomes old. Fresh becomes boring./ The pink cammy gets switched for grey cotton … /All that tear-your-clothes-off sex? Forgotten" (p. 36).

Alvita comes back to the topic of ownership in marriage. We have previously seen her ironic comments on bodily ownership when it comes to sexual pleasure. However, in the following lines she talks about freedom and ownership. She is no longer talking about sex but about personal freedom as an individual who is willingly sharing their time with someone else. She tells her husband Elridge:

ALVITA: You psych yourself out, stressing about who owns me, while you keep your junk under lock and key. And try to keep me home. But we don't own each other. I don't check up on my phone, or use GPS to see where you are.

(Smith, 2021, p. 38)

Husband Elridge verbally attacks Alvita for her way of dressing, hence evoking the misogynist stereotype of a prostitute wearing inappropriate clothing: "Please don't use, my brother,/One type of woman to cuss another./We are all sisters" (Smith, 2021, p. 41). Not all men behave as Alvita's husbands[29] nor can all women be reduced to a label. Sisterhood enables women to fight and debunk patriarchy. A healthy relationship within and outside the feminine world where mutual respect and inclusion provides a safe space for women.

The Prologue proceeds, and Alvita continues defending and protecting the concept of womanhood. Husband Winston compares love given by a woman to the pits of hell: "To love you is hell –/It's like I'm thirsty and you're a dry well" (Smith, 2021, p. 42). Alvita's love is compared to a fiery place; for consumed by fire is how Husband Darren and Husband Ian feel. Alvita is also compared to woodworms that consume and destroy trees from inside.[30] This destructive criticism sets an utterly catastrophic tone by which females are reduced to devastation and rottenness.

In the following paragraph, Alvita is pointing towards an imbalance in how we judge certain behaviours. In this case, she opens the debate to whether it is reasonable to be unfaithful when you are no longer appreciated in the relationship. She expostulates and blames patriarchy for those restrictions on women. According to her, her husband had an affair, but she could not even think she was being neglected. And, if she dared, she would be called a *bad wife* or a *shrew*, both derogatory terms. Furthermore, she declares that she did not cheat but she found pleasure in flirting. On the other hand, he is depicted as a chronically jealous person, and this unfounded jealousy made his life utter hell:

ALVITA: Why're you groaning? You wanna get with me? Mi deh yah[31] – I'm right here. Now, you see, fact is this pum-pum[32] could have a good time somewhere else – don't mean to kill the mood – But apparently if I cheat on you that would make me a *bad wife* and *a shrew. Lawd!* The patriarchy! It's like I'm caught in a trap and it's all your own damn fault! Oh, we'd have a lot of these little chats ... Let's move on. Fourth Husband. We'll get into that: My fourth husband was a proper player. We were married but he had a lover. And I was young, and really feeling myself.

(Smith, 2021, pp. 46–47)

Alvita presents her own journey, through different seasons of womanhood. She talks about her *sweet May*, being *in September* now. But also, she acknowledges in a very crude way the heavy burden of growing old and its physical manifestations "Now I'm old. Boobs hang low. Lost my bum" (Smith, 2021, p. 48), facts which are presented in a crude yet realistic manner and that realistic simplicity may resonate with a female audience.

The description of Alvita's relationship with her fifth husband is the harshest, and her evocative telling of physical violence may be distressing. This is, without a doubt, a very contemporary example of what is happening in many households. Surprisingly, she does not wish him to rot in hell despite the fact that he has mistreated her. Alvita, aware of the gravity of the situation, proclaims that it would be the first and last time this ever happens to her. She is not blindfolded in any way and she is able to address the issue and be willing to stop it. However, she also sympathizes with those who might find it difficult to put an end to it. Thus, she reckons the difficulty in distancing oneself from a partner with a powerful sexual connection. In this destructive loop,[33] she understands how easy it is to feel trapped. She claims that this irrational attachment to the other person is hard to eliminate even though one is conscious of its deceiving nature:

ALVITA: That's the first and last time I'll let that happen, I swear. He hurt me here, there, oh, everywhere ... And yet in bed he was so fresh, so fine, gave head with such skill, the man took his time, So even when I was aching from old bruises, I could turn his base love to gold. Can it be I loved him more than the rest because he always gave me so much less?

(Smith, 2021, pp. 50–51)

This fifth husband is portrayed as an Oxford student who is doing his Master's.[34] His alleged superiority lies in his intellectual background. She happened to meet him at her fourth husband's funeral. She evokes the scene and declares that she behaved as was customary for widows: "I got my weep on, and really did look/Gutted, like a proper sad widow should" (Smith, 2021, p. 55), but we all know this is far from the truth; she could not possibly feel sadness for someone who was unfaithful to her.

The scene, which is rather lugubrious, is turned into an utterly comic scene where Alvita is sexually aroused when she sees Ryan (Husband no. 5):

ALVITA: And God help me, but I was like *wow* He's fit, you know! Nice body, tight round bum … He was twenty. I could have been his mum.

(Smith, 2021, p. 55)

She is not ashamed of her own desires. Although she is in her forties, her sexual appetite and bodily desires are something of a youngish nature. She acknowledges her own nature and accepts her inclination to utter physical attraction: "Like Venus gave me lust and passion,/But Mars made a woman of action"[35] (Smith, 2021, pp. 55–56). This straightforward and sincere confession of her inner passions can be problematic if taken too seriously. She is being open about her own nature as a sexual being. Perhaps she delights herself too much in using coarse language or she presents an inability to restrain herself. Ultimately, this genuine manner of relating what is not politically correct is what makes her speech unhackneyed. She leaves us a thoughtful speech about her inclusive appetites:

ALVITA: I'm all instinct. It's whatever feels right. He can be tall or short or black or white – I'm not bothered, as long as he feels me. Don't have to be rich, or have a degree … What can I say?

(Smith, 2021, p. 56)

Examining this declaration leads us to two possible reasonings. Either we consider Alvita to be a man-eater who really does not have a preference due to her lust, or Alvita comes across as someone who does not pay attention to physical traits, social status, or race. Ultimately, she seeks true passion as her emotional response to her lover. As she puts it: "as long as he feels me" (Smith, 2021, p. 56).[36] This problematic view is also found in Chaucer's text, where Alisoun's ambiguity so challenges our preconceptions and judgement as to leave the reader at a loss or heavily reflecting on it.[37]

She proceeds with her tale and how things changed drastically when they got married. Alvita tells how she is half deaf because Ryan exerted control over her by means of physical violence. The reason of this domestic violence episode is that Alvita tore a page from a book he was reading. Physical violence cannot be justified in any shape or form, the reason for this aggression is utterly deplorable.[38]

She feels trapped in this marriage. He even controls her movements; she says that he has the right to do so as a husband. His authority, he finds, is validated in different texts.[39] These texts are *ad feminam* abusive texts written by male authors giving instructions about how to treat or, to put it another way, how to control wives.[40] These books indoctrinate readers in the treacherous and perversive nature of women. This fanatic view of looking at women transforms their relationship into one of hate and, blame. Alvita is compared to Eve, the first one to be blamed in history, for she was responsible for the damnation of humanity.

Husband Ryan proceeds in his expostulation, arguing there were more doomed women in the past. He enumerates all the *bad wives* of history: Delilah betrayed Samson and cut his hair, thus leaving him devoid of strength; Hercules' second wife Deianira unintentionally poisoned him; Xanthippe's abusive behaviour towards her husband Socrates.

These sexist comments infuriate Alvita. She continues the thread of examples of different wives in history who allegedly mistreated their husband in one way or another.[41] Alvita has had enough of this never-ending loop of misogyny. She puts her foot down and faces her husband in an act of desperation:[42]

ALVITA: Can you imagine how much it hurt me to listen to this pure misogyny? And when I saw him about to restart reading that damn book.[43]

(Smith, 2021, p. 67)

Zaire explains how Alvita tore three pages of the book. This book is composed of different contemporary sexist books. Smith provides a contemporary literary background[44] for Husband Ryan's prejudices against women. This sexist propaganda becomes "his Bible" (Smith, 2021, p. 59), as Alvita puts it. As precisely introduced by the narrator, the re-enactment of a vital scene takes place at a point where Alvita's exhaustion leads her to destroy the object representing the abuse. An object which contains a mystification of wifehood. Thus, the act of physically tearing the sheets of the book apart becomes the debunking of the myth itself. She also strikes him across the face and he lands on the fireplace. This humiliating scene causes the husband's choleric comeback and provides a harsh and violent domestic scene.[45]

Patriarchy replies with a fit of rage in the shape of physical violence. Husband Ryan "chose/To get up and strike (her) upside (her) head" (Smith, 2021, p. 68). She receives a very violent blow; she lies on the floor as if she were dead. There are tragic overtones in this scene where it seems Alvita is not superior enough (either physically or intellectually) to match her misogynist husband. Alvita regains consciousness and her husband, who was about to run away from the crime scene, kneels and asks for forgiveness.

HUSBAND RYAN: I love you, darling Alvita, I swear to God I will never beat yer. Though it was sort of your fault that I did,[46] I hope you'll find it in your heart to forgive.

(Smith, 2021, p. 69)

She is reluctant to accept the apology, but in the end, his husband complies with her wife's exigencies. She becomes the master of the relationship; she owns her own property and he finds himself unable to function without prior consent of his wife. She upends her place in the relationship, from feeling trapped to re-emerging on top. On the other hand, her husband changes to the submissive type whereby his wife's own volition conditions his own behaviour. This denouement seems to conclude a marital war where both powers have been tested. Alvita's supremacy over her husband occurs when he becomes servile and accepts her conditions:

HUSBAND RYAN: Oh, my amazing wife, do whatever you want with your own life; What's best for you is clearly best for me.

(Smith, 2021, p. 70)

Alvita leaves us with a reflection to finish her Prologue. Notwithstanding the final crisis between her and her husband Ryan, both reach a consensus on what is best for their marriage to succeed. She acknowledges from that moment onwards that he behaves as a dutiful husband.

The Wife of Willesden's Tale

The Tale provides a question and an answer to the Wife's own tribulations. Zadie Smith sets the Tale in a different scene to that of Chaucer: 18th-century Jamaica. The author finds this setting more suitable for her adaptation than Arthurian times. In both stories, the male in charge (the King) delegates to the Queen[47] the decision on the destiny of a man accused of rape.[48] In the text by Smith, we encounter Queen Nanny, who was the leader of the Maroons in 18th-century Jamaica.[49]

Queen Nanny had a young Maroon in her army. This military man allegedly raped a young woman.[50] Darren (Husband no. 2) and Kelly (Alvita's niece) perform the outrageous deed. In the text we find two pauses. The first pause is placed before the rape takes place. The omission of information reflects the inability to describe what is about to happen. The absence of information enables the reader to fill the gap and imagine the horrendous scene:

A virgin, with no interest in this guy, But he wouldn't stop. *Pause.* He thought his strength gave him the right. *Longer pause.*

(Smith, 2021, p. 77)

The Queen believes death is not enough as a punishment for this *bad bwoy*. She does not deny the possibility of such an outcome, yet she would like to employ a different manner to punish him:

QUEEN NANNY: Yuh nuh outta trouble yet! Mi might still Kill you. But capital punishment will only go so far. I'm interested in restorative justice. Understanding who you hurt and why.

(Smith, 2021, p. 78)

Queen Nanny, in her wisdom, acknowledges that the death penalty would be insufficient. She goes beyond the natural impulse of revenge for such an atrocious deed; she claims she is more interested in restorative justice. As Queen and head of the community, her interest lies in the reformation of this man and luring him into the pursuit of repentance.[51]

Queen Nanny's resolution is that he should embark upon the adventure of finding what women most desire:

QUEEN NANNY: So here is my deal: You'll live – *if* you can tell me what *we* feel – I mean we women. What *we* most desire. You tell me that? I won't set you on fire.

(Smith, 2021, p. 78)

The words in italics accentuate the fact that what Queen Nanny really wants is that he comprehends the necessities of women. When he raped the young woman, he did not grind to a halt when he saw she was not eager to have sexual intercourse. In the text, his physical superiority is what enables him to take advantage of her. Thus, his duty is to focus on women's desire, which implies a complete abnegation of the man's own needs. The restorative justice she imposes on him is just the execution of a selfless act.

The impossibility of finding a consensual answer is a parody in itself. This is reflected in Smith's work where Husband Winston, Husband Ian, Auntie P, Zaire and Husband Elridge discuss the matter as a parallel story to the Tale itself. Husband Winston claims that what women most desire is money, to whch Aunti P replies that she is *personally* [52] fond of jewels. According to Husband Ian, it is power which women are most drawn to; yet for Husband Elridge, sycophantic praise is what satisfies women. Zaire, on the other hand, pinpoints that it is not material things women want but carnal satisfaction. She speaks up: "Women want actual orgasms, you fools!/And to have multiple partners – unjudged" (Smith, 2021, p. 80).[53]

They agree on freedom as the essential desire or need of women. A longing for liberation so they would be able to seek their own appetites and wishes, freed of patriarchal criticism and absolute judgement.[54] They are exhausted from listening about their failings, their lack of common sense and their irrationality – personality traits which have long been attributed to women in the most general sense.

Alvita proceeds with her Tale. The young man encounters a "troll-like old Obeah woman" (Smith, 2021, p. 87) along the way.[55] She encourages him to tell her what he is seeking. This Old Wife[56] claims she can aid him in his errand, for "Dere's tings only ol'women unnerstan" (p. 87). When the Young Maroon comes back to court, complying with Queen Nanny's command, he gives an account of what the Old Wife taught him:

YOUNG MAROON: Queen Nanny, who rules this place with iron fist: The thing women want is basically this: They want their husbands to consent, freely; to *submit to their wives' wills* – which should be natural in love; for we submit to love. *Pause.* To keep power, and have no man above them – all women want this. And you can kill me, but I speak the truth. Do what you will.

(Smith, 2021, p. 90)[57]

The audience was highly satisfied by the young man's words.[58] Nonetheless, the Old Wife came to obtain her reward for revealing to the man the genuine truth. She claims he agreed on espousing her providing he survived. Thus, when Queen Nanny and the wise women in the audience consider that he does not deserve death, she claims her right and demands he be consistent with his words.

The Young Maroon is utterly terrified of this deed. He is eager to bestow her with riches and possessions yet what she cannot possess is his body: "But please leave my body! *It's my body*" (Smith, 2021, p. 92).[59] This desperate request echoes the previous rape episode. Although the rape scene is not explicitly described in the story, we might imagine a similar rejection of pliancy and submission on the young woman's part.

The Old Wife is ultimately more interested in the young man's love. Marriage is the conduct through which her wish is granted: She is not so much seeking to satisfy her sexual appetite. This whimsical behaviour of hers is a reaction to her own desperation for genuine love (Smith, 2021, p. 92). Whereas the Young Maroon is preoccupied with the maltreatment of his virility and the use of his body as the old lady's recreational facility, the Old Wife is complaining about his rejection. The reason for that rejection is her old, ugly, low-born and poor nature, so she is treated as a commodity with little or no value.[60]

The Old Wife commences an intellectual game in which she demonstrates sovereignty. Her new husband despises her because of his inability to change his present state. Yet he insists on her making up for the sacrifice he made in marrying her. The Old Wife, in her shrewdness, provides two alternatives to ease her husband's pain. Either she remains old and ugly but with the certainty she will never be unfaithful to him; or she becomes a young and beautiful woman in her prime, yet with the risk of her becoming too popular in the city.[61]

Eventually, he acknowledges it is a dead end and the Wife's mastery is something he cannot compete with. Finally, "*experience, though noon auctoritee*" prevails, and thus it validates what Alvita conveyed in her Prologue. She has learnt through experience with each of her marriages and through each of her husbands, to eventually resolve the tangle and comprehend what it is that she truly desires. She encapsulates feminine sovereignty through the lens of wifehood.[62]

Smith's sublime adaptation of the ending to contemporary needs is one which addresses body positivity. Whereas in Chaucer's Wife, the Old Wife transforms into a beautiful young woman who swears to be true and faithful,[63] Smith's Old Wife transforms into Alvita, a middle-aged woman in all her middle-aged beauteousness (Smith, 2021, p. 103), thereby busting the myth that beauty goes hand in hand with youth.[64] Both parties agree on pleasuring each other, thus achieving a reconciliation within the relationship. They are equally involved and committed to their life in common.

Concluding Remarks

What Alisoun presented in her Prologue and Tale is still a contemporary issue. Equality is not yet internalized due to hundreds of years of male-biased constructs. *The Wife of Willesden*'s value is not only found in the masterly crafted retelling of Chaucer's *Wife of Bath*, but its value also lies in the bringing back to the fore contentious topics which are sometimes neglected or overlooked. In this work, they find a way to reach a broad and inclusive audience, especially addressing young women who due to lack of experience may have more uncertainties about sexuality or femininity in a broader sense.

In the Tale we are given the question and the answer. What do women most desire? Nonetheless, there is a previous hint in the Prologue with which I would like to conclude this chapter. This answer is crafted in the form of a feminist manifesto, a declaration of intent, a request for freedom and a demand to regain agency. She demands sovereignty for women to govern themselves as they please.[65] Your own sovereignty equals your own freedom, and this is what Alisoun and Alvita pursue and demand on behalf of womankind. Smith's work pushes the boundaries,[66] and it continues Alisoun's task, encouraging women to develop critical thinking[67] which in turn can enable them to redefine her own view on femininity according to contemporary values and needs.

ALVITA: Women like me, we can't love control freaks. We want to travel, to live, to seek fresh pastures, possibilities, new worlds. We're women. Not children. Not little girls.

(Smith, 2021, p. 39)

Notes

1 See Part III, "Approaching Canterbury: Prologue for a historical introduction to the Tales", in Marion Turner's *Chaucer: A European life* (Princeton University Press, 2020).
2 See The Ellesmere Manuscript (*The Canterbury Tales*) c. 1400–1410. It is one of the most famous and earliest manuscripts. Their pages are also beautifully

illustrated. MS EL 26 C 9, The Huntington Library, San Marino, California. For an introduction see The British Library. Medieval collection items. The Ellesmere Manuscript (The Canterbury Tales), https://www.bl.uk/collection-items/ellesm ere-manuscript. See also William Caxton's *Geoffrey Chaucer, The Canterbury Tales*, 2nd edition, printed for the first time in 1476 and a second edition in 1483. G. 11586. Both editions are fully digitalized and available at https://www.bl.uk/trea sures/caxton/search.asp.

3 See page xii in Zadie Smith's *The Wife of Willesden* (2021) for an introductory explanation of the medieval pilgrimages to visit St Alban's shrine or the Black Madonna in St Mary's Willesden.

4 I will be using Harvard University's translation into contemporary English. The purpose of using modernized spelling is to reach a broader audience. Throughout the endnotes, The General Prologue will be hereafter cited as GP, The Wife of Bath's Prologue as WBP and The Tale as WBT. Zadie Smith's *The Wife of Willesden* will be hereafter cited as *WW* for notational purposes.

5 Marion Turner (2022) devotes a chapter in her biography of The Wife of Bath in which she praises among others Zadie Smith's work describing it as "a hugely dramatic adaptation of the Wife of Bath's Prologue and Tale … Like the original, it is long and luxuriant" (p. 231).

6 "A triumph of dramatic creativity, this slim volume is a total delight", in Herbert E. Shapiro (2023) Review of Smith, Zadie, *The Wife of Willesden* (p. 87).

7 The Windrush generation was a group of people who arrived in the UK from Caribbean countries during the years 1948 to 1971. They were key in providing support to help the post-war labour shortage. For more information check Colin Grant's *Homecoming: Voices of the Windrush Generation* (Vintage, 2019) as well as contemporary fiction like *The Lonely Londoners* by Sam Selvon (Penguin, 2021).

8 For a postcolonial reading of the text, see Marion Turner, *The Wife of Bath: A Biography* (Princeton UP, 2022), especially Chapter 10, "Black Alisons"; and Mohamed Karim Dhouib (2023), "Re-Telling Chaucer in Zadie Smith's *Wife of Willesden*", *New Chaucer Studies: Pedagogy and Profession, 4(2)*, 21–41.

9 WBP, ll. 446, 447, 453, 456, 457, 468.

10 *Woman's Hat (Isicholo)*. Art Institute Chicago. https://www.artic.edu/artworks/229886/woman-s-hat-isicholo

11 My own emphasis.

12 Compare with WBP, ll. 460–461: "She had (married) five husbands at the church door,/Not counting other company in youth".

13 British slang for "friend". Check entry for more information about the origin. http s://www.collinsdictionary.com/es/diccionario/ingles/bredren.

14 Compare with WBP, ll. 474–476: "In fellowship she well knew how to laugh and chatter./She knew, as it happened, about remedies for love/For she knew the old dance (tricks of the trade) of that art".

15 As Turner (2020) puts it, "The Wife's life as an authority outside her own tale is without parallel in Chaucer's corpus: he makes her an 'author' in a way that he does for no other character" (p. 458).

16 Compare this to a less straightway remark in WBP, l. 46: "For truly, I will not keep myself chaste in everything".

17 As Dhouib (2023) puts it: "The two women stress the corporeality of the human being and celebrate sex in a culture that sees it as sinful and aberrant" (p. 30).

18 This debate about the purpose of genitals is found in WBP, ll. 115–123.

19 It is assumed that Chaucer's Wife may be childless since she does not mention it. Turner (2022) also points out that we can find "a phrase in the General Prologue (line 475) description of her that may imply her familiarity with contraception and abortion. The narrator tells us that she knows well the 'remedies of love'" (p.

221). See also Alison Buckett Rivera (1998), "Motherhood in the Wife of Bath", *Selim, 6,* 103–116.

20 Compare to WBP, ll. 135–137: "But I say not that every person is required,/That has such equipment as I to you told,/To go and use them in procreation".

21 Compare to WBP, ll. 149–150: "In wifehood I will use my instrument/As freely as my Maker has it sent".

22 Compare to WBP, ll. 152–153: "My husband shall have it both evenings and mornings,/When it pleases him to come forth and pay his debt".

23 A reference to a non-judgemental approach to sex in Chris Donaghue (2015): "Sexual activism, sexual health, and sex positivity are about a perspective and a lifestyle of not perpetuating or creating 'norms' or policing the borders of what is 'acceptable' when sex is consensual, non-damaging, and pleasurable" (p. 5).

24 Compare to WBP ll. 158–159: "I have the power during all my life/Over his own body, and not he".

25 Alvita's disappointment is relatable to the experience told by Chaucer's Wife. See WBP, ll. 198–202.

26 See Andrea Waling (2023), "Inoculate boys against toxic masculinity: Exploring discourses of men and masculinity in #Metoo commentaries", *The Journal of Men's Studies, 31*(1), 130–156, and Carol Harrington (2020) "What is 'toxic masculinity' and why does it matter?" *Men and Masculinities, XX*(X), 1–8. DOI: 10.1177/1097184X20943254.

27 Compare Alvita's rebuttal with that of Chaucer's wife in these absolutely brilliant lines in WBP, ll. 248–256: "Thou sayest to me it is a great misfortune/To wed a poor woman, because of expense;/And if she be rich, of high birth,/Then thou sayest that it is a torment/To put up with her pride and her angry moods./And if she be fair, thou utter knave,/Thou sayest that every lecher wants to have her;/She can not remain chaste for any length of time,/Who is assailed on every side".

28 Compare to WBP, ll. 282–284.

29 See p. 35 in Smith's work. Alvita says: "For some men it's awful/If a woman is rich or hot or fine/Or smart of talented or sweet or kind". The use of *some men* negates the generalization.

30 Compare this imagery to WBP, ll. 371–378: "Thou also compare women's love to hell,/To barren land, where water may not remain./Thou compare it also to Greek [inextinguishable] fire; The more it burns, the more it has desire/To consume everything that will be burned./Thou sayest, just as worms destroy a tree,/Right so a wife destroys her husband;/This know they who are bound to wives".

31 "Patois meaning 'Everything is good, I'm here, I'm okay'" (*WW*, p. 47). This note is found in the original work by Zadie Smith.

32 "Patois: crude term for 'vagina'" (*WW*, p. 47). This note is found in the original work by Zadie Smith.

33 Compare to Chaucer's Wife (WBP, ll. 508–514).

34 In Chaucer's Wife, the fifth husband is Jankin, a former clerk at Oxford, a book keeper and accountant to a previous husband.

35 "Sturdy boldness" (WBP, l. 612) in Alisoun's words.

36 Compare to Alisoun's words: "I never loved in moderation,/But always followed my appetite,/Whether he were short, or tall, or black-haired, or blond;/I took no notice, provided that he pleased me,/How poor he was, nor also of what rank" (WBP, ll. 622–626).

37 This dichotomic nature is also commented by Alexandra Melville: "The Wife's self-awareness of her own socially outrageous behaviour does, however, create a layer of irony around her character, leaving it ambiguous as to whether she is a virago, a figure of ridicule and disgust, or a satirical tool for Chaucer" (Melville, 2022).

38 Mary Carruthers (1979) considers that Jankyn is not an eccentric but "a very young man who has suddenly been given control of the entire estate of a formidable older wife and who feels understandably inadequate to the task" (p. 215).

39 See Richard McCormick Houser (2013), "Alisoun takes exception: Medieval legal pleading and the Wife of Bath", *The Chaucer Review, 48*(1), 66–90; for an insight into Chaucer's exploration of clerical authoritative texts and the risks of literal interpretation.

40 The fictious *Book of Wicked Wives* is the name Alisoun uses (WBP, l. 685). She addresses how all this material was written by male authors giving their own and biased perspective in how a wife should behave. Jerome's *Adversus Jovinianum* is one of the literary sources for this book. See Turner (2020, 452), Warren S. Smith (1997), "The Wife of Bath debates Jerome", *The Chaucer Review, 32*(2), 129–145; and Theresa Tinkle (2010) "Contested authority: Jerome and the Wife of Bath on 1 Timothy 2", *The Chaucer Review, 44*(3), 268–293. Also Ralph Hanna III and Traugott Lawler (Eds.) (1997), *Jankyn's Book of Wikked Wives. Vol. 1: The Primary Texts*, University of Georgia Press. To explain her point in WBP, she makes a reference to Aesop's fable *The Lion and the Man* in line 692 ("Who painted the lion, tell me who?"). See Robert M. Correale and Mary Hamel (Eds.) (1995), "Romulus, Fable 44: The Man and the Lion", *Sources and Analogues* (2: pp. 382–383), D. S. Brewer. The representation of the lion subjugated to men is just another example of the male gaze and humankind's supremacy. It is purposely represented in such a way because man's agency is put into a position of power. She reckons the same process took place with this representation of "bad" wives. Had female authors written those stories, we would have had more stories about male wickedness in our archives. See Mary Carruthers (1979), "The Wife of Bath and the painting of lions", *PMLA, 94*(2), 209–222; and Marjorie M. Malvern's (1983) "Who peyntede the leon, tel me who?": Rhetorical and didactic roles played by an Aesopic fable in the 'Wife of Bath's Prologue'", *Studies in Philology, 80*(3), 238–252.

41 She talks about Pasiphaë, goddess of witchcraft and sorcery. Cursed by Poseidon, she fell in love with a bull and after having sexual intercourse gave birth to the Minotaur. Clytemnestra, for example, together with her lover Aegisthus murdered Agamemnon. Eriphyle who persuades her husband to take part in a daunting enterprise and his foreseeable death in exchange of a necklace. Livia, third wife of the Roman emperor Augustus, who was suspected of poisoning the emperor and caused his death. These are but a few, but many women have been described as despicable wives. Robert A. Pratt (1963) talking about Chaucer's Wife states: "Thus Alice, in the latter portion of her Prologue, tells of two villains, two wicked clerks, Jerome and Jankyn – and we are hard put to choose between them: the writer of these scurrilous defamations of wives, and the bad husband who read the stories with such 'devocioun'" (p. 322).

42 See Anne McTaggart (2012), "What women want? Mimesis and gender in Chaucer's 'Wife of Bath's Prologue' and 'Tale'", *Contagion: Journal of Violence, Mimesis, and Culture, 19*, 2012, p. 51.

43 This "damn book" refers to the "Book of Wicked Wives" in WBP.

44 The following books and authors are mentioned: Jordan Peterson (2018), *Twelve Rules for Life: An Antidote to Chaos*, Allen Lane; Warren Farrell (1993), *The Myth of Male Power*, Simon and Schuster; Neil Strauss (2007), *The Game: Penetrating the Secret Society of Pick-Up Artists*, Canongate; Steve Moxon (2008), *The Woman Racket: The New Science Explaining How the Sexes Relate at Work, at Play and in Society*, Imprint Academic. These are the "saints" Husband Ryan refers to at p. 60.

45 Compare WBP, ll. 788–802. This scene represents a revolution against the literary misogynist cannon. See Turner (2020, p. 459).

46 Both wives are to be blamed for their respective husbands' ill-treatment. According to them, their behaviours trigger their husband's brutal fit of anger and therefore they must be pardoned. See WBP, ll. 804–806.

47 "The 'Wife of Bath's Tale' stages exactly this scene of male kingly violence being neutralized by queenly abjection and pleas for peace" (Turner, 2020, p. 71).

48 Compare to WBT, ll. 897–898.

49 See Karla Gottlieb (2000), *The mother of us all: A history of Queen Nanny, leader of the Windward Jamaican Maroons*, Africa World Press.

50 This scene is just but a line (888) in WBT.

51 The moral of the tale encompasses the achievement of equality by means of restorative justice: "The 'Wife of Bath's Tale' is thus a very serious tale indeed, a tale that forcefully puts forward the position that women and men of all ages and estates are moral equivalents" (Turner, 2020, p. 464).

52 My own emphasis.

53 Compare to WBT, ll. 925–930: "Some said women love riches best,/Some said honor, some said gaiety,/Some rich clothing, some said lust in bed,/And frequently to be widow and wedded./Some said that our hearts are most eased/When we are flattered and pleased".

54 Compare to WBT, ll. 935–944.

55 Compare to WBT, l. 999.

56 I concur with Susanne Sara Thomas (2006) in her view about avoiding the use of the term "hag" to describe the old woman. She does not agree on the use of this pejorative term because although "is usually used by critics discussing the tale ... not a term the tale itself uses, and because it is such a painfully sexist term that its usage should be discouraged" (p. 88).

57 Compare to WBT, ll. 1037–1041.

58 The Queen and women's sovereignty is also articulated in this scene where their good judgement is demonstrated. "The queen and ladies of the 'Wife of Bath's Tale' ... demonstrate equitable judgement and use their intelligence and reason to deflect violence" (Turner 2020, p. 360).

59 Compare this utter desperation to WBT, ll. 1058–1061: "This knight answered, 'Alas and woe is me!/I know right well that such was my promise./For God's love, choose a new request!/Take all my goods and let my body go'".

60 Compare to WBT, ll. 1062–1066.

61 Compare to WBT, ll. 1019–1027. As Anne McTaggart (2012) claims: "the purpose of asking him whether he would prefer a wife who is ugly but true or beautiful but possible unfaithful is not to see if he has learned the lesson of inner merit per se, but to see if he has learned the humility to know that it is not his place to decide what 'woman' is and how she should be for his sake" (p. 58).

62 Compare to WBT, ll. 1028–1035.

63 Compare to WBT, l. 1251: "That she so was beautiful, and so young moreover". As William F. Woods (2008) points out: "this old 'wyf' is like the Wife herself, her youth vanished, having to devise some way of continuing the 'olde daunce' of marriage – and life itself – in the no-man's land between what women want and what men want" (p. 129).

64 As Marion Turner (2022) puts it: "Beauty is again decoupled from age as, in a move of which Alison would surely have approved, Smith emphasises that ageing should not make women invisible or remove them from a world of sexual activity and attractiveness" (p. 246).

65 As Chaucer's Wife who was a pioneer in "exploring narratives of the self" and provides her audience with "a particular kind of revelation of the inner life" (Turner 2022, p. 4).

66 In a similar vein, Turner (2022) agrees on this fact when she explores Alison's Tale: "Part of Alison's project is to shine a light on the fact that there is usually no place in stories like

this for reasonable older women – and certainly not for older women to have acceptable sexual desires, or to be the ethical heart of the story" (p. 44).

67 So does Chaucer's Wife, as Turner pinpoints in her biography (2022): "Far more than an embodiment of antifeminist stereotypes, Alison and her text here encourage us to critique those source materials and to think about individual experience rather than official authority" (p. 17).

References

1 Corinthians, 7:9. (1975). In *Holy bible: New King James version*. Thomas Nelson.

Art Institute Chicago. *Woman's hat (Isicholo)*. https://www.artic.edu/artworks/229886/woman-s-hat-isicholo.

Buckett Rivera, A. (1998). Motherhood in The Wife of Bath. *Selim*, 6, 103–116. https://doi.org/10.17811/selim.6.1996.104-117.

Carruthers, M. (1979). The Wife of Bath and the painting of lions. *PMLA*, 94(2), 209–222. https://doi.org/10.2307/461886.

Chaucer, G. (1977). The Wife of Bath's prologue and tale. In G. Chaucer, *Selected tales from Chaucer* (J. Winny, Ed.). Cambridge University Press.

Correale, R. M. & Hamel, H. (1995). Romulus, fable 44: The man and the lion. In *Sources and Analogues* (pp. 382–383). D. S. Brewer. https://doi.org/10.1080/00138380802130865.

Dhouib, M. K. (2023). Re-telling Chaucer in Zadie Smith's Wife of Willesden. *New Chaucer Studies: Pedagogy and Profession*, 4(2), 21–41. https://doi.org/10.5070/NC34262323.

Donaghue, C. (2015). *Sex outside the lines: Authentic sexuality in a sexually dysfunctional culture*. BenBella Books. https://doi.org/10.1080/0092623X.2016.1176833.

Gottlieb, K. (2000). *The mother of us all: A history of Queen Nanny, leader of the Windward Jamaican Maroons*. Africa World Press.

Grant, C. (2019). *Homecoming: Voices of the Windrush generation*. Vintage.

Hanna III, R. & Lawler, T. (Eds.) (1997). *Jankyn's book of wikked wives. Vol. 1: The primary texts*. University of Georgia Press.

Harrington, C. (2020). What is toxic masculinity and why does it matter? *Men and Masculinities*, XX(X), 1–8. http://doi.org/10.1177/1097184X20943254.

Malvern, M. M. (1983). "Who peyntede the Leon, tel me who?": Rhetorical and didactic roles played by an Aesopic fable in the Wife of Bath's prologue. *Studies in Philology*, 80(3), 238–252.

McCormick Houser, R. (2013). Alisoun takes exception: Medieval legal pleading and the Wife of Bath. *The Chaucer Review*, 48(1), 66–90. https://doi.org/10.5325/chaucerrev.48.1.0066.

McTaggart, A. (2012) What women want? Mimesis and gender in Chaucer's Wife of Bath's Prologue and Tale. *Contagion: Journal of Violence, Mimesis, and Culture*, 19, 41–67. http://doi.org/10.1353/ctn.2012.0000.

Melville, A. (2022, 22 Aug). Female "soveraynetee" in Chaucer's "The Wife of Bath's Prologue and Tale". British Library. https://brewminate.com/female-soveraynetee-in-chaucers-the-wife-of-baths-prologue-and-tale/.

Pratt, R. A. (1963). Saint Jerome in Jankyn's Book of Wikked Wyves. *Criticism*, 5(4), 316–322.

Selvon, S. (2021). *The lonely Londoners*. Penguin.

Shapiro, H. E. (2023). Review of Smith, Zadie, The Wife of Willesden. Drama. *Library Journal*, 148(1), 87.

Smith, W. S. (1997). The Wife of Bath debates Jerome. *The Chaucer Review*, 32(2), 129–145.

Smith, Z. (2021). *The Wife of Willesden*. Penguin.

Thomas, S. S. (2006). The Problem of Defining "Sovereynetee" in the "Wife of Bath's Tale". *The Chaucer Review*, 41(1), 87–97.

Tinkle, T. (2010). Contested authority: Jerome and *The Wife of Bath* on 1 Timothy 2. *The Chaucer Review*, 44(3), 268–293. https://doi.org/10.5325/chaucerrev.44.3.0268.

Turner, M. (2020). *Chaucer: A European life*. Princeton University Press.

Turner, M. (2022). *The Wife of Bath: A biography*. Princeton University Press.

Waling, A. (2023). "Inoculate boys against toxic masculinity": Exploring discourses of men and masculinity in #MeToo commentaries. *The Journal of Men's Studies*, 31 (1), 130–156. https://doi.org/10.1177/10608265221092044.

Woods, W. F. (2008). *Chaucerian spaces: Spatial poetics in Chaucer's opening tales*. State University of New York Press.

8

DUMBING DOWN OR PLAYING UP?

Directing Shakespeare for Young People

Leonard Love

Introduction

I once had a conversation with a group of 17-year-old performing arts students who were highly enthusiastic and passionate about theatre. They talked a lot about the shows they had seen and what expectations they had of the shows they were prepared to see. We began chatting about how theatre is so expensive nowadays and that getting a ticket for one of the big West End productions would be impossible because of the wages that these young people obtained by serving fries or stacking shelves. I then explained that the Globe Theatre offers way cheaper tickets than other venues in London and that this would give them an experience of live theatre at a mere fraction of the cost of a West End musical.

This suggestion went down like a cup of cold porridge.

The appeal of seeing a Shakespeare play compared to that of a musical or other popular form of production was evidently clear. Shakespeare, apparently, was not high on the agenda when it came to being entertained by something fun or *sick*, as *da yoof* proclaimed. Back in the lecture theatre I brought the question up again in the hope of confronting my learners with the idea that Shakespeare may possibly be entertainment. This encouraged enthusiastic debate while, frustratingly, little was decided as an outcome, but interestingly, when I asked the students to describe what their prejudices were, it became majorly clear that Shakespeare was deemed *posh* and *arty-farty* and, allegedly *out of touch with real people* and most importantly, young people. Shakespeare, according to the group, was for snobs and the Bard's work seemed to be inappropriate or redundant and unable to appeal to the sensibilities and tastes of teenagers living in 21st-century Britain. Especially the ones who were sitting in front of me. It was then that I decided

DOI: 10.4324/9781003470434-10

that as our next major project we should produce and perform a Shakespeare play. Accordingly, this made me an utter bastard but as much as it would seem cruel and vindictive to thrust my own theatrical know-how onto the mindsets of a snap-chatting cohort, I felt it would be entirely fresh and invigorating to not only interpret the text for performance, but make the play appropriate, both culturally and socially, to 21st-century young people too. What this chapter hopes to discuss are the perceptions that are inherently abundant in Shakespearean performance and an account and exploration of why and how they helped to develop creative ideas for the purpose of appropriation and adaptation for my young learners. Throughout the chapter I will analyse and discuss how notions of highbrow and lowbrow entertainment are a clear dichotomy in British theatre, and associate these ideas with my own practice as a director for young people's theatre. The hope is that perceived ideas of cultural hierarchies that are clearly embedded inb the UK's schools and are reflective of the dichotomous appreciation of theatre (especially with regard to economic and social contexts) will be decimated through an open and liberating approach to Shakespearean text that not only enthuses young people but empowers them. The chapter will also attempt to define specific aspects of Mikhail Bakhtin's theory of the carnivalesque in which he presents an idea of using *shared laughter* that suspends or subverts *official* orders or hierarchies. These ideas will be argued as beneficial in exploring Shakespeare's texts not only in the classroom, but also in performance processes.

As a teacher and practitioner, I can assert that Shakespearean performance proportionately carries with it a stigma which associates itself with highbrow culture and not, it would seem, with room full of young people somewhere in the West Midlands of England. As a practitioner who works exclusively with young people and who is aware of current trends in popular, youth culture, how is it possible to not only enthuse the performers with the idea of exploring Shakespeare, but more importantly, empower them with their own sense of identity when interpreting the texts for performance? It would seem appropriate at this point to discuss how and why Shakespeare is the epitome of highbrow theatre and does not charm the likes of the working-class teenagers whom I have the joy to educate. Martin Van Dijk (2001) claims that Shakespeare is deemed as an "elitist bard" by many students and that his work is "inaccessible because of his language, resented for his status as set text, and treated with hostility for his irrelevance to popular culture" (pp. 163–164). Stephen Purcell (2005) claims that "the Shakespearean audience has been predominantly bourgeois, as have the values that the Shakespearean canon is perceived to uphold" (p. 81) and Douglas Lanier (2002) offers a whole chapter that traces why Shakespeare's plays were transformed from "ephemeral popular entertainment to centrepieces of the literary canon" (p. 22), a process which he titles "Shakespeare's un-popularization" (p. 22). Shakespearean performance therefore seemingly conforms to a notion that alienates itself from current ideas of mass entertainment. These ideas open a debate on the credibility of lowbrow forms of theatre against its highbrow counterpart. It was also a debate for Theodor Adorno and other members of the Frankfurt School who believed that "culture needed to be protected from the threat of popular forms of theatre such as variety and operetta" (Davis, 2016, p. 9). The post-Marxist theorists claimed that "high culture" could be turned into a "form of subjugation when absorbed into the cultural industry" (Davis, 2016, p. 10) by discouraging audiences from developing a broader, more historical and more critical perspective on their own social and political status. In the words of John McGrath (1996) whose manifesto for *A Good Night Out* argues that conventions of mass entertainment are integral to a working-class, popular theatre, Adorno's concerns could be symptomatic of a "well-fed, white, middle class, sensitive but sophisticated literary critic" (p. 2). According to Adorno and the Frankfurt School of thinking, the two notions of high-art and mass entertainment should never be *absorbed* into each other as this could ultimately contaminate a system of high culture and turn it into a form of *subjugated* popularity. On the other hand, Douglas Lanier (2002) claims that "Shakespeare remains an important symbolic site of struggle between stratified, cultural institutions" (p. 49). He goes on to state that the striving to keep Shakespeare and pop culture as diametric concepts is shared by those who argue that pop culture displaces cultural heritage and those who "champion popular culture as the people's alternative to an elitist literary canon" (p. 3). It is this symbolic site of struggle which will be linked to carnivalesque theory and the justification of this investigation. Never more so was this struggle apparent when I was trying to discuss the same point to a class of teenagers who argued that Joey Essex could be an *amazing* Hamlet.

Personal Refection: The First Readthrough

The first process that I encourage all my young learners to participate in is a group reading of the text. This gives us opportune moments to not only absorb some of the contextual aspects of the play, but more importantly obtain a deeper knowledge and understanding of the plot and characters. I usually involve the whole cohort in this process before the auditions so that each learner can explore, devise and ask questions. It's also an opportunity for me to share some enthusiasm for the play:

ME: Are there any questions?
    (Silence)
ME: Anyone?
X: What time is lunch?
ME: Very good. Anything about the play?
    (Silence)

ME: Anything at all? The characters? Plot? Language?
X: Upon what timeth ist thou having lunch, my lord?[1]

The highly popular *Britain's Got Talent* semi-final in 2016 created a backlash of discourse when the head judge, Simon Cowell, made an assuming statement about a participating entrant in the vastly popular TV talent show. He claimed that there was something *untouchable* about the opera quartet Zyrah Rose's performance and that the singers were the culinary equivalent of *caviar* but what the British people wanted was *spaghetti bolognaise*. This comment sparked an outpouring of opinions from the tweeting public who wrongly or rightly claimed that Cowell is partly responsible for the dumbing-down of Britain. Cowell's metaphorical claim could certainly be argued as highlighting a snobbish regard to entertainment or maybe even wedge a further divide into a class system which emphatically uses culture as a prominent feature of its identity. To be fair to Cowell, I love spaghetti bolognaise and, I must admit, have dabbled with a bit of caviar in my time, but as an ex-entertainer-turned-academic I find myself torn between the two worlds of both *bolognaise* and *caviar*, or translated as such: highbrow and popular entertainment. As a practising teacher of young people in 21st-century England and someone who possesses a fondness for directing Shakespeare, it has become fundamental in my work to create a metaphorical caviar/bolognaise dish, of sorts, that not only embraces the intrinsic qualities of the text, but also a sense of populist entertainment that the participants can associate or empower themselves with. Therefore, I always anticipate that the process and performance carry with it the opportunity to hybridize a style and form that resonates with a cultural slant towards the *carnivalesque*. The carnivalesque is an ideological term which was pioneered by the literary critic Mikhail Bakhtin. In brief, he traces the history of this kind of representation back to a late medieval era when carnival was used as a celebratory time when orthodox expectations were subverted and social boundaries were broken. According to Bakhtin this took place "in the minor low genres, on the itinerant stage, in public squares on market day, in street songs and jokes" (Vice, 1997). Bawdy behaviour and grotesque realism were conventions that were intrinsic to the carnival and ultimately, have had an influence on how mass entertainment and popular culture are regarded even though Bakhtin (1984a) claimed that theatre had no place within carnivalesque ideology because the carnival "does not acknowledge any distinction between actors and spectators" (p. 7) and that the carnival is a time when "the viewer is also participant" (Bakhtin, 1984b, p. 18); "Carnival is not a spectacle seen by the people; they live in it, and everyone participates because its very idea embraces all the people" (Bakhtin, 1984a, p. 7). It's easy then to associate the carnivalesque with lowbrow, *spaghetti bolognaise* entertainment and establish its opposite in the form of highbrow *caviar* theatre, an association iwhich will be explored later in this chapter.

Perceptions and the Problem of Entertainment

Young people undoubtedly perceive Shakespeare's plays as highbrow theatre in comparison to their experience and knowledge of popular entertainment. This idea was the primary discussion which prompted me to explore the idea further through practical work with my learners. But what is it exactly that creates this factionalism between the Bard's work and young people's eth- nology in 21st-century Britain? Stephen Purcell (2005) claims that Shake- speare "does not speak" to a modern audience "in the popular idiom" as "he is a symbol of elite culture" that carries the "predominately bourgeois values that the Shakespearean canon is perceived to uphold" (p. 81). Dou- glas Lanier (2002) agrees when he states that Shakespeare's plays were given canonical status when they were put into print as the First Folio in 1623 and (paraphrasing Ben Johnson somewhat) were regarded as "literature rather than popular culture" of which the result is that we now "routinely associate Shakespeare with high culture" (p. 21). However, when discussing the con- cept of theatrical entertainment, Jim Davis (2016) supplies an inclusive definition by presenting the lyrics from the 1953 musical number *That's Entertainment.* In this song we learn that entertainment can make us cry as well as laugh and that it can involve "The clown with his pants falling down/or the dance that's a dream of romance/or the scene where the villain is mean" (p. 3). Furthermore, it could be Oedipus Rex "where a chap kills his father/and causes a lot of bother" or "some great Shakespearean scene/ where a ghost and a prince meet/and everyone ends in mincemeat" or "the bride with the guy on the side/or the ball where she gives him her all" (p. 3). According to the lyrics of the song, high art such as Sophocles and Shake- speare full under the remit of popular entertainment but, "nevertheless", claims Davis (2016), "entertainment is often perceived as the antithesis to serious theatre, as if audiences can only be entertained if they are not over- stimulated intellectually or emotionally" (p. 4). There is also an idea that popular entertainment caries with its sense of spectacle and escapism that is conducive to modern tastes and technologies. One only needs to recognize the appeal of AI and CGI effects in cinema to appreciate this idea. The RSC's version of *The Tempest* at Stratford in 2017 was an example of hybridizing state-of-the-art technology with a live Shakespeare performance, which was critiqued for over-using such technology. With regard to using technical conventions of mass entertainment such as contemporary use of lighting, music and sound effects, there was a discourse surrounding Emma Rice's departure as artistic director of Shakespeare's Globe in 2016. While Rice's first summer season at the London venue had been a massive revenue success, the CEO at the Globe claimed that Rice's creative vision was not compatible with the boards (I emphasize the word "board" and not "bard" as the irony would be too entertaining!). Rice's use of lighting effects, pop culture, music and sound accordingly did not correlate with the Globe's authentic use of shared lighting, which promptly created a swathe of commentary from various sources. When discussing Rice's interpretation of *A Midsummer's Night Dream* Professor Michael Dobson claimed (2016) that the venue had been turned into a "sixth form disco" (Furness, 2016, para. 16) while Richard Morrison (2016) of *The Times* claimed that what he found alarming about the play "was the perversity, incongruity and disrespect of mounting it at the Globe" (para. 2). A most recent review of Daniel Kramer's *Romeo and Juliet* at the Globe was more concerned with the "visceral crudity of the production" that included lavish death masks and a raucous routine to the Village People's *YMCA* which ultimately warranted the article's title: "The Globe's perverse show vandalizes Shakespeare" (Billington, 2017). Emma Rice herself has been quoted several times claiming that Shakespeare made her sleepy and that listening to *The Archers* on Radio 4 was easier to digest. Surely, then, it is reasonable for a director of her integrity to utilize style, form and components of modern entertainment within her artistic tenure to not only affront the perceived, highbrow aspects of Shakespearean text, but also make the plays more universal in appeal, especially to young audiences, rather than embed the text with archaic and historic ideologies of performance that were clearly expected by her critics. The debate over whether the Globe is a theatre or a museum is ongoing, and one with which this chapter will not ingratiate itself. Although it's arguably a shame that Rice was made to leave the Globe as early as she did. I loved my sixth form disco!

Young audiences, and audiences in general, carry with them their own perceptions of what is high art and what is popular entertainment, and in doing so they will observe and react to a performance accordingly. This unwritten understanding of the player–spectator relationship is discussed by Jacky Bratton (2003), who coins the term *intertheatricality* to describe the process. Bratton's theory observes the "elements and interactions that make up the whole web of mutual understanding between potential audiences and their players" (p. 37) and ultimately it "posits that all entertainments, including the dramas, that are performed within a single theatrical tradition are more or less interdependent" (p. 37). John McGrath (1996) discusses the elements that are "beyond the text" (p. 7) and "even beyond the production" (p. 7) in *A Good Night Out; Popular Theatre: Audience, Class and Form* in which he also establishes the idea that in the "choice of venue, audience, performers and the relationship between performer and audience" (p. 7) all maintain the language of theatre. Evidently, the interdependency lies inherently in audience perceptions and concepts of the performance and in doing so, establishes the text as either highbrow or otherwise. Therefore, it could be argued that enjoying the canonical status as they do, Shakespeare's plays will hold a plethora of intertheatrical expectations such as long posh words; men in tights spitting a lot and comedies that are only funny if you understand the language. Is it possible, however, to blur the lines between these expectations by metaphorically shoving a custard pie in the face of these assumptions, which will mutate the text into a shared experience of carnivalesque entertainment conducive to the propriety or cultural identity of young people in 21st-century Britain?

With regard to the entertaining appeal of Shakespeare, it can be assessed and debated how the objective and subjective merits of the plays are seemingly popular as far as box-office appeal and the longevity of their productions are concerned. However, there is an inadequate academic community that focuses on *entertainment* in the UK, with, at the time of writing, only two universities offering B.A. degrees in Events and Entertainment Management. However, as a theatrical concept or theoretical approach to performance, there is a dearth of literature that analyses it as such. A theoretical analysis of entertainment is sparsely mentioned in academic writing and is mostly associated with its dismissal, with neo-Marxist critiques from the likes of Horkheimer and Adorno (1972) who claim that entertainment induces a "stunting of the mass-media consumer's powers of imagination" (p. 126). One example from the extraordinarily limited research on the topic is *Only Entertainment* (2002) by Richard Dyer, although Oliver Double's history of variety theatre in *Britain Had Talent* (2012) provides an historical account of variety entertainment and examines techniques used by the industry's performers and the fundamental conventions utilized to appeal to mass audiences. Mass audiences, accordingly, are associated with trends or movements that are inherent in popular culture or are reflective of a society's tastes and ideology vis-à-vis specific examples of cultural forms. From a Marxist perspective then, popular culture has focused primarily on the appeal or mass consumption for the purpose of gaining an audience for funding. According to Alan McKee:

> Popular culture isn't the same thing as entertainment. It is a catch-all category, defined as the "lack" of high culture. Everything from entertainment to working practices to tattoos to cooking has been brought under the title of popular culture. While it has served an invaluable purpose in creating a space for universities for studying everything that isn't Art, it is limited as an analytical category.
>
> *(McKee, 2012, p. 9)*

Culture and its relation to populism or popularity can easily be dissected with regards to social and economic contexts, but it is abundantly clear that popular entertainment is the lesser regarded aspect of theatre performance from the point of view of an intellectualism that alleges it to be "a failure to be art" (McKee, 2012, p. 18). "Any piece of entertainment that serves no other function than to be great fun is dismissed as unimportant because it is not *serious* or *quality*" (p. 18). This idea is in direct contrast to the plays of Shakespeare that have arguably been studied and scrutinized by academics as a British theatrical tradition for centuries. Michael Bristol (1989) agrees on this point when he states that the popular element of Shakespeare's work "has either been ignored or been treated as yet another instrument of political and cultural domination" (p. 6). Charles Marowitz asserts his opposition to the disparity between popular culture and Shakespeare by stating:

> But what it must never become is the exclusive property of academics. I would make Shakespeare available to everyone – except the traditional academics, those semiotic vampires whose vocation is to suck him dry, and index him out of existence.
>
> *(Marowitz, 1991, p. 31)*

He goes on to declare what theatregoers want to see and experience from a production of Shakespeare:

> What we want most from Shakespeare today is not the routine repetition of his words and imagery, but the Shakespearean Experience, and, ironically, that can come from dissolving the works into a new compound – and that is, creating that sense of vicissitude, variety and intellectual vigor with which the author himself confronted his own time.
>
> *(Marowitz, 1991, p. 31)*

Adapting the works into popular forms using conventions of lowbrow entertainment including slapstick comedy, pop music and dance not only applies the vicissitude and vigor mentioned by Marowitz but also establishes the plays as a confrontation and usurpation, as it were, of their own literary status. To adapt the works of Shakespeare using popular forms of entertainment could be a direct contestation of their canonical status or *officialdom*. John Drakakis elaborates on this idea further by saying that this kind of adaptation "systematically challenges" the authority and

> serves as a means of giving the process of mythologising Shakespeare a specific historical context and promotes the idea of Shakespearean texts as sites of contestation, as opposed to being repositories of cultural wisdom.
>
> *(Drakakis, 1997, p. 165)*

Drakakis uses the term demystification to outline the idea of Shakespearean appropriation that utilizes popular forms of theatre, such as parody, suggesting that it serves to deconstruct the iconic reverence of such cultural elitism. The deconstructive rationale behind this idea suggests a carnivalization akin to Bakhtinian ideology, which requires further discussion.

Carnival as Practice

Bakhtin's theory of the carnivalesque is embedded in the traditions that were sustained throughout medieval and Early Modern carnivals and festivals. The festivities were usually bacchanalian affairs that were primarily linked to archaic religious folklore or specific aspects of feudalism that were officially observed. The festivities themselves were essentially focused on dissembling any sense of "officialdom" through shared laughter and an "indissoluble collectivity" (Bakhtin, 1984a, pp. 222–223) that subverted or transgressed the social and cultural hierarchies. In doing so carnival was the embodiment of a collectivist subversion of opposites, the rich and the poor, the young and the old, the common and the dignified. Carnival time supplied a temporary suspension of reality by making fools into kings, kings into fools and the common folk of the marketplace into a preeminent voice. Michael Bristol (1989) brands the idea of common folk as *plebian* in direct contrast to the hierarchies or *official* cultures that were prevalent in these societies, such as ruling class, the clergy and royalty. During the carnival festivities Bakhtin (1984a) explains how the *plebs* (for want of a better term) directly opposed the official social hierarchies through parody, laughter, irony, humour, elements of self-deprecation and grotesque realism that temporarily de-crowned the ennobled language of official ideology. However, the essence of carnival theory is the idea of rejuvenation that is the result of such degradation. Accordingly, for the common folk of the marketplace, carnival was the celebratory escape from the "drabness of everyday existence" (p. 19); but Leesa Fanning (2003) explains the ideology further by stating:

> The carnivalesque is not just a celebration, but, like the grotesque, it is a factor in texts and art, a liminal space where "the law" is overturned. More than just parody, the carnivalesque is genuine transgression, an aspect of the semiotic/grotesque, a space where non-exclusive oppositions collide.
>
> *(Fanning, 2003, p. 258)*

If one assumes, then, that Shakespeare's plays are termed as official as opposed to their lesser official counterparts inherent in popular entertainment, is it possible that these *non-exclusive oppositions* can be hybridized to essentially transgress perceptions or preconceptions surrounding their cultural identities?

Bakhtin describes the unification of binary ideas as *carnival mésalliances.* "Carnival brings together, unifies, weds, and combines the sacred with the profane, the lofty with the low, the great with the insignificant, the wise with the stupid" (Bakhtin, 1984b, p. 123). Simply put, carnivalesque can be the culmination of juxtaposing binary ideas or notions that are either contradictory or incongruous to say the least. In 20th-century popular entertainment this idea was the basis of many comedy duos, such as Laurel and Hardy, Abbott and Costello and Morecambe and Wise, whose acts were essentially built on the idea of having the straight guy juxtaposing the comedy stooge. This dynamic can also be attributed to theatrical plays and even Shakespeare with characters such as Puck opposing Oberon in *A Midsummer Night's Dream* and the Fool who incongruously establishes King Lear's faults in the titular play. The functionality of such juxtaposition is remarkably like Brecht's alienation effect in the way that it encourages the audience to critically assess the action by drawing attention to the expressive means and conventions onstage first and then subsequently questions its agenda or intentions. The process of associating these contradictions or juxtaposition of directives with characters can easily be played out in a style and form which is often also comical in nature. According to Bakhtin (1984b) this generation of laughter becomes unified or creates a "carnivalistic familiarization" that "however lofty or 'important' becomes truth itself" (p. 132). In association with this idea, Brecht's revelations of truth were based on conventions that sometimes laughed at or debased those lofty or important ideas using humour. By using elements of surprise and contradiction incongruous with the underlying social aspects of his plays, Brecht would often confront officialdom using popular forms of entertainment in his plays that at the same time highlighted social and cultural issues. A potent demonstration of using such incongruous conventions is evident in *The Resistible Rise of Artruro Ui* (1941) in which Brecht uses Shakespeare's Julius Caesar as an analogy of Hitler's rise to power. The play incorporates parody, slapstick and song and becomes a stimulus for laughter:

> The gangster, Hitler-Ui, is given acting lessons by a superannuated old ham using "Friends, Romans, countrymen", as an example of study. The scene as a whole is almost slapstick comedy until the end, when Ui is left alone to demonstrate his command of the speech. As the lights fade, with not a word of Shakespeare changed, the audience has the chilling experience of seeing Hitler's Nuremburg-rally gestus appropriating Shakespeare with devastating effect.
>
> *(Van Dijk, 2001)*

Personal Reflections: "Going to Hell in a Handcart!" *Rockbeth* (2019)

Rockbeth is a rock-musical version of Macbeth using songs from the likes of AC/DC, Led Zeppelin, Alice Cooper and Iron Maiden – completely self-indulgent, but highly appropriate to the style and form of the show, as well as the play itself, I believed. On the first initial reading of the text and after I had eventually got the cohort round to getting on board with a Shakespeare production, we began to associate various contextually cultural and social factors.

The numbers in the show and the varying style and form of the production were all related effectively to the action onstage and, arguably rather tenuously, to the text. (For example, when the Doctor and the Maid are commenting on Lady Macbeth's insanity and impending suicide, the scene ends with an uproarious rendition of Van Halen's *Jump*.) At the end of Act 1, I wanted the audience to recognize the downfall of Macbeth as a national hero and his moral descent into the corrupt dictatorship that he embodies throughout the rest of the play. An idea was brought about through discussing the rise of Macbeth's power that was wrought with political controversy akin to that of political dictatorships such as Stalin's regime, the Khmer Rouge and Hitler's Third Reich. As a musical it needed a substantial number to emphasize this. Suggestions included *We Are the Champions* by Queen, *Paradise City* by Guns N' Roses and *Back in Black* by AC/DC. The song chosen was *Anarchy in the UK* by the Sex Pistols, a song that not only established the political ambitions and anarchistic intent of Macbeth's rise to power, but lyrically also gave the text the added fusion of anti-establishment sentiment that the students seemed to admire, especially with regard to performing Shakespeare.

However, I suggested that we could potentially strike a double whammy with this number. The style and form of the Pistols' version could be easily recognized and in the final scene play into expectations that would be wholly appropriate to the text; however, would it be possible to give the audience something that would not only subvert their perceptions of Shakespeare, but also their perceptions of punk rock and its antagonistic appeal?

One of the learners was a keen tap-dancer (and exceptionally talented), and suggested the idea of maybe creating a tap-routine to the number that resembled the lavish musical shows from the golden age of Broadway. Resulting from a conversation with the musical director and choreographer, Act 1 climaxed with a toe-tapping rendition of *Anarchy in the UK* along with a camp chorus line who high-kicked/goose-stepped their way through the routine dressed as Gestapo officers. The spectacle involved a swastika-like banner made up of hands holding daggers being lowered onto the stage alongside a chirpy Macbeth who gaily sang about being an *anti-Christ* and an *anarchist*. One of the learners told me that I was going to hell in a handcart. I told them that at least I'd be doing it with a curtain-call!

Getting Cheeky with It

Brecht effectively unifies several binaries creating the carnival mésalliance: lowbrow slapstick and highbrow Shakespeare; vaudeville and Nazism; the fool and the dictator. Van Dijk (2001) redefines this form of theatre as simply "cheek" as in, one can assume, being cheeky. He claims that theatrical styles derivative of forms such as commedia dell'arte, carnival, satire, parody and the like, maintain a "resistance to authority" (p. 161). As a practitioner of young people's theatre, there is one thing that I can be confident in proclaiming; young people will always be resistant to an authoritative ideology, no matter how tenuous, rebellious or ideological. Cheek, it would seem, is a way in which authority can not only be resisted, but more importantly confronted. Van Dijk clarifies this idea further, stating that "Cheek has served consistently as a multifaceted, irreverent, oppositional utopia, where ebullient artifice could interrogate entrenched structures of power, genre and tradition" (p. 161). Admittedly, it is this idea of cheek and irreverence that has become the stalwart impetus to adapting Shakespeare with my ensemble of young actors, which is why the juxtaposition of a Broadway-esque chorus line, Nazi symbolism, the Sex Pistols and Shakespearean text was questioned, but ultimately embraced by them.

Brecht clearly demonstrates this transgressive appeal by not only juxtaposing one of Shakespeare's politically driven speeches with comedy, but more importantly by portraying Ui's analogical stance of Hitler as a fool or buffoon. Der Führer and Nazism, it would seem, are applicable for bit of cheek? The 2001 Broadway musical *The Producers* explicitly draws on the knowledge that Nazism and Hitler's rise to power is a taboo subject in modern popular culture, therefore by presenting this as an outrageously camp and purely ostentatious spectacle, it not only unifies these binary symbols as incongruous humour but deconstructs the officialdom of the subject through laughter. Steve Cohan (2005) points out the show's incongruities: "From its jaw-dropping, eye-popping combination of Ziegfeld showgirl line and offensive Nazi symbolism to the leading man: the director himself takes on the starring role at the last minute and performs Hitler by channelling Judy Garland" (p. 341). The disparate pairing of Nazi symbolism and lavish, Broadway musical relentlessly give the show chances to not only reinforce cultural stereotypes and historical context, but more importantly debase or uncrown hierarchical figures such as Adolf Hitler, by placing the character centre-stage as an overtly camp, musical theatre performer. It is the combination of the sacred and profane, lofty and low, great and insignificant and wise and stupid that make the show a unifying experience. Audiences recognize the taboo nature of the topic and appreciate the spectacle of the form but the complete incongruity of both combined sardonically subverts any seriousness or *officialdom* and it is this carnivalesque approach to theatrical form that will purposefully unify and empower young people when tackling the works of Shakespeare.

Personal Reflection: Language of the Marketplace (*Romeo & Jools*, 2022)

We have been rehearsing the scene in which Nurse approaches the Montague gang behind the Odeon in Birmingham. (I changed the setting from Renaissance Verona to mid-90s Birmingham.) She has come to deliver the news to

Romeo that Juliet is available and that, should he never upset her under any circumstances, he will be her husband. The conversation then segues into the raucous scenes of banter between Mercutio, Benvolio and the gang, much to the annoyance of Nurse, who is a very moralistic, working-class matron of pride. At the start of the scene, it was important for Nurse to get more agitated by the gang so that the transition into the song didn't feel tenuous or glib. The words are spoken clearly ("Here's goodly gear", "For the bawdy hand of the dial is upon the prick of noon", etc.), but there lacks an empathy or an attempt to make these lines sound dirty or intimidating. The actors were too busy trying to get their heads around the archaic language rather than the bullish banter which was highly appropriate for the scene. From the rehearsal notes (2022):

> For some reason, you ALL find it hard to recognize the social status of your roles. These are young kids who hang around shop doorways. Nurse is a working-class woman who may not have the best education but has common-sense and a heart of gold. The Montague gang are the sort of youngsters that you would avoid if you saw them at a bus-stop. The way that you are playing, it seems as though you've gone to the same school as Mary Poppins! Lighten up.

After the notes we attempted to add some of the actors' *own* interpretations of what they would say. I will not repeat in this chapter exactly what was said, but the actors soon found not only the motivation, but the joy in what they were saying and how they were re-acting to each other. The youngsters needed a target. "Nurse" was the target. For example:[2]

NURSE: (To Romeo) Sir, I need some confidence with you.
BENNY: Oooh! She invites him round for supper!?
MERCUTIA: The brazen whore!
BENNY: Bet she likes a bit of finger-lickin-chicken!
MERCUTIA: I've heard a Twix fits.
BENNY: What's for dessert?

The improv led to Mercutio grabbing Romeo by one arm and Nurse grabbing the other like a human tug of war.

NURSE: You bloody hooligans! I've got acute angina!
MERCUTIA: I hope so! Your tits are shit! (#Song[3])

Power of Profanity

A barrier to the bard's work for many uninitiated theatregoers (especially young people) is the language and its meaning in contemporary popular culture. Shakespearean language and its relation to the cultural identity of modern teenagers is agreed to be redundant. Shakespearean text and its use of verse, archaic form and pentameter are all merely annoyances in the minds of weary school children in British society today. From an auto-ethnographic perspective, I have this idea securely entrenched. When discussing the contemporary reception of Shakespeare's plays, Andrew Kocsis (2016) attempts to investigate the performative aspects of Shakespeare for the purpose of establishing new meaning for modern audiences. In his thesis entitled "Revising Shakespeare: Demystifying the meaning construction of Shakespeare's dramatic text for the pedagogic and performative engagement of the modern viewer", he outlines the possibilities of revising Shakespeare's work, identifying choices that encourage a "shift in the viewer's comprehension, ultimately enabling the active participation of the viewer through an explicit mediation of the performative text" (p. 3). Kocsis claims that the "introduction of a performative text improves the dramatic transmission of the text and encourages the active meaning construction of the viewer" (p. 3). In other words, performing a play creates new meaning for an audience rather than just reading it can. Kocsis (2016) focuses on the relationship between the language of the text and audience, claiming that "it can impede on the viewer's ability to interpret and understand" and "obstruct their comprehension of the drama" (p. 8):

> Performances of Shakespeare's plays can, therefore, at times be difficult for the modern viewer to comprehend, as the constant need for explanation and possibly the translation of the unfamiliar rhythms of the language may impede full comprehension of the text. As a result, in the moment of a performance, the viewer may not be an active observer or an active constructor of meaning, but rather a passive participant.
>
> *(Kocsis, 2016, p. 3)*

As much as Kocisis argues that the performative text improves the transmission of the written, he also still claims that the incomprehension or unfamiliarity of the language could create a passive or less active observer. I would most certainly argue that this outcome is the legacy of how and why Shakespeare is normally taught in schools. I will elaborate on this point later in the chapter but, seemingly, it is the language that binds the young reader or performer to a lack of unanimity with the popular appeal of Shakespeare's work. Assuming that Shakespeare maintains the canonical status of British literary and theatrical tradition and that the 400-year-old plays should be followed to the letter for the purpose of adaptation, I would suggest that this risks any appropriation or creativity conducive to young people in the 21st century. Stephen Purcell (2005) forbodes that exploring the texts with such reverence would "close them off from further interpretation" and act "to hermetically seal them from interrogation by the modern world" (p. 81). As a practitioner of young people's theatre, I agree. Shakespearean productions must assume to be progressive by cultivating a healthy apathy towards the *official* nature of the text. The integrity and highbrow associations with Shakespeare have now become a symbol of elite culture in opposition to the popular. The plays have attracted a predominately bourgeois audience along with values that they perceive themselves to uphold, and in an ever-changing cultural and social context it would seem entirely appropriate to subvert and transgress these values for the purpose of conforming to the identity of young people in 21st-century Britain. As many may argue that this affront to Shakespeare's work could mean an essential dumbing down of the text, I would most certainly argue that it categorically plays up to the idea of Shakespeare's work as being popular and regenerates them as entirely new phenomena, akin to Bakhtin's idea of liberation from dogmatism, fanaticism and pedantry (Bakhtin, 1984a, pp. 122–123). Primarily, the truth is in the language. Please appreciate the following piece of adapted text as an example of how this idea was put into practice through workshops and improvisation:

A Midsummer Night's Dream

Helena:
How happy some o'er other some can be!
Through Athens I am though as fair as she.
But what of that? Demetrius thinks not so;
He will not know what all but he does know.
And as he errs, doting on Hermia's eyes,
So I, admiring of his qualities.
Things base and vile, holding no quantity,
Love can transpose to form and dignity.
Love looks not with the eyes, but with the mind,
And therefore is winged Cupid painted blind.
Nor hath love's mind of any judgement taste;
Wings, and no eyes, figure unheedy haste;
And therefore is love said to be a child
Because in choice he is so oft beguiled.
As waggish boys in game themselves forswear,
So the boy Love is perjured everywhere;
For, ere Demetrius looked on Hermia's eyne,
He hailed down oaths that he was only mine,
And when this hail some heat from Hermia felt,
So he dissolved, and showers of oaths did melt.
I will go tell him of fair Hermia's flight:
Then to the wood will he, tomorrow night,
Pursue her; and for this intelligence,
If I have thanks it is a dear expense;
But herein mean I to enrich my pain,
To have his sight thither, and back again.
(*Exit*)

(*Shakespeare, 2004, pp. 224–251*)

A Mid-80s Night's Dream (2023)[4]

HELENA: Oh happy some others in love can be! In Athens I am thought as fair
as she. But what of that? While Mia and Sander hear Cupid's bow ringing,
Demetrius thinks that I'm fucking minging! Love looks not with the eyes
but with the mind, and therefore is winged Cupid blind. For before Demetrius looked into Mia's eyes, he swore to me that he was only mine. He
whispered sweet nothings and told me I was fit. Then he ran off with Mia,
the cheating shit! And I wallowed and wept and got myself plastered as I
watched the two-timing lecherous bastard, go off with my bestie and put a
ring on her finger … but wait … a plan in my head doth linger! I will tell
Demetrius of fair Helena's flight then into the woods he will go in the night.
He will pursue her with me by his side, and I will surely turn loves lost
ebbing tide. And through the woods and through bushes and as the moonlight flickers, I'll get Demetrius back in my knickers!

The dialogue that was devised and performed was subsequently the product
of getting the young actor playing Helena to question *why* she was standing
in the middle of a town talking to herself. The actor gave a highly comical
response to this question involving cultural references to *bunny-boilers* and
that women are driven mad by men who are bastards. They also resisted the
poetic notions of *Love* being an actual *boy* and argued that the truth behind
Helena's heartache was probably the result of sexual vanity or pride. This was
the idea that spawned the speech that was eventually performed, with great
aplomb.

The ability to allow young actors to interpret the text accordingly not only
establishes and demonstrates an understanding of the character, plot and
meaning but more importantly, empowers the young actor to truly explore
their own identity and knowledge of performance. It is arguable that many
young actors refuse to feel trapped by the linguistic or literary merits of
Shakespeare's plays so being able to interpret, adapt and create through their
own vernacular allows them to proudly proclaim their own understanding of
the plays which have been intrenched in heritage, tradition and cultural elitism. An amalgamation of incongruous humour, contemporary issues and an
affiliation with popular, youth culture creates a collective consciousness for
the actors that makes Shakespeare a source of personal agenda. If we imagine
that young people are at the border between childhood and adulthood,
maintaining and embracing an identity that allows them to freely communicate their own wants, needs, passions and politics will give them opportunities to gain a sense of self. To do a great thing, it would seem, one must do
a little wrong and if that means Friar Lawrence smoking a spliff and calling
Romeo a bell-end for gallivanting with Jools, so be it! As much as the dramatic implications are questionable, the entertainment factor is enhanced.

Dumbing Down or Playing Up?

In the process of adapting the script and workshopping scenes, the young actors whom I have directed have always managed to take ownership of their own character in development. Whether creating back stories, physical traits or behavioural habits for specific roles, the idea of creating a character that they have interpreted from text has given them a sense of pride and knowledge that empowers them as, for want of a better term, Shakespearean actors. What I have found remarkably interesting, however, is that the young actors have always seemed to apply their performance skills towards appeasing an audience rather than critically evaluating and applying an academic attitude to playing the text. In today's social media culture where having a number of online followers or getting an amount of *likes* for various posts makes you popular, it is easy to consider why the young people I teach are seemingly aware of audience reception and disposition towards their work. Therefore, throughout the rehearsal and development process of producing the play, it is crucial that the young actors are versatile in utilizing imagination, energy, interplay and, more importantly, enjoyment. By focussing on these facets, the young actors cultivate their confidence in playing with Shakespeare rather than inferring the text for the purpose of assessment, and in doing so there is direct link to creating meaning and entertainment for the spectator.

As the director Declan Donnellan claims: "In the beginning was the imagination, which longs to communicate with others", and then goes on to state, "What I love to see is the actor's imagination making various events and words inevitable" (Berry, 1989, p. 207). As a practitioner I would argue that the events and inevitability of any production lie in its entertainment value as a spectator. As mentioned previously, the dearth of academic literature based around the conceptual factors of entertainment make it difficult to associate it with Shakespearean performance, but what I have found intrinsic to developing ideas with young actors is their insatiable need to entertain, especially when it comes to performing the Bard's work. The fact that Shakespeare as a topic is compounded with associations of an "idealized past" or an "icon of modern elite culture" (Purcell, 2005, p. 76), it has seemingly become the prime objective for my learners to create a style of performance that is intrinsically built on subverting these ideas; decrowning the official, as it were and applying their own criterion of entertainment in the hope of making Shakespeare popular. Stephen Purcell (2005) makes us aware that "the charge most frequently levelled is that in the process of being made to appeal to a popular audience, the integrity of the Shakespearean text is betrayed" (p. 76). Charles Marowitz (1991) confirms Purcell's allegation when he insists that "accessibility and populism almost invariably usher in facile, oversimplified results because there is a complexity in classics which resists reductive reasoning" (p. 63). It is difficult to not accept Marowitz's accusation without feeling disenfranchised from highbrow theatre, but what is important is establishing that there is a stark difference between the popular notion of theatre and entertainment as a cultural entity and popular as in a commercial sense of the word; which Stuart Hall (1998) contentiously describes as being "quite rightly associated with the manipulation and debasement of the culture of the people" (p. 446). However, if mainstream Shakespearean performance is inextricably linked to academia, the middle classes and highbrow theatre, then surely any attempt to forge its appeal to those outside of this elite culture should be embraced and applauded. Marowitz's and Hall's objections are founded in the ideas that anything that qualifies as a *dumbing down* of the text lies outside the legitimacy of Shakespeare's work. This idea is irrational when it comes to collaborating with creative young actors.

If it is useful to establish how young people could intrinsically explore the idea of entertainment for the purpose of appeasing an audience, it would also be important to discuss the underlying factors that comprise audiences, especially between the binary ideas of highbrow and lowbrow culture. In doing so, it would be useful to re-iterate the original performance contexts of Shakespeare's theatre. The Globe was set on the south bank of London's river in the "bad, bold world of Southwark, amid the brothels, bear pits and pleasure gardens" (Davies, 2018, p. 23). Historically the theatre itself was a throng of noise and debauchery that opened its doors to a universal audience. Ironically, the authorities within the City wall of London were against theatre and the immoral implications of the performances that were produced for the crowds. It seems, then, that this idea has culturally shifted as the idea of watching a Shakespeare play in such a way seems inappropriate. A level of decorum and expectations of conduct are components of audiences that are appropriate to their comprehension of the style and form of the show they are watching. One only needs to appreciate how audiences for a live version of *The Rocky Horror Show* differ from those watching *La Bohème*, for example. The same can be said of expectations for a Shakespeare performance. As much as the current climate at the Globe is attempting to establish a sense of archaism that is fundamentally linked to the original performance context, audiences are still aware that they are watching, spectating and appreciating a Shakespeare play. Their behaviour and their reverence for the text is clear even with Emma Rice's controversial adaptations.

In 2001 the comedy troupe The League of Gentlemen drew attention to the behavioural habits of those who appreciate Shakespeare and those of football spectators. The results culminated in a hilarious sketch which not only emphasized the bawdy culture of the football terrace, but also how comical it would seem to associate Shakespeare with it. The sketch sets itself up with two characters wearing the appropriate colours for their teams, sat watching a game. After some pre-match banter the audience begin to realize that the two characters are watching a live performance of *Hamlet*. This gag is made abundantly clear when one of the spectators, played by Steve Pemberton, gets to his feet and shouts "Come on Hamlet! Make your fucking mind up! Jesus!", quickly followed by Mark Gatiss' character who responds, "Stop soliloquising, you Danish poof![5]" What the sketch effectively does is emphasize the binary between highbrow theatre and working-class culture represented in the football stand. This point is inextricably demonstrated at the end of the sketch when in the dying moments of Hamlet's demise:

GATISS: Ah! Fatal indecision!
PEMBERTON: Fatal!
GATISS: He wants to do it when he's drunk asleep or in his rage!
PEMBERTON: Or incestuous pleasure of his bed; at game of swearing or about some act that hath no relish in it.
GATISS: Yeah! (beat) Cunt.

$$(2001)^6$$

Gatiss and Pemberton's sketch can be easily associated with the carnivalesque by the fact that they do not condemn the works of Shakespeare as a subject of mockery. Nor do they condemn the uncultured ethos that can be associated with football terraces. Their characters are the voices of the people; their utterances applaud their own loyalty to Shakespearean text but at the same time degrade it. Bakhtin's affiliation with this idea is explained when he claims:

The man who is speaking is one with the crowd; he does not present himself as its opponent, nor does he teach, accuse, or intimidate it. He laughs with it. There is not the slightest tone of morose seriousness, in his oration, no fear, piety, or humility. This is an absolutely gay and fearless talk, free and frank, which echoes in the festive square beyond all verbal prohibitions, limitations, and conventions.

(Bakhtin, 1984a, p. 167)

The openness of the language of the *marketplace*, as Bakhtin defines it and the ritualistic expectations of the football match and theatregoer within the sketch signify the carnival elements of working-class culture which not only confront the content of Hamlet, literally, but also highlight the discrepancies between highbrow theatre and popular culture. This becomes the dialogic bridge between the two concepts and one that is very much unified with Bakhtin's notions of folk-humour and communal laughter, which I believe are theoretically central to an idea of lowbrow entertainment.

Conclusion

What this chapter has hopefully helped to understand is a rebuttal of the accusation of "dumbing-down" Shakespearean text with regard to adapting the plays for young actors. I have attempted to qualify how young people assert their own sense of identity and contextual understanding to the plays that, as much as being clearly incongruous to audience expectations, result in a form of theatre that applies itself effectively to the realm of popular entertainment and not to highbrow theatre practice. What is evidently clear from my experience of directing young people is their ability to appreciate and *play-up* to an audience's idea of entertainment and at the same time apply a deeper appreciation and understanding of the Shakespearean text that empowers them as actors. To apply these ideas to Bakhtin's carnivalesque, it could be conceivable to discuss the idea of how Bakhtin's ideology has been linked to theatre practice, primarily grotesque realism, in pursuit of synthesizing the ideas to establish a framework for practice.

The Russian theatre director, Vsevolod Meyerhold, frequently turned to popular performance forms such as circus and commedia dell'arte in his bold and brave theatre adaptions. The thought behind his process lay in his abandonment of Russian realism which placed the audience in a privacy of otherworldliness via the convention of the metaphoric fourth wall. "The popular, because of the participatory nature of these forms, might break these artificial barriers down" (Price, 2016, p. 33) and "facilitate more active responses from spectators" (p. 33). Accordingly, Meyerhold (1998) claimed that dramatic realism "forces the spectator to adopt an ambivalent attitude" (p. 139) to the action onstage in contrast to the carnivalesque or grotesque realism which emblematically tries to "switch the spectator from the plane he has just reached to another which is totally unforeseen" (Braun, 1991, p. 139). In his own words, Meyerhold (1998) claims that "the grotesque mixes opposites, consciously creating harsh incongruity and relying solely on its own originality" (p. 138). He goes on to clarify:

> The grotesque has its own attitude towards the outward appearance of life. The grotesque deepens life's outward appearance to the point where it ceases to appear merely natural. Beneath what we see of life there are vast unfathomed depths. In its search for the supernatural, the grotesque synthesizes opposites, creates a picture of the incredible and invites the spectator to solve the riddle of the inscrutable.
>
> *(Braun, 1991, p. 139)*

This theatrical style allegedly "plays with sharp contradictions and produces a constant shift in the planes of perception" (Gladkov, 1997, p. 142). This theory is put into practice with my young actors in not only shifting their perceptions of Shakespeare, but also how they attempt to shift the audience's perceptions too. Jonathan Pitches (2008) acknowledges Meyerhold's attempt to subvert the audience's perceptions of a predictable or comfortable form of theatre. He distinctly identifies a list of practical approaches and critical perspectives that should be applied to embed the idea of grotesque realism and carnivalesque theatre:

- It mixes opposites: tragedy and comedy, life and death, beauty, and ugliness.
- It celebrates incongruities.
- It challenges our perceptions.
- It is naturally mischievous, even satirical.
- It borrows from different (and unlikely) sources.
- It always has a touch of the diabolical, the "devil's influence".
- It stretches the natural to the extent that it becomes unnatural or stylized.
- It revels in fantasy and mystery.
- It is constantly transforming things: objects, figures, landscapes, and atmospheres.   *(Pitches, 2008, pp. 61–62)*

This carnivalesque attempt to subvert theatrical expectations is subsequently reasonable in young people's theatre practice and, more importantly, it can also be applied in a classroom setting when tutoring young people. Po-Chi Tam's (2010) research identifies how Bakhtinian ideology can be used as a pedagogic tool for drama teachers. The study uses carnival theory to argue that the power of drama pedagogy relies on the "playfulness, plebianism and fictiveness at its heart, potentially capable of resisting the authoritarian, monolithic and exclusive modes of learning in the classroom" (p. 190) that can arguably be said of the teaching and learning of Shakespeare required for assessment according to the National Curriculum.

The playfulness, openness, plebianism and imaginativeness abundant in the work of my young performers reconceptualizes highbrow theatre as a transgressive and pedagogical form that is firmly rooted in carnival, popular culture and entertainment. Their work is sometimes contradictory and multivalent, that gives the audience an opportunity to re-evaluate their own conceptions of highbrow theatre in a style that includes carnival elements and conventions. As Jim Davis (2016) argues, "entertainment is a condition of all theatre that holds or occupies our attention" and adds that "it cannot be simplistically dismissed as a euphemism for capitalist manipulation of the masses nor used as an easy label for intellectually undemanding theatrical experiences". He goes on to question this theory, asking, "who decides which theatrical experiences are intellectually demanding, anyway?" (p. 79). A question which was also part of the discussion I had with my young cast at the very start of this process. Inevitably, they very quickly dismissed any suggestions of answering it and constructed their own ideas for making the text appropriate to their understanding. What is refreshingly clear about subverting expectations and ideas of highbrow theatre for the purpose of appropriating the text for young actors, is that the young actors themselves have a confident appreciation of entertainment. Instinctively, they can associate their own ideas of character and dialogue that not only translate the work according to the dramatic meaning, but also entrench their own cultural identity as young people. Rather contentiously I have asserted that Bakhtin's own ideology is questionable in that he dssociates his ideas from drama. This research has effectively argued that performance aspects and specific forms, conventions and styles of performance that are associated with lowbrow entertainment can easily be attributed to carnival either theoretically or contextually. It can be assumed that models or frameworks of processes can be devised that can be explored or investigated in the production or teaching of Shakespearean text, especially for the purpose of making it *popular*. The work that my young companies produce recognizes the authenticity of the plays, and they capitalize on this in their understanding of creating meaning, but paradoxically they also subvert and convert the expectations of Shakespearean theatre in a way that is conducive to their own perceptions of entertainment which creates new meaning. The officialdom of Shakespeare is de-crowned, but the text is regenerated. As an avid believer in establishing a form of theatre that is wholly ingrained in young people's social and cultural ideology for the purpose of constructing a sense of identity, carnivalesque theory conceptualizes theatre practice but maintains a front of reasoning that redeems it from being simply *dumbing down*. Charles Marowitz polemically forwards his own ideas about regenerating Shakespeare in a chapter entitled *How to Rape Shakespeare*. What this present chapter has hopefully established is a system of ideas and theories that could joyously fuck him with consent.

Notes

1 Unpublished rehearsal notes.
2 Unpublished rehearsal notes.
3 Unpublished rehearsal notes.
4 Unpublished workshop notes.
5 Unpublished reflection.
6 Unpublished sketch notes.

References

Bakhtin, M. (1984a) *Rabelais and his world*. Indiana State University Press.
Bakhtin, M. (1984b). *Problems of Dostoevsky's poetics*. University of Minnesota Press.
Bendelack, S. (director). (2001). *The League of Gentlemen: Live at Drury Lane*. DVD. Universal.
Berry, R. (1989). *On directing Shakespeare*. Hamish Hamilton.

Billington, M. (2017, 28 April). Romeo and Juliet review: The Globe's perverse show vandalises Shakespeare. *The Guardian.* https://www.theguardian.com/stage/2017/apr/28/romeo-and-juliet-review-globe-shakespeare.

Bratton, J. (2003). *New readings in theatre history.* Cambridge University Press.

Braun, E. (1991). *Meyerhold on theatre.* Methuen.

Bristol, M. D. (1989). *Carnival and theatre: Plebian culture and the structure of authority in Renaissance England.* Routledge.

Cohan, D. (2005). *Incongruous entertainment: Camp, cultural value, and the MGM musical.* Duke University Press.

Davies, O. F. (2018). *Performing Shakespeare.* Nick Hern Books.

Davis, J. (2016). *Theatre and entertainment.* Palgrave Macmillan.

Double, O. (2012). *Britain had talent: A history of variety theatre.* Palgrave Macmillan.

Drakakis, J. (1997). Shakespeare in quotations. In S. Bassnett (Ed.), *Studying British cultures: An introduction.* Routledge.

Dyer, R. (2002). *Only entertainment.* Routledge.

Fanning, L. (2003). *Willem de Kooning's women: The body of the grotesque in modern art and the grotesque.* Cambridge University Press.

Furness, H. (2016, 5 May). Shakespeare's Globe risks wrath after installing sixth form disco. *Telegraph.* https://www.telegraph.co.uk/news/2016/05/05/shakespeares-globe-risks-wrath-after-installing-sixth-form-disco/.

Gladkov, A. (1997). *Meyerhold speaks, Meyerhold rehearses.* Harwood Academic Publishers.

Hall, S. (1998). Notes on deconstructing the popular. In J. Storey (Ed.), *Cultural theory and popular culture: A reader* (pp. 227–239). Pearson Education.

Horkheimer, M. & Adorno, T. (1972). *Dialectic of enlightenment.* Continuum.

Kocsis, A. W. (2016). *Revising Shakespeare: Demystifying the meaning construction of Shakespeare's dramatic text for the pedagogic and performative engagement of the modern viewer.* Murdoch University.

Lanier, D. (2002). *Shakespeare and modern popular culture.* Oxford University Press.

Marowitz, C. (1991). *Recycling Shakespeare.* Applause Theatre Books.

McGrath. John (1996) *A good night out: Popular theatre: Audience, class, and form.* Nick Hern Books.

McKee, A. (2012). The aesthetic system of entertainment: Pornography as case study. In A. McKee, C. Collis & B. Hamley (Eds.), *Entertainment industries: Entertainment as a cultural system* (pp. 9–20). Routledge.

Meyerhold, V. (1998). *Meyerhold on theatre.* Routledge.

Morrison, R. (2016, 30 Sept). Richard Morrison: The Globe has been a success story – and Emma Rice is wrecking it. *The Sunday Times.* https://www.thetimes.co.uk/article/richard-morrison-the-globe-has-been-a-success-story-and-emma-rice-is-wrecking-it-xrrgxz3ml.

Pitches, J. (2008). *Vsevolod Meyerhold.* Routledge.

Po-chi, T. (2010). The implications of carnival theory for interpreting drama pedagogy from research in drama education. *The Journal of Applied Theatre and Performance*, 15(2), 175–192.

Price, J. (2016). *Modern popular theatre.* Palgrave Macmillan.

Purcell, S. (2005). A shared experience: Shakespeare and popular theatre. *Performance Research*, 10(3), 74–84.

Shakespeare, W. (2004). *A midsummer night's dream.* World Scholastic Publishers.

Van Dijk, M. (2001). "Lice in Fur"; The aesthetics of cheek and Shakespearean production strategy. In M. Bristol, K. McLuskie & C. Holmes, *Shakespeare and modern theatre* (pp. 160–180). Routledge.

Vice, S. (1997). *Introducing Bakhtin*. Manchester University Press.

9

BRING BRITISH YOUTH THEATRE OVERSEAS

A Case Study on Routes to China

Xiaolin Huang and Yiming Wang

The creative puppet show *Cloud Man*, created by Ailie Cohen and Lewis Hetherington and produced by Scottish Theatre Producers, has often been found in regular tours around big cities in China throughout the last decade. The collaboration was started after its first performance at the 2011 Edinburgh Fringe Festival. During that time, one person among the audiences, Ms Forrina, who served as general director of the ASK (Art Space for Kids) Theatre Company, foresaw the great potential in bringing British youth theatre works to international audiences. She was keen to introduceng *Cloud Man* to Chinese stages afterwards. Eventually, in 2014 when *Cloud Man* was performed at BangWan theatre at the Wuzhen International Theatre Festival as a guest performance, having great success and much appreciation from peers and spectators. After that, *Cloud Man* toured over ten cities in China, including Shanghai, Beijing and Xian annually. The artistic choices made by the theatre groups, in both their scripting and their staging, were based on their shared understanding of the lives and backgrounds of their audience (Durden, 2022). According to Durden, though there are major cultural differences between Chinese and UK, Ailie and ASK's experiment proves that children of both countries can enjoy the same performance.

After realizing the success of ASK, more Chinese state-owned theatres and private companies have started to experiment with international collaborations; theatre owners are not only targeting British youth shows but also starting international co-creation attempts between theatres, as opposed to original importations. For example, another leading Chinese theatre company, The Little Player Theatre, collaborated with Sweden's Bananteatern Björn Dahlman to present a multimedia children's play, *My Dad Is a Dinosaur*, in 2017, which received great spectator response but toured for only a short time; due to the costs not being able to equal the profits, it never

DOI: 10.4324/9781003470434-11

appeared on stage again. The Little Player Theatre's attempt represents the result of most international collaborations before the pandemic. Meanwhile, in terms of the share of the children's theatre market, in 2014, local Chinese productions accounted for 94% of the market, with British shows such as *Cloud Man* accounting for 4%. International collaborations took 2%, whereas by 2016 this data changed significantly, with the share of local performances falling to 81%. The share of foreign-imported plays reached 17%, while the share of international collaborative plays remained unchanged (*China Securities Journal*, 2016). During the same period, the overall size of China's youth theatre market grew steadily at an annual rate of about 6%, while in that year, the number of under-18 audiences exceeded that of adults for the first time in terms of national figures, with 5.68 million and 5.14 million people respectively. Even with China's population base, this record is still beyond imagination and difficult to replicate in other parts of the world.

In the context of globalization, the rapid growth of the Chinese market and the demand for theatre performances by underage audiences provide a lower bar for increasing exchange and collaboration between Chinese and British children's theatres. As mentioned in *Theatre for Young Audiences: Opportunities in China*, published in 2016 by BOP Consulting under the commission of the British Council, both audiences' demand and the demand for commercially viable content are fundamental driving forces in the development of theatre for young people in China at the moment described (*China Now*, n.d.). But it has to be noted that, in addition to market demand, what should not be overlooked are intercultural and cross-national collaborations, content that is successful in both countries and more importantly, fits the process of rehearsal and adaptation by overseas theatre companies within mainland China, and should be considered by practitioners and researchers in addition to market data. From 2014 to 2016, despite the accelerated introduction of overseas children's theatre in China's first-tier cities, theatres rapidly captured 10% of the overall market share. While making money, they failed to produce performances that had good reviews and could start a tour in mainland China, such as *Cloud Man*, and the majority of the overseas productions were merely showcased, paraded around from city to city and then disappeared, not giving emerging British theatre artists an excellent chance to be seen. Especially after the pandemic, while theatre industries in both countries are slowly recovering, the zeitgeist of the once-successful productions and creators is coming to the fore. In the summer of 2023, when Chinese children are on summer vacation, Ailie Cohen's team is touring China again.

Therefore, this research will introduce the Chinese children's theatre market in the context of globalization, provide a case study of the inter-cultural process of *Cloud Man* and collate the possibilities and cultural barriers for the future development of British youth theatre's journey to the East.

Decoding the Chinese Youth Theatre Industry

Domestic Performing Arts Industry Markets

As mentioned, the size of the youth theatre sector in China has steadily increased in the past decades. Based on the data collected by BOP consulting, it was particularly successful in 2014, the same year that *Cloud Man* was first introduced to the Wuzhen stage. Statistics show that the Chinese stage hosted 37% more shows on stage than the previous year, leading to a 24% growth in box office profits. After becoming the largest theatre sub-sector in 2016, the target spectator party for children's theatre productions grew. On the one hand, as *victims* of the Chinese One-Child policy, middle-class families today who are roughly aged 30–40, as China's post-1980s generation (those born after 1980) have become parents, they have driven increasing recognition of the important role of theatre in the education and entertainment of their young children (Zou, 2015). The same group of parents are willing to have their second or even third kids to compensate for their loss of the right to have siblings.

On the other hand, the financial situation for urban families in third- or fourth-tier cities improved in the past few years until the pandemic hit; extra income allows parents to invest in kids' after-school activities where youth theatre companies in Beijing or Shanghai started to expand their range and begin Theatre in Education programmes. In 2020, after theatres were shut down due to the impact of the pandemic, the theatre market reached £70 million, more than the entire British theatre industry in the same year. However, even though overseas productions have already taken over more than one-third of the market, international content meets different theatrical contexts in China, leading to various results due to a slightly complicated theatre organization system. Also, though generally youth theatre can be seen as theatre made either by youth, with youth, or for youth, its appearance in China varies (Durden, 2022). Subsidized theatres, private theatres, independent theatre companies and performing arts agencies have different working methods, especially when importing foreign productions or holding international collaborations. Managed by state-affiliated art organizations, theatres such as the China National Theatre for Children have the highest ranking, in the performance of which they also undertake the corresponding task of publicity and the production of children's programmes representing the highest level of performance in China. Theatres such as the China National Theatre for Children have the highest rank. At the same time, they have the task of promoting and producing children's programmes that represent the highest level of performance in China. Therefore, in terms of content, the China National Theatre for Children is inclined to tell traditional Chinese stories and stage performances that include traditional Chinese performing arts such as opera and shadow puppetry. Though in 2004

Ukaegbu (2004) proposed that "what is needed is not a new concept or definition but the re-introduction of production strategies and collective concerns that created the traditional performances that audiences attended as participants instead of as detached spectators" (p. 53). However, on the Chinese main stage, the actor–spectator relationship would typically be divided by an invisible wall, even in youth theatre. In recent years, in line with the needs of propaganda and government policy, the theatre has also increased the proportion of stage interpretations of stories about the outstanding Communist Party during the founding of the PRC, many of which have taken place in children's lifetimes. At the same time, the theatre prefers to invite foreign troupes to perform traditional plays such as those of Shakespeare and Wilde, and pays more attention to whether the plays or authors are in the classic genre. Compared to other theatres, the China National Theatre for Children and other local children's theatres have a significant advantage regarding commissions and production costs, as the theatre's operating funds come directly from the government's direct management. However, as a state-run performance unit, tickets for performances will be more affordable while giving little consideration to box office profits. This mode of operation makes this type of theatre appealing to lower-income and regular middle-class families in first-tier cities, who will bring their children to experience theatre because of the affordable ticket prices.

Thinking in terms of broadening the audience for theatre in China and exposing an underrepresented group to the performing art form, as well as allowing children to learn about another country through children's theatre, British children's theatre companies working in partnership with such theatres can see that in addition to the children of elite, white-collar families in Beijing and Shanghai, there is also an audience of teenagers from working-class families or less-developed cities.

Theatre companies like ASK are the backbone of Sino-British children's theatre cooperation. Compared to theatres, they do not have their own stages and those with multi-functional rehearsal rooms are already relatively well-developed, with more companies working with external venues to complete rehearsals and compositions of British productions when they come to China. At the performance stage, these companies use their venues for commercial performances on a rental or co-production basis through partnerships with major theatres such as the Shanghai Cultural Square, Shanghai Grand Theatre and Beijing Tianqiao Art Centre. As the plays introduced in the UK are primarily performed in fringe theatres, their stage design is not suitable for grand Chinese theatres where the audience often exceeds 2,000 and the multi-functional halls (whose size is about the same as a fringe theatre, but which also host conferences and evening parties, etc. and therefore have a name not closely related to the theatre in China and are located on the second-floor periphery of the theatre), while at the same time, the company will use their venues for commercial performances by renting or co-producing them. At the same time, from 2016 to the present, the residency has been challenging to realize in both big and small theatres in China. The reason is that based on the performance market in China, residency in big theatres is at a high level, with increased investment in production costs, and small theatre performances need to be estimated at around 80 performances to achieve profitability due to seating capacity constraints, and this is also the reason why foreign companies such as *Cloud Man*, represented by the case study in this chapter, can be considered to be the most profitable theatre form in China. This is why foreign theatre productions like *Cloud Man* in this chapter's case study chose to tour mainland China while cooperating with ASK. It is worth noting, however, that there are differences between this kind of tour and the more common tours in the UK. First of all, in terms of cooperation, a domestic theatre company such as ASK acts as an intermediary in communicating with the theatre of the tour destination. Generally speaking, the domestic company will also ask the theatre of the destination to pay a performance fee and in this way it will avoid the loss of box office revenue during the tour as much as possible.

Therefore, when a UK theatre company leaves a first-tier city such as Beijing, Shanghai, Guangzhou or Shenzhen and enters a second-tier or second-tier city such as Xi'an or Chengdu, they often find that the performance venues, the stage equipment, the audience's cooperation and so on are beyond their expectations. The production team need to make adjustments in a very short time. Due to the lower education level of the whole city, the children will not be able to enjoy the performance as much as they would in big cities under the all-English, cross-language performance language environment. Due to the town's lower education level, the children need help in understanding the play.

As the popularity of foreign productions in the Chinese theatre market continues to grow, more investors, theatre companies and theatres are travelling to the UK to find suitable British productions to introduce. In addition to their capital position and commercial understanding of the market, the way they select productions and the opportunities for those they have already signed up to enter the Chinese market is unique in international cross-cultural theatre practice. In addition to children's theatre, musicals from the West End and Broadway are another vein of foreign theatre introduction. For musicals, Chinese business people choose the hottest, highest box office-grossing shows of the year for commercial introduction or Chinese version development, often with their award-winning reputation playing a significant part. In 2023 for example, SMG and the Shanghai Cultural Plaza made an unprecedented move to introduce a Chinese version of *The Phantom of the Opera*, which has toured major Chinese cities to great acclaim. They are touring major cities in China with great success. It is a different story in the children's theatre market: first, in the Chinese market, shows modelled on Disney's classic animated movies in secondary creations, such as *Frozen*, etc., are very popular in second- and third-tier cities, The cost of such shows is lower. The production standards could be better, not for the audience's consideration, but entirely to make money in cities, with the actors and actresses wearing costumes similar to those in Disneyland to perform loosely onstage. However, such shows have exploited legal loopholes and appropriated the images of animated characters that are popular with young children, damaging the children's theatre market to a certain extent. Therefore, theatre companies would only put a little thought into recreating classic IP on the stage when looking at UK shows. Still, instead, they would prefer to see a form of performance that is not currently available in China, one that is more interactive with the audience and one that can be used for commercial promotion.

Once the target is chosen, international theatre festivals in China are often the best time for these children's theatre productions to make a name for themselves, create a good reputation and build an audience base for subsequent tours in mainland China. Mainstream theatre festivals such as the Wuzhen International Theatre Festival, Anaya Theatre Festival, etc., all have a separate section for overseas productions, which attract a large enough audience and thanks to the rapid development of China's social media, stage photos and show promotions are spread rapidly from the audience's point of view through media platforms such as Red, Weibo and so on. The audience's point of view is spreading rapidly, attracting parents who do not have the opportunity to go to theatre festivals in the cities. After the festival, the creators use their time in China to scout for similar productions, target theatres, etc., and then begin adapting and rehearsing in China.

In addition to theatre festivals, another way is to collaborate with English language education institutions, thanks to the support and promotion of English language education in China since the reform and opening up of China. At present, the proportion of language training institutions in cities of all levels, their degree of development and their access to schools and parental resources are far better than that of theatre or performing arts and theatre education institutions, so for the performance and promotion of children's theatre, cooperation with these institutions is necessary for the specific environment of China. There are two models of collaboration between the two: one is that the language school will disseminate information about the play to parents and when feedback is collected from families in the tens of thousands, a theatre company such as ASK will rationalize the profitability of the play it has on hand in the Chinese market and these family units will naturally become the first loyal audience for the play it introduces. In contrast, in the post-epidemic era, when China ended its lockdown, expensive theatre camps became the new choice for summer family trips. At last year's Edinburgh Fringe Festival, at least five or more camps were going to Edinburgh to experience theatre arts, and when the children watched the plays, the parents, like Ms. Forrina back then, saw the charm of the fringe theatre performances and at the end of the camps, the parents who took the young Brits' books were able to enjoy the theatre. At the end of the camp, parents with the contact information for young British practitioners are very likely to invite British theatre companies to perform in China in a joint venture. From the author's perspective, this can be developed into a transnational support programme for young artists with long-term development potential. In the context of globalization, online platforms during the epidemic have reduced the difficulty of transnational communication to a certain extent and, at the same time, have given the world more opportunities to see children's theatre performances that would otherwise only have a regional impact in the UK through the artists' homepage or the theatre company's video broadcasting platforms, outside of the mainstream online theatre platforms in the UK such as NT Live, and spreading the impact of outstanding works across continents. The effect of the theatre can be felt across continents.

Comparison of British Youth Theatre with Chinese Performances

Cloud Man, a performance in which the actor interacts with a puppet to interpret the role of a non-human creature, is a part of the foreign theatre repertoire, which, of course, has much to do with China's training system for theatre actors. At the drama school level, puppetry, drama performance and applied theatre are three different disciplines and teaching systems. This results in a more traditional or oriental approach to training while students are still in school. Therefore, after graduation, when they embark on applied theatre practice in the community or primary and secondary school campuses, or when they participate in children's theatre productions, the combination of various theatre techniques is not well exploited by them compared to theatre practitioners in the UK. But more importantly, in the significant urban children's education system, TIE, DIE and similar theatre education paradigms generated by China's unique education system, drama studies have created models of local children's theatre forms, contents and rehearsal methods in the theatre performances in which under-aged children perform as actors during the school education stage.

In contrast to a more open-minded approach, such as Ailie Cohen's expectations at the time of creation, the original play's main characters are the colours of the rainbow, each colour representing a different emotion and in the course of the performance, she will, through the way she acts, allow the underage audience to see the power of faith and the importance of emotional detoxification, peace of mind and the creation of something more representative of British children's theatre. One of the aims of colorful characters is so that every individual can represent group of people; as Nicholson (2011) says, what applied theatre should discover is how to "touch the lives of others" (p. 4). The Chinese Drama Etude performance system is different and based on a series of plays written for Chinese primary and junior high school students by its creator, William Huizhu Sun, who holds a Ph.D. in Performance Studies at New York University. In addition to the text, this paradigm provides rehearsal methods, staging and costume design that can be used as a reference by general school teachers without theatre training. This paradigm also provides an assembly line model for rehearsal, staging, costume design and other aspects of the rehearsal process that ordinary teachers can use without theatre training. Professor Sun first adapted classic texts, such as *Les Miserables*, in choosing the scripts. He deleted any content of *Les Miserables* that was not suitable for minors, and at the same time simplified the core conflict in the story and found the educational significance of the story, such as Jean Valjean's salvation and self-awakening, etc., to integrate the educational function of children's theatre into the performances. "Sun's 25-minute-long adaption of portions of *Les Misérables*, one of five, features Jean Valjean stealing Bishop Myriel's silverware only to run into two policemen right away" (Shen, 2021, p. 131). To simplify the difficulty of the lines, he has modelled it on traditional Chinese opera texts, in which the last word of each sentence is pronounced in a rhyming character, increasing the performability of the lines. Safety is another crucial element in Drama Etude, mentally and physically. As a result, Sun reduced dynamic body movements and reduced the potential of causing physical damage in stage direction. The betweeness of story, like theatrical distance, is without actual dimensions. It takes a place wherever people feel safe enough to face the danger of putting themselves in the place imagination has cleared for them – whether this be in a play in a story, in a theatre, or by a fireside (Duggan & Grainger, 1997).

In addition to Western classics, Sun also chooses to write traditional Chinese stories such as the legend of Confucius. Based on China's population base, a class in a primary school can often have 40–50 children, so to give each child a more equal chance of performing, he breaks the script into multiple acts, with each act performed by different children. A Drama Etude such as *Les Miserables* can run for about 50 minutes, which is close to a children's theatre piece in terms of performance length. At this stage, compared to the co-creation of TIE, Drama Etude wants students to receive theatre education in a fixed rehearsal mode, which reduces teachers' difficulty in forming performances. As he mentioned, Drama Etudes, like Music Etudes, allow all students to practice in the classroom, divided into small groups and guided by their teacher (Huizhu Sun, 2018). By encountering Etude plays, students can best experience and understand theatre. But at the same time, as William Sun's work progressed, he created fragmented performances based on Chinese idioms and poems, which could be kept to less than 10 minutes, to enable students to learn about traditional Chinese culture and the literature they would be taught in Chinese classes in a more lively and relaxed theatre atmosphere. But when his updated model was rehearsed and performed in 2023 in Shanghai's inter-community cultural centres with community residents, combined classroom drama with community theatre, performed by residents, who undoubtedly are amateurs, received funds from certain community councils which are in line with Coon's four key elements of community theatre: "(1) they are local, (2) the company's beginnings or their essence must be amateur, (3) they both expose a community to theatre performance as well as engender participation, and (4) they depend upon their community for their survival" (Coon, 2015, p. 6). Spectators of these short plays were mainly Shanghai school children and their parents, the same audience as for the introduced plays in Shanghai. From the researchers' observations, we can compare and conclude that for Chinese children's theatre audiences today, British plays written from a child's point of view are more appealing to them despite the difficulty of understanding the language. Parents' reactions show that, for plays of an educational nature, where the content for adults is *de-intellectualized* to make it easier for children to understand and where idioms with only four words and ancient poems with 28 words are expanded and then dramatized, there is still a discussion of the moral concepts or traditional codes of behaviour embedded in the play, which are essentially the same. However, they are theatre performances discussing the moral concepts or conventional codes of conduct embedded in them. Instead of attracting the attention of parents, who subconsciously think that this is a compulsory subject for their children to receive, they play with their mobile phones or doze off while watching the performance and fail to connect with their children concerning the content and thus gain something from the theatre performance.

Coincidentally, *Cloud Man*, with the assistance of creators Ailie and Lewis' newly formed theatre company Constellation Points, has worked with Theatre in Schools Scotland to develop the For Nursery (4+) – P3 Pupils in Schools classroom drama course programme, which commenced operations on 23 October 2023. In common with Drama Etude, the programme lists stage dimensions, performance length and maximum audience size, and instructions to guide students in the making of puppets in the classroom and how to work with them to deliver the performance. The creator has also provided the following teaching themes for the performance: Science: the natural world, observation and experimentation, respecting ecosystems and environments; Independent Learning: care and respect for other living things, patience and diligence, the rewards of putting another being's welfare above your own, kindness and curiosity. However, when comparing the content of the script with the design of the lines and what the children were expected to learn through the theatre performance, although the scripts were provided, Ailie, in addition to the synopsis, mentioned in her note to the classroom teacher that it was possible to leave it up to the children to creatively develop their interpretations of the main character in the story, Mr Cloud, which are two of the first steps. This is the most significant difference between the two types of theatre that move from the stage to the classroom, from professional actors to children acting in a story for children.

Moral lessons and traditional cultural learning are necessary under the Chinese value system; through observing the audience's behaviour, the author maintains that the Western view of applied theatre, created for children, performed for children and communicated by children, is of intercultural value.

In September 2023, a children's theatre performance competition was held at the Chinese Children's Art Theatre and the Drama Etude performance *Qiangwa*, adapted from *Les Miserables*, was joint winner with a play modelled on the creative style of contemporary British children's theatre. In the parental feedback session after the performance, the children's theatre that focuses more on mobilizing the attention of the underage audience through dramatic, exaggerated actions and, at the same time, guides the children to the stage to throw paper aeroplanes left under the seats in advance, constantly encouraging the children to interact with the actors and raising the awareness of environmental protection among the minors in the course of fun, has gained a greater tendency to be chosen as the play for the family-based group activity. The two plays indicate the trends of the whole market. The introduction of plays accounted for little long term increase in the trend of box office revenues; whether from the content, performance form or audience choice, it is said that from the point of view of the audience group, the children and the family on the choice of theatre-going behaviour is the same, and because of the different cultural backgrounds, the influence of the other languages is limited. However, the theatre's introduction in the post-epidemic era still has room for development and it has become the aim of young British artists to support international exchange.

However, from the difference in content, it is easy to see that when a play is introduced to China, it still has to go through the necessary cross-cultural adaptation process, whether from the content of the script or from the director's point of view, to assist non-English-speaking audiences to understand better the performance of the necessary adjustments, which is crucial for the creators, theatre companies and the audience, so the following is a description of the process of cross-cultural adaptation and touring of children's theatre in 2014, with reference to the adaptation of *Cloud Man*.

The Intercultural Adaptation Process of *Cloud Man*

Creation of **Cloud Man**

Cloud Man tells a story about faith. Scientist Cloudia is obsessed with research and firmly believes a creature commonly called Mr Cloud must live in the sky. To find this mysterious man, she climbed the mountains, travelled all over the wilderness and searched for Mr Cloud for her whole life. One day, Mr Cloud comes to her house by mistake for an adventure; suddenly, Cloudia captures him with a set-up and starts her scientific research. However, after she senses Mr Cloud is unhappy about being caught, Cloudia sends him back to nature. The script came from a brainstorming session between actor Ailie Cohen and writer Lewis Hetherington, which was inspired by puppets (Anonymous, n.d.). Ailie, who used to work for a puppet-making company, believes that each puppet has its characteristics and energy, and using puppets to represent another self while the actor is performing creates excellent potential for on-stage communication. These two creators grew up in Scotland during the same period, developing a fascination with back-to-nature themes and then making an artistic decision to create a story told through puppetry. The first draft was "Rainbow Man", a seven-coloured character with different personalities depending on the colour, and the first character created was Mr Cloud, a shy and socially awkward white man, after which *Cloud Man* was born. Lewis mentioned the following in an interview with the author: "As a playwright, I am very good at telling stories through words, but I prefer to complete the expression of visual storytelling through the combination of puppets and lines for a performance designed for children, the situation that can be entered quickly is the first condition for playwriting".[1] Since both characters in the performance are performed by Ailie herself, a clear distinction must be made regarding the characters' portrayal, with a natural conflict between an obsessive science nerd, Cloudia, and a shy Mr Cloud.

The stage design is all handcrafted by Ailie herself – the puppets, the clouds and the mountaintop hut where Cloudia lives. Although the colour scheme is simple yet full of mechanical design, it brings magic on stage. As Ailie said, during an interview with the author, her previous experience in children's theatre started with acting in fairy tales, which gave her a magical experience onstage and made her work credible to youngsters. This was combined with her excellent craftsmanship to create *Cloud Man*. *Cloud Man* is not only for children but also for their parents. Ailie hopes *Cloud Man* becomes a performance that makes lovely family memories, helping parents to start conversations and revisit children's education from a different angle. As a typical youth theatre performance, the creation of *Cloud Man* is by, for, with and about young people is often seen to be more instrumental, less sophisticated,and have less value in professional theatre settings and is thus regarded by theatre researchers and even some practitioners as being less sophisticated than the "real thing" (Busby et al., 2022).

Difficulties Encountered in Localized Adaptations

Cloud Man has several excellent qualities that are conducive to its introduction into China: first, it is concise, with a performance length of about 55 minutes, which is conducive to children's concentration; second, the text is not too long, and conveys the maximum amount of information through concise language; and third, the stage scenery can be reproduced, as the performers themselves made the first version of the show's choreography and set-up and although it is complex in structure, it is not too big, so it can be transferred to China and reproduced on-site according to the drawings. Before this process started, another issue concerning representatives is about whether or not Chinese children's voices can be heard in an intercultural context, and whether, if the story doesn't meet the concerns of local families and children, it would be as effective and influential as the production in Edinburgh. Actually, rather than "giving a voice" we should think more in terms of amplifying voices (Busby, 2022, p. 117). When Ailie and ASK look back to what initiated the collaboration, showing Chinese children a performance and encouraging them to speak in their their true voices is what drives them here. The first version of the show was handmade by the actors and although the structure was complex, it needed to be more significant to be transported to China or otherwise reproduced on the spot according to the drawings.

One of the most pressing problems in China was the language barrier. The premiere theatre was chosen in Wuzhen, which coincided with the opening of the Wuzhen Drama Festival, a folk festival of children's games. Even though most of the participants came from Shanghai to participate in the event and had a certain degree of English language proficiency, ensuring that the audience would receive 100% of the information was impossible. The idea was to have subtitles, but the Chinese subtitles were also a barrier to reading for the younger audience. In the end, we chose to have a Chinese actor, who also played the voice of Cloudia, translate the lines into Chinese and repeat them in conjunction with the performance. We arranged an internal testing ground to test the stage effect before the rehearsal hall.

Bringing *Cloud Man* to China was a groundbreaking decision, as Chinese children's theatre is limited in style, with most of the fairy tales being performed in a lively manner, with exaggerated gestures of the characters and animal roles. Leng Jiahua, deputy director of the Wuhan People's Art Theatre, once pointed out that nowadays, most people who come to see children's theatre are pre-schoolers and to mobilize the atmosphere, many of the plays allow children to come on stage and join in the interaction in the middle of the performance. Regardless of whether that is a good thing, as long as the small audience is happy, parents are satisfied and have peace of mind (*China News*, n.d.). With all the jubilation on stage, the offstage audience is relatively quiet. It does not form an immersive relationship with the performance, which is usually a mingling of the stage and the audience, with the main focus being on the hustle and bustle. But the production is just the opposite; it is a quiet play requiring total concentration and dedication. The character of Mr Cloud is a 13cm tall puppet with a tiny presence on stage, blending in with the clouds in the background and sometimes requiring concentration to look for it carefully; so no one knew before the premiere whether the Chinese children's audience would receive it well after travelling so far across the oceans. Fortunately, the attempt reaped great success and since its premiere in 2014 it has remained active on the Chinese children's theatre stage, having toured China's major cities for over a decade. After that, more British children's theatre entered the Chinese market, contributing to the prosperity of the Chinese children's theatre market.

Different Geographical Feedback for Premieres and Tours

The ten-year tour of *Cloud Man* in China has covered all major cities, and been mainly divided into three routes: the first one is the series of major cities in Jiangsu, Zhejiang and Shanghai with Shanghai as the centre, the second route is to the northern cities of Beijing and Tianjin and the third route is the northwest route which starts at Shanghai and passes through Luoyang, Xi'an, Lanzhou, Yinchuan and Urumqi. In this way British Children's Theatre has walked out of the silk road on the map of China.

Audience feedback varies slightly from city to city, with first-tier cities Shanghai and Beijing showing a common response. In Shanghai, for example, preschool children are generally educated in English. The language environment is more favourable than that of other Chinese cities, so most of the children can read and understand the content of the play independently and don't need to get the information indirectly through the Chinese interpreter and can usually interact with the British actors directly in the performance process. Some children in Hangzhou rely on interpreters to help them with their lines, but more than half the audience can interact directly. The performance effect is similar to that of the first-tier cities. The first-tier cities have rich experience in children's theatre; many children are familiar with theatre etiquette and understand the performance process due to their parents' theatregoing habits, forming a potentially cultivated audience group.

There is a big difference between the audience in Northwest China and and those of the northern cities. *Cloud Man* toured the Silk Road through five western provincial capitals, China's third-tier cities according to their economic classification. The children in these cities seldom have the opportunity to go to the theatre to enjoy a children's play, lack experience in watching theatre, lack psychological preparation for watching theatre, and the English language is not widespread, so it will take more time to spend more money on the process of managing the theatres. Audiences need to spend more time getting used to the theatre situation, and they rely more on the Chinese interpreter to understand the lines and react only after the Chinese interpreter has supplied the translation. However, due to the need for more theatre experience in the region, parents and children were more interested in children's theatre from the UK. They participated more actively in the interactive shows and workshops and various peripheral activities after the play, which were more interactive experiences.

It is worth mentioning an exceptional performance, a charity performance prepared by the introduction team for the left-behind children in a working children's primary school. Because it was a public welfare performance, the performance cost was reduced as much as possible and the venue was not in a theatre in Hangzhou. Still, it was provided for free by the Buddha Hall of a temple, which is usually a place for the temple abbot to conduct pujas and preach sermons. As it was a public service venue, people associated with the show were welcome to sit in the audience on the day of the performance, so the audience was made up of monks from the temple and children from the children's primary school, with the children's ages ranging from 6 to13 years old. In contrast, several monks were adults in their 20s and 50s. Ailie said in an interview that it was a performance she would never forget and that the venue and audience were unprecedented. This production tells a story of faith and the stage was set in a religious sanctuary. The primary setting of the show created a sacred atmosphere, with the majority of the audience being children from a particular category of children in China whose parents have taken them away from their hometowns to work in the cities and who have arrived in a city that is far more economically advantaged than their hometowns, but do not have the same level of entertainment and access to resources as the big city children. Most seldom watch TV or even have access to electronic devices such as mobile phones and tablets, and have never had the opportunity to go to a theatre to watch a performance. Therefore, the British children's play staged in Foton was their first theatre experience and they showed more concentration and curiosity than other children of the same age. They held their breath and were entirely focused on the stage throughout the play. It was also the first time that several of the monks, who have spent much of their lives in the service of their faith, had seen a theatre performance and for the first time, they were able to see how to pursue their *faith* from a third-person perspective. After the performance, one of the monks said that he had seen the power of faith, interpreting *Cloud Man*'s message as "If you have Buddha in your heart, you will see Buddha everywhere".[2]

It is is a very quiet and peaceful show and the feedback from this performance was particularly quiet and focused, with the audience onstage probably being the best audience for this play for that reason. The theatre atmosphere in the venue was so immersive that the puppet on stage, Mr Cloud, was even more animated and alive. Ailie said it was one of the most focused and immersive experiences of her acting career, one which still impresses her and has had an enormous impact on her future creations and performances.

The Influence of British Youth Theatre in China

English Teaching and Cultural Communication

British children's theatre is be greatly welcomed in China for several reasons. First, Chinese original children's theatre is still in the process of development and there is still much room for progress in the selection of themes, script writing and production presentation, while British children's theatre is relatively mature and has a diversity of themes so that it can be directly transferred to the Chinese stage. Second, Chinese primary and secondary schools have begun to pay more attention to English education in recent years and children's theatre is a perfect opportunity for practice, which can not only test the effect of English education but also increase children's interest in English through the fun of the play. *Cloud Man* was so popular on the Silk Road in Northwest China because, after the show, the children were given a workshop on making Mr Cloud in conjunction with an English class. The actors and English teachers encouraged the children to use their imaginations to recreate the process of making *Cloud Man*, creating an English language environment for the younger children and teenagers. The workshop created an English language environment for the children and enhanced their hands-on skills. The auditoriums were packed during the tour and the workshop after the play was always overcrowded. Children in Northwest China rarely have such an opportunity to learn English, so compared to first-tier cities, parents and children in Northwest China showed a more active attitude to participation.

Meanwhile, based on the British playwright's life experience and personal expression, *Cloud Man* creates a fairy tale with a philosophical element that is not too deep. This type of story can be used as a blueprint for accumulating British culture, which differs from traditional Chinese mythological stories. With the help of the elements and literary conjectures of British culture, it presents Chinese children with a new and strange cultural experience. Chinese theatre creation is often confined to the rituals and rules of traditional culture. In contrast, children's theatre selections are primarily derived from mythological stories and classic fables, such as *Mulan's Story*, which emphasizes filial piety and personal growth, and *Tadpole Looking for Mummy*, which focuses on independence and perseverance, the starting point of which is to play a role in children's ideological education through children's theatre performance, and the purpose of indoctrination will be implanted in the scripts from the very beginning of the creative process. The script of *Cloud Man* is based on elements of freedom, faith and return to nature, which are characteristic of the West. The performance focuses on enlightenment, guiding the audience to use their imagination and think independently, but does not want to convey a positive truth in too obvious a fashion. For domestic practitioners, creating stories such as Mr Cloud, which aims to build an emotional connection and encourage its audience, brings a fresh angle to Chinese children's theatre. Also, it allows the audience to re-examine the role of children's theatre from the perspective of cultural differences.

Driving the Development of Chinese Youth Theatre

With Ailie's production as the first introduced work, the theatre company ASK subsequently introduced several British children's theatre groups,s and with the revenue and audience feedback of *Cloud Man*, it created China's first "parent-child micro-theatre" concept. "Before this, the audience of children's theatre was limited to children and teenagers, with parents playing the role of companion and guardian" (*China Now*, n.d.). However, *Cloud Man* is an example of a family-based show where parents and children enter the theatre as audience members. When the play was first introduced in 2014, the auditorium was designed for parents and children to sit together because we worried that Chinese children could not be fully immersed in the play. However, after dozens of tests, we found that the children were very focused during the play and did not need any special care, so we decided to adjust the auditorium to have the children sit in the front area for a close-up view.

In contrast, the parents sat at the back to watch the play so the parents and children were separated. This was to create a theatre environment for large and small audiences. In this way, parents generally gave feedback saying that this form of experience was perfect; parents and children can focus on the show, but also take part afterwards in the parent–child exchanges and discussions, which invariably creates a new mode of theatre.

Stimulating the Development of Local Productions

China's local, original children's theatre has long been under-powered. Taking the 2016 annual performance survey as an example, 258 children's theatre productions were staged locally in Shanghai in 2016 (including multiple rounds of performances by the same organizations), of which 192 were adaptations and 66 were original productions. Of the 192 adaptations, Grimm's *Fairy Tales* and Hans Christian Andersen's *Fairy Tales* were the most favoured blueprints, with 60 shows, with 60 and with 17 children's theatre productions choosing to adapt and reinterpret these works. The proportion of original foreign productions was much higher than that of mainland China.

The proportion of original works among those performed by foreign performing groups in Shanghai was 59%, which is the highest among the three types of local performances in China, so the introduction of plays has increased year by year, which side by side also reflects China's lack of originality. More than half of the shortlisted productions in the "Top 10

Chinese Children's Theatre Box Office [successes] in 2017" (Idaolue, 2019) are children's theatre productions imported from foreign countries such as Hong Kong, Macao and Taiwan. In particular, creative plays that have won awards at various international arts festivals go viral in first-tier cities. Statistics also show that 2017, 77 plays were imported from Hong Kong, Macao, Taiwan and other countries.

In 2017, of the national children's theatre performances, 77 plays were imported from Hong Kong, Macao, Taiwan and other countries, with a total of 2,097 performances, a year-on-year increase of 16.8%, and box office revenues amounted to 96,665,000 yuan, a year-on-year increase of 37.6%.

According to 2023 statistics, the size of Chinese children's theatre audiences exceeded 3.15 million people, with the introduction of children's theatre from overseas leading to the growth of box office sales, and despite the impact of the pandemic the children's theatre market is still developing rapidly. The development of Chinese children's theatre in terms of a historical process can be roughly divided into four phases. The first phase came before the founding of the country in 1949 – this historical period started from scratch and gradually established the process of Chinese children's theatre; the second stage came after the founding of the country and lasted until the reform and opening-up period; the integration and development of the past and the future, this stage combined with the needs of China's national conditions to give birth to the creation of works like the *Treasure Boat* created by Lao She as well as the *Maranhwa*. The third stage runs from the reform and opening-up to the early 21st century – a period of prosperity and stagnation, especially at the end of the 20th century as the world entered the information age; children's art and culture were affected by the diversified development of the information wave and a large number of novel and richly animated films emerged via television, films and the internet. The cross-pollination of film media and the internet structure, as well as the high-speed interactivity and timely dissemination of modern communications, are widely favoured by children and young people, dramatically impacting the children's theatre market. Although it cannot be said that children's theatre around the 20th century had no development or progress relative to the developments and changes of Chinese society, it needed to reflect the progress of the times in many aspects. *The Daughter of the Sea* and *Snow White* still haven't been adapted for the stage, while creative rethinks of children's theatre and market-oriented operations are lagging behind and insufficient to a certain extent. The fourth stage is the introduction of overseas children's theatre into China after 2010, especially after British children's theatre entered the market in the form of family theatre in 2014, which has created incentives for positive competition in the original market. Many state-run theatre troupes have had to create original works to improve their attractiveness at the box office.

To promote the development of children's theatre, a series of original children's theatre competitions have been organized, led by the China Children's

Art Theatre and the Shanghai Children's Art Theatre of the China Welfare Foundation, to stimulate Chinese children's theatre from the original scripts to the quality of production. The China Children's Art Theatre organized two incubation programmes for children's and young people's stage artworks in the wake of the pandemic. A total of 22 works were shortlisted, including *Girl with Pearls*, which was based on an opera, and several children's theatre productions modelled on Western examples combining music, light and shadow, and magic. China Theatre Publishing House and the Children's Theatre Committee of the China Children's Literature Research Association also chose three original children's scripts for the *Golden Eyebrows* in 2021–2023, from a collection of more than 600 original and outstanding works.

The company that introduced *Cloud Man*, ASK, has presented excellent children's theatre productions such as *The Polar Bears Go Up, the Anatomy of the Piano, We Dance Wee Groove, Boing*, and so on, to further broaden the Chinese market after opening it up with *Cloud Man, Boing* and other outstanding children's theatre productions, and further widening the Chinese market since the first introduction of British children's theatre in 2014. The company has been profitable for ten years and Shanghai, Hangzhou, Suzhou, Beijing, Tianjin and other first-tier and second-tier cities in China have independent theatres and occupy a particular share of the children's theatre market. Subsequently, the company will expand its repertoire to Europe, Australia and other regions, and introduce more outstanding overseas productions to China.

China's children's theatre market demand is increasing year by year; overseas children's theatre still occupies more than half of it by proportion; British children's theatre still has a lot of room for development in China and is known for its ability to attract parents and children to the theatre; and for the second- and third-tier cities, because of the demand there for English language education, British children's theatre is more attractive than domestic children's theatre. From the point of view of profitability and artistic standards, British children's theatre is still ahead of mainland original children's theatre.

Notes

1 Unpublished interview notes with Lewis Hetherington, interviewed by Huang Xiaolin, 2023.
2 Unpublished reflection notes.

References

Anonymous (n.d.). Cloud man Ailie Cohen. In *Made in Scotland Showcase*. https://www.madeinscotlandshowcase.com/shows/cloud-man-ailie-cohen/.
Busby, S. (2022). *Applied theatre: A pedagogy of utopia*. Bloomsbury Methuen Drama.

Busby, S., Freebody, K. & Rajendran, C. (2022). Introduction. In S. Busby, K. Free-body & C. Rajendran, *The Routledge companion to theatre and young people* (pp. 1–15). Routledge. https://doi.org/10.4324/9781003149965-1.

China News. (n.d.). The 2nd China children's theatre festival seminar. *Sina News.* https://news.sina.com.cn/o/2012-08-27/001525039732.shtml.

China Now. (n.d.). Theatre for young audiences in China report. https://chinanow.britishcouncil.cn/research/theatre-young-audiences-china-report/.

China Securities Journal. (2016, 10 Dec). Children's theatre market grows rapidly: Speaking loudly through good performances. EastMoney Securities. https://finance.eastmoney.com/news/1355,20161210692325854.html.

Coon, S. M. (2015). Crossing the aether-net: Community and the theatre of Team Starkid. Ohio Link ETD Center. http://rave.ohiolink.edu/etdc/view?acc_num=bgsu1429204552.

Duggan, M. & Grainger, R. (1997). *Imagination, identification, and catharsis in theatre and therapy.* Jessica Kingsley.

Durden, E. (2022). "Home Grown" productions for their own young people. In S. Busby, K. Freebody & C. Rajendran, *The Routledge companion to theatre and young people.* (pp. 153–169). Routledge. https://doi.org/10.4324/9781003149965-12.

Huizhu Sun, W. (2018). *Drama etudes for the classroom: Training, scripts and acting.* Shanghai Jiao Tong University Press.

Idaolue (2019, 23 Aug). *Children's drama annual report: Market growth slows down, parent-child micro-theatres.* Idaolue.com. http://www.idaolue.com/Data/Detail.aspx?id=1646.

Nicholson, H. (2011). *Theatre, education and performance.* Bloomsbury.

Shen, L. (2021). Drama etudes. *TDR: The Drama Review,* 65(2), 131–149. https://doi.org/10.1017/s1054204321000125.

Ukaegbu, V. (2004) The problem with definitions: An examination of Applied Theatre in traditional African contexts. *National Drama,* 3, 45–54.

Zou, R. (2015). How can China's children's theatre market have its cake and eat it too? *China News.* https://www.chinanews.com/cul/2015/05-21/7292500.shtml.

PART 3

Local, National and International Voices

10

IMAGINING BEYOND THE BARBARISM

Richard Holmes and Ben Ballin

A State of Barbarism

The adult world does terrible things to its young, with each new generation of adults finding new ways to do more terrible things to the next generation. This abuse is endemic and the germ of the abuse stems from the defence of private property, defence of privilege and the defence of the power by those who have it. The defence of their wealth and power requires an *offence* against the rest.

Over the last twenty years, politics in the UK – and a great many other countries across the globe – has deepened this systematic attack on the defenceless, especially on the young. We are seeing governments around the world turning to *"common sense"* solutions to the cultural and economic crisis we face, solutions which encourage and train the powerless to abuse each other and themselves.

Conditions for the Young

In his 2015 speech to the UK Tory party conference, then-prime minister David Cameron famously said that he wanted his time in power to be remembered as "a defining decade for our country … the turnaround decade … one which people will look back on and say that's the time when the tide turned … when people no longer felt the current going against them but working with them" (as cited in Settle, 2015, para. 5). He also asserted that the Tory party would "finish the fight for real equality and wage an all-out assault on poverty" (as cited in Wintour & Watt, 2015, para. 1).

In reality, Cameron drove the country into a Brexit-shaped iceberg, before leaving the sinking ship. The consequences are that now, eight years later,

DOI: 10.4324/9781003470434-13

many people are drowning in debt. (Meanwhile, Cameron, now elevated to the position of unelected peer Lord Cameron, is back as the country's foreign secretary).

In reality, the "common sense" solutions proposed by Cameron and his successors have constituted an *offence* against the young.

Poverty has not been *assaulted* but has deepened. According to the report *UK Poverty 2022* (Joseph Rowntree Foundation, 2022), 14.5 million people live in poverty in Britain today. The report goes on to say there are more than 4.3 million children (almost a third of the entire child population in the UK) who are living in households on less than 60% of the average income and the number is rising. With a predicted two-year recession on the horizon, things will only get worse.

The *offence* has displaced the young from their sustenance and their homes. Since Cameron's speech, food bank usage has doubled, with one in every six households in the UK using them. The soaring cost of energy has led to a rise in warmth banks and *warm spaces* as well. Poverty has risen by 62%, because of high rents, rapid inflation, cuts in welfare and the lack of affordable housing, resulting in 36 people a day becoming homeless since 2015, and this isn't showing any sign of slowing down. According to the *Homelessness Monitor England* report (Crisis, 2022) there were 282,000 people without a permanent home in 2022, including 120,000 children. That was an increase of over 100,000 since 2015.

The *offence* has also been against the bodies of the young. In February 2024, the Academy for Medical Sciences reported an "appalling decline" in the health of children under five, including a significant increase in infant mortality (Academy for Medical Sciences, 2024). The report's co-chair (2024) outlined "an appalling decline in the health of our children, which makes for an even more bleak outlook for their future." And yet, he continued, "There is clear evidence in the report that tackling childhood health conditions, addressing inequalities and providing early years social support can change the future of health and prosperity" (PA Media, 2024).

In writing about this attack on children for National Drama (Holmes, 2023), Big Brum's Artistic Director Richard Holmes was "reminded of Lorna Jackson, the head teacher from a primary school in London" who in 2018 had reported finding two of her children sleeping behind a bin: "Mum, Dad and the two little children were all sleeping on a mattress they'd found. The family had been evicted and the children had very little to eat" (Ferguson, 2018, para. 1).

This head teacher's experience was not unique. Since her interview, teachers from all over the UK talk regularly about feeding hungry children in their classes or schools, contributing to funeral costs for students, or where schools have set up food and clothes banks, offering support to parents unable to help themselves. Big Brum meets many of these teachers, parents and children on a regular basis. Indeed, the local community has set up a food bank on the premises that we work from.

Our young are living through these most hostile of conditions. Poverty and the threats from it are a real presence in their lives. Children come to school hungry, tired or inappropriately dressed. They may leave homes of substance abuse, violence, disorder, mental illness, neglect and Victorian-type squalor. For some, the conditions are qualitatively better – for others they are inconceivably worse.

So, if those are the conditions faced by the young, what did David Cameron really mean by "an all-out assault on poverty?" (as cited in Wintour & Watt, 2015, para. 1).

In 2012, a radical, right-wing, Conservative parliamentary faction calling themselves the Free Enterprise Group sent out a manifesto entitled "Britannia Unchained" (Kwarteng et al., 2012). Their manifesto laid out plans for a "harsh medicine", which this think tank believed Britain needed to take, in order to be more competitive on the global economic stage.

At the heart of this collection of essays was an advocation of "Austerity Max"[1], part of which called for a loosening of regulations covering the employment of children. The members of this group were Dominic Raab, Kwasi Kwarteng, Priti Patel, Elizabeth Truss, Andrea Leadsom, Jacob Rees-Mogg, Rory Stewart, Kit Malthouse, Robert Buckland, James Cleverly and Christopher Pincher.

In 2012, this group of self-confessed Thatcherites and neo-Thatcherites were backbenchers. Boris Johnson was an advocate of this group's thinking, so much so that he made them all influential cabinet members after his election as Prime Minister. Later, Elizabeth Truss and her finance minister Kwasi Kwarteng attempted to implement some of its key policies during their short and disastrous tenure in office, thereby deepening the financial crisis in the process and plunging many families even deeper into debt. Other notable supporters of these radical thinkers were Michael Fallon and Sajid Javid (later Chancellor of the Exchequer for Boris Johnson, though for less than a year).

Cameron's "Age of Austerity", coupled with the deregulations allowed by Brexit, have paved the way for the radical right in the UK to implement the harshest of conditions against the poor. "The talented and hardworking have nothing to fear" (as cited in Hope Not Hate, n.d., para. 48), threatened Dominic Raab, while Jake Berry, another Tory MP, while serving as Chairman of the Conservative Party, told Sky News (2022) that the solution for the millions of families up and down the country struggling to pay their bills was for "people (to) know that when their bills arrive, they can either cut their consumption or they can get a higher paid salary, higher wages, go out there and get that new job" (as cited in *BBC News*, 2022, para. 4).

Ever more young people and their families in the UK are forced to choose whether to eat or to stay warm (we are sure that this is true of many other places, too). This state of affairs is proof of how detached, dispassionate and disinterested politicians have become.

Trusting the Young

These are the barbarous conditions that young people find themselves in when Big Brum encounters them.

The reason Big Brum works with young people is because they are remarkable. They feel most profoundly the world and its movement. But however remarkable young people are, they can't apply this to their own enthusiasm, needs, or even creativity, without a shared space to help them do it. Drama is a collective and social activity and the theatre Big Brum creates provides young people with the space to articulate their felt experiences.

The work of Big Brum has always been audacious. Given the current social, political and cultural crisis in the UK and worldwide, to create work today that continues to offer such a space, is in itself audacious. This audacity runs through the company's practice and artistic output, but also its policies and its strategic plans.

A young person's nature is to question, to be tender and social, to be creative and imaginative; but there is a danger that this is being knocked out of them as a matter of course. Schools, colleges and universities (which are themselves facing the "harsh medicine" prescribed by government) are increasingly under pressure to "get results", rather than to engage in subjects such as the arts which delve deeper into the human condition (Ball, 2018; 2003; O'Toole & O'Mara, 2007; Samuels, 2019).

As set out in its Artistic Policy, Big Brum proceeds "from the premise that children are not undeveloped adults but human beings in their own right, with specific experiences that go to the heart of being human" (Big Brum, 2011). This places young people, their needs and their experiences, at the heart of the company's practice, policy and strategic thinking.

The company "uses theatre and drama to work alongside young people to make meaning of their lives and the world around them" (Big Brum, 2011). For Big Brum this means taking a position which is radically opposed to that of the barbarism outlined above: it means trusting the young, trusting the child. We therefore "use the art form to enable young people to educate their own minds not in *what to think* but *how to think*" (Big Brum, 2011). Big Brum therefore creates spaces that make it possible for audiences to think for themselves how best to lead their lives.

Given the barbarism of our times, it is perhaps not surprising that some people have wondered if Big Brum's plays and programmes might make too many demands on young audiences. We have already noted that we are in a political culture where young people are systematically undervalued … and worse. We are also living with an educational culture that too often sees young people as "empty vessels" to be filled with authorized knowledge and achieve approved results, where "the children only [learn] what could be turned into data" (Rosen, 2018, para. 1).

We know from experience that our plays and programmes don't make too many demands. Rather, they open up areas that young people are aware of, fundamental aspects of reality that hardly anyone speaks to them about, or more importantly spaces where they can be heard. The plays of Big Brum *ought to* be the work Big Brum does, because its work creates such spaces. They have never been more necessary.

Big Brum's Practice: "In Defence of the Child"

Big Brum was established in 1982 to provide Theatre in Education for secondary schools in Birmingham, the UK's second-largest city. Over 40 years later, this remit has been extended to include many different settings, such as universities, primary and secondary schools and to work in a wider geographical area.

However, the common feature of all its work is a fierce commitment to bringing the highest quality of artistic work to those least likely to receive it. Big Brum usually takes 2–3 original pieces of theatre each year to 80–100 venues, performing to audiences of around 7,500 young people. Since 1982, the company has produced well over 100 original programmes of work, bringing a richly varied experience of theatre to an audience of over 300,000 young people. From Shakespeare to original plays by Edward Bond, from Greek myths to fairy tales, this body of work has earned it a local, national and international reputation for creating work of the highest artistic and educational quality.

> The work of Big Brum proceeds from the materialist philosophical premise that the world is knowable and that Art, like science, is a mode of knowing this world in which we live. Art cognizes life truthfully. But the truth is not fixed immutable knowledge, it is knowing in the present moment and therefore subject to change. Like evolution, artistic production is a process of becoming, born out of the need that human beings have to know and re-know themselves, individually and socially. Art is social imagination, which functions through a synthesis of feeling and thought with implications for future action in life.
>
> *(Big Brum, Artistic Policy, 2011)*

In 2023, Big Brum set out a five-year programme of work which was designed around the title "In defence of the child: Creating human space for the displaced".

War, poverty and climate change-related disasters have left more people presently displaced from their home than at any other time in history. As well as those literally displaced, there is an increasing number of people who have become metaphorically displaced from their homes, their family and friends, jobs, even themselves. The uncertainty in the world has created uncertainty in us. We set out some of the ways in which this happens at the start of this chapter.

We can see this process of displacement in the increase in mental health issues and suicide amongst the most vulnerable in our society, especially the young. Big Brum, like all artists, has an obligation to take a relationship to the *displaced*, whether working with young audiences in schools, within our local community or with the community of fellow artists we help to develop.

Drama compacts reality and resonates for an audience on both a conscious and unconscious level. Image enables us to cognize apparently different aspects of reality in their essence and in relation to each other. This resonance is the intuitive starting point for the gleaning of new knowledge that can be conceptualized and categorized. The power of this mode of knowing is that the image resonates in the mind long after facts have been forgotten. So what does this work look like in practice?

The Monuments Trilogy

What follows is an outline of an ambitious programme of work, *The Monuments Trilogy* and how this has been realized in practice. This trilogy was created between 2020 and 2023 and was built around William Shakespeare's *Romeo and Juliet*. The trilogy was comprised of: the digital monodrama *Socially Distant*, which was set in the present day (during the Covid-19 lockdown); a hybrid (live/filmed) adaptation of *Romeo and Juliet* (which took us back to Jacobean England and the birth of capitalism) and the play and TIE programme *Over the Balcony* (set in a dystopian near-future).

Part 1: Socially Distant

Socially Distant was Big Brum's first attempt at film drama for schools. This digital resource was produced during the first Covid lockdown in 2020 and included a substantial programme of work designed to support drama teachers. The activities were designed to accommodate any year group and the material had an emphasis on drama/performing arts but could be used as part of Personal Social and Health Education (PSHE).

The aim of the digital TIE programme was to provide students and teachers with material to explore fully the content and context of the story and the people in the story, while providing a stimulus for thinking and reflecting on their own lives, safely through the fiction. We provided teachers with a multitude of tasks to help steer their student's experience around the programme's central concepts of isolation, disconnection and repression, with the key question being: *Living in this world has made us socially distant from ourselves and each other, where lies and greed conceal our true nature. How then can our true selves be revealed in such conditions?* That central question has not gone away, but gained an additional significance during the experience of lockdown.

The programme and the drama aimed to provoke young people into finding their own relationship to these central concepts, while working in an integrated, connected and expressive manner: in short, working in the opposite way to the world the drama was set in.

In the programme, the young people are asked by a socially considerate non-governmental organization called Humankind to help them understand the suicide of a teenage boy, which has occurred during lockdown in a location close to the young people's school. A local community action group has commissioned Humankind to explore the event, in order to offer a design for a monument or memorial; one that holds the meaning of the incident; to help the family and community at the centre of the situation move on from the tragedy.

The fictitious NGO Humankind contacts the young people, via their teacher, first by letter and then through a filmed request directly addressed to the young people: *This monument should not just be for now but to help all those in the future to understand and never forget what happened here. We believe that you are the right people to help in creating the monument and hope that you might offer proposals for what it should be. We at Humankind want the final monument to be all about the voices of young people.*

Over the last few years, the company has moved away from putting the young people in "role", but rather invites them to experience the situation as themselves. Big Brum has steered away from putting them in the shoes of others, adopting a more "stepping into our own shoes" approach and giving ourselves the chance to experience the given situation from *us*.

One could also say that, working in the crucible paradigm, we are "building the shoes together" that we will all stand in. Alongside the film, teachers were provided with a collection of activities designed to be spread over a term, in the form of a publication called "Socially distant", which also included the playscript (Big Brum TIE, 2021; Cooper, 2020;).

Part 2: Romeo and Juliet

In recent times, the news seems to have been awash with people saying "We weren't expecting it to happen" or "It happened so quickly we weren't ready". Think back to the Brexit result; the Grenfell Tower tragedy in London; Covid-19; the retaking of Afghanistan by the Taliban; climate-related fires and floods; and the economic crisis that broke out in 2008 and was soon exacerbated by ideologues like Truss and Kwarteng.

However, while politicians and the media scratch their heads trying to catch up, people's lives are turned upside down … or they are losing them. This is not new. Shakespeare's *Romeo and Juliet* unfolds over four days, taking place two weeks before Juliet's 14th birthday. At the end of the story, all the adults are shocked, struggling to make sense of the tragic events that have overtaken them.

Though set in Verona, Shakespeare was reflecting on his England, a nation in transition from Roman Catholicism to a sovereign Anglican Church, part of the Reformation that enabled the birth of capitalism in the UK and the country's journey towards Empire. Shakespeare's story also foreshadows the coming English revolution, 40 years after his death.

Verona (Shakespeare's England) is a society obsessed by power, position and property. The desires of the adults, however, leave young people disconnected from the adult world, fractious, fractional and frustrated by the status quo. The story sees the murder of three young people and the suicide of two more. None of the adults would have imagined that such a thing could be possible. But why are they so surprised? And who or what is truly responsible?

Our production of *Romeo and Juliet* offered a mix of live and filmed moments. The live moments concentrated on the Romeo and Juliet story, performed by our touring company, while the film focused on the broader social and political context. The filmed elements were performed by non-professional actors, teachers, social workers, a scaffolder, students, etc. The material on film therefore has the feel of the laboratory, being experimental and explorative. The film's conceit sees the return of the fictitious human rights organization Humankind, which is now made up of members of *the community*. The young audience are asked to watch and listen to the story and reflect on where the responsibility for the suicides of Romeo and Juliet really lies:

> We want to invite you, to join us, to help us shape this work in progress. We want to know what you think. We want to know from you, who or what is responsible for this bloody mess. We need your feedback and it's our hope that with the assistance of your teachers you will be able to give us that. So, please, attend to this story with your hearts and minds as you attend to your own stories, to see what we can learn for Humankind.

Part 3: Over the Balcony

> These violent delights have violent ends.
> *(Friar Lawrence in William Shakespeare's* Romeo and Juliet *(Act 2, Scene 6)*

The combination of the three parts of *The Monuments Trilogy* explores fundamentally the world we live in now. But more importantly, what does being a human mean today?

All three parts relate to the story of *Romeo and Juliet*. Part 1, *Socially Distant*, begins during the Covid crisis, amidst the unfolding logic of late capitalism. It connects to the story of the Montagues, who – like the protagonist of the monodrama (and like Shakespeare during the plague) – have lost a son. *Romeo and Juliet* takes us back four hundred years to Jacobean England and capitalism's birth, to see today from a different perspective. Part 3, *Over the Balcony*, is set in 2064, in our near future. It toured secondary schools in summer 2023 as the final episode in the trilogy.

Together, the three stories reflect and resonate with the lives of young people today, bridging universal experience through time and space and connecting our young audiences with people and stories of the past; with themselves in the same class and world today; and with those that are yet to be born. To explain more about how Big Brum's practice uses and engages imaginations to meet the needs of young people in the barbaric circumstances that we have earlier described, we will now go into greater detail about Part 3, *Over the Balcony*.

Tragedy, Drama and Young People's Needs

> Tragedy shows what is perishable, what is fragile, and what is slow moving about us. In a world defined by relentless speed and the unending acceleration of information flows that cultivate amnesia and an endless thirst for the short-term future allegedly guaranteed through worship of the new prosthetic gods of technology, tragedy is a way of applying the emergency brakes.
>
> *(Critchley, 2019, p. 3)*

Humans have a want and need to know themselves and re-know themselves, individually and socially. This has been one of the defining aspects of our history. The societies and cultures we have built are testimony to that. Unfortunately, as we have noted earlier – and as *Over the Balcony* poignantly depicts – the modern world ideologizes and commodifies human want and need for us to the point where we are unable to see the reality of our condition, like wallpaper pasted to our faces.

Tragedy peels the wallpaper from our eyes. Tragedy penetrates the trappings of the modern world, revealing their triviality, so we "come face-to-face with what we do not know about ourselves but what makes those selves the things they are" (Critchley, 2019, p. 3).

The drama of Big Brum aims to create tragedy and we set out to do so powerfully with *Over the Balcony*. Such drama evokes, as Edward Bond suggests, "Accident Time" (Bond, 2005): the experience that people describe when in an accident, where time slows down and we witness events with a newfound clarity. In *Over the Balcony*, as in other programmes, Big Brum gives space and time for the young audiences to be both in the event (the tragedy of the protagonists Rae and Blake) as it unfolds on the stage, while being able to witness it with this newfound clarity.

The plays Big Brum creates for young audiences, even when set in the future like *Over the Balcony*, are about today. That is how and why they resonate so powerfully with an audience. A play like *Over the Balcony* speaks to them about their reality, their lived experience, in all its complexity and with all its contradictions, in order to move them or for them to connect with it. As we witnessed during this tour and with a wide range of young audiences, this transcends all cultural boundaries. It moves and connects us to ourselves and each other. Rae and Blake's story is one that young people recognize themselves within.

Dramatizing human experience has for millennia been at centre of creating culture. Drama is the interface between self and society, and society and self and it is through this process that we begin to decide who we are and how we want to live. As we have noted already, young people need drama more than ever. That is why we offered them *Over the Balcony* and – we think – why they have responded so strongly to it.

Over the Balcony: A Centre, a Void

Big Brum uses Bond's concept of *centre* in its work:

> The central problem of all drama is justice [not all plays have a centre]. Particular plays deal with the centre in relation to specific situations. The play's main metaphors and similes reflect its centre. Its patterns are based on structures extended from the centre.
>
> *(Bond, 2005, p. 88)*

What was the centre of the story of *Over the Balcony* and where did it resonate with the centre of young people's lives, today?

> Far from being the autonomous dictators of our destinies, genes are controlled by their environment, and without environmental signals they could not function. In effect, they are turned on and off by the environment; human life could not exist if it weren't so.
>
> *(Maté, 2018, p. 238)*

In preparing for *Over the Balcony*, Big Brum became intrigued by Gabor Maté's (2018) concept of the "void" (p. 52). This great word struck us as beautifully evocative, but also terrifyingly expressive of nothingness. In political and legal terms, things become null and void; scientifically, it is a space that lacks, a state of emptiness where all has been drained away; for individuals, it can be a feeling of want or hollowness – a feeling we have all had at some point.

Sensory stimulation is so necessary for the human infant's healthy biological development that babies who are never picked up simply die. They stress themselves to death.

(Maté, 2018, p. 223)

For Maté (2018), the void dwells in each of us, in everything that surrounds us, it directs and determines every aspect of our lives, it is unavoidable. As a psychologist, he proposes that the void is the cause of our individual deep pain, pain that is caused by living in the modern world. He also suggests that the modern world's solution to the pain deepens the void, whether that solution is extreme, like drugs and drink, or a more acceptable *addiction* such as consumerism or workaholicism. This insight holds for both adults and young people.

Where does the void come from? While this relates to contemporary circumstances, it can – like everything – be traced and understood historically. We would argue that an understanding of our history is the real solution to the condition of living in the void.

Over the Balcony: *The Play*

The story of *Over the Balcony* (Cooper, 2023) is set in 2064 and unfolds over a day. The two protagonists, Rae (15) and Blake (16) are holed up in a dilapidated apartment situated towards the top floor of a block of flats. The place is run down, dirty and empty, a hideout provided by traffickers.

It is a world that was recognized by many of the young people we worked with. "It smells like a flat I visited, run down … I know people who live there" (young person in North Solihull, looking at the set for *Over the Balcony* and imagining how the apartment would smell[2]).

In the story's imagined 2064, governments have vanished and been replaced by corporations. The future that young audiences were presented with was not the dystopian future that Orwell's *1984* paints, but more of a Huxleyan *Brave New World*. To paraphrase Huxley (2004), this is a future where people have become deprived of their autonomy, maturity and history; where no one wants to read and truth is drowned in a sea of irrelevance; one where culture is awash with the trivial that panders to man's almost infinite appetite for distractions; a society where people have come to love their oppression, while adoring all the technologies that function to replace the capacities to think; and one where decadence has reduced people to simple passivity and egoism, a civilization that is controlled by inflicting pleasure.

Rae and Blake wish to escape this world and have absconded from their parents, looking to cross the *border*, to freedom. Rae is desperate to not be like her mother or father, corrupted by money and power. She sees how lonely and isolated her parents are from themselves and each other, these voids filled by their addiction to money and power. She also sees how Blake's parents have damaged him – he is perpetually scared, only safe when taking his prescribed (and unprescribed) drugs.

RAE TO BLAKE: They want to control us. That's why they sent us to their clinic. That's why they prescribed pills. We're better than all of them. Right? We don't need their world. Their corporation. It takes over everything – everywhere.[3]

However, Rae's mother is not interested in letting them be together and she pursues the young couple to the apartment.

RAE'S MOTHER TO BLAKE: You need to know my family won't let you be together. Yours too no doubt. I will find you.[4]

The Theatre in Education Programme for *Over the Balcony*

The programme for *Over the Balcony* explored the questions:

- How do you truly free yourself when you aren't sure you're trapped?
- Where are the safe places for young people to learn to live?

It explored these question through the frame of young people living today. This is something today's young people are experts in, when viewing life four decades from now. We felt this both offered a safety for them, while connecting them to the reality that what we do today will materially affect the future.

To aid this exploration we used the binary concepts of:

- Free – Imprisoned/trapped
- Alone – Together
- Stress full/filled – Stress free
- Blind/unseeing – See/seeing

In the following quotes from young people in North Solihull, we can observe them stepping into their own shoes through the power of drama.

- "His internal thoughts are trapping him" (about Blake)
- "She's stuck in this place, can't go forward or backward" (about Rae)
- "Temporary freedom is not freedom, it's confinement" (advice to Blake)

Imagining Beyond the Barbarism – Changing Lives in North Solihull

It is one thing to rehearse, perform and facilitate a powerful drama that creates spaces for young people to explore their lives and their world through the power of imagination. But what if it were possible to offer that experience to every child and young person in a geographically distinct area who had historically been denied it? Can we imagine what that would look like? Can we conceive of what it might mean for those young people, their schools and their whole community?

That is the challenge that Big Brum set itself when setting out on ambitious and strategic plans for working with every young person in North Solihull, one of the poorest areas in England, in a programme which intends to make a significant difference to their lives: creating space for the imagination, fostering community and nurturing young and emerging artists. This strategic plan is supported through Arts Council England's National Portfolio. For the plan, Big Brum has identified three key priorities:

Schools of Recovery

Big Brum is currently running a model of Schools of Recovery, working with six primary schools in areas of deprivation. This is funded by the Paul Hamlyn Foundation. This model places a strong emphasis on young people's creative and personal agency and in doing so aims to bring about a cultural change in the participating schools. Rather than a one-off or short-term engagement in schools, the model involves intensive and extended collaboration with teachers, supporting their use of drama in order to improve creative and cultural education for children and young people. In this way, Big Brum and the teachers are not only creating but extending the imaginative spaces made possible through TIE and in the very places where the attack on children is most acutely experienced.

Building on this, Big Brum has gone to large funders to implement the Schools of Recovery programme in North Solihull, seeking support for its collaboration with Solihull Council and local school networks. Big Brum's ambition is to bring world class theatre and drama to every school and every special educational support setting in North Solihull, eventually reaching an audience of over 12,000 children and young people. Every child, aged between 5 and 15, will experience a live performance at least once each year and each school will receive multiple copies of a company-produced picture book or graphic novel, based on the plays performed – an enrichment of our work that has proved extremely successful in the past. This process has already started.

The choice of North Solihull is not accidental. It is the community which sits directly on the company's geographical doorstep. North Solihull is a discrete area on the edge of the city of Birmingham and the relatively affluent borough of Solihull. It has experienced historical marginalization by politicians, planners and the providers of resources and the arts. North Solihull is part of the UK Government's "Levelling Up" programme for areas of deprivation and people of all ages, including the young, experience high levels of unemployment and poverty but low levels of arts engagement.

The Schools of Recovery model that Big Brum has been developing in the six primary schools is already demonstrating an approach that will bring about a cultural change within schools and can hugely boost the social and cultural capital of a community. The company believes that such sustained and regular access to live art in North Solihull will excite interest in the hearts and minds of the area's young people. This in turn incites a desire to become involved, to engage in arts activities in and out of school. As a Year 6 teacher from one of the six primary schools told project evaluators, "We'd struggled to get much from the children, but ... they really went for it ... Drama is the perfect device to move children on in their thought process and their understanding of the world we are living in: it is just a phenomenal way to do it".[5]

We do not yet know what the cumulative effect of working in this way with 12,000 children young people in a single community will be, especially when built up and sustained over several years, but we do believe that it will be transformational: it offers the dialectical opposite to a culture of barbarism.

Community of Recovery

While Schools of Recovery offers the initial incentive to become involved in the arts, the accompanying plan for a Community of Recovery ensures the continued provision of these artistic opportunities for the young people of North Solihull. With Arts Council support, Big Brum is planning a much widened and improved range of creative and artistic opportunities for young people, based in the community beyond the school gate. Big Brum will ensure that the young people's creative and cultural education is deepened and enriched through a Theatre Makers Group, a Film Makers Group and a Visual & Digital Art Makers Group; through visits to galleries, exhibitions and theatres; through projects like a recent "Trains of Thought" project with very young children – playing and painting trains, hearing train stories, going on an actual train trip, meeting station masters and train drivers and finally sharing children's thoughts through huge bright banners at the local station.

The Community of Recovery programme seeks to create many such opportunities for groups to share their work, ensuring that they have prospective audiences for it. This goes beyond traditional venues in order to reach the widest possible audience, most firmly rooted in the community. As well as the station, Big Brum envisages that such venues might include pop-up galleries in shopping centres, performances in libraries or community centres, film showings in elderly care homes.

Through the Community of Recovery programme, young people will have opportunities to work alongside industry professionals and students from Big Brum's partners, such as theatre makers at Birmingham City University, film makers at Birmingham Film School and Worcester University, digital artists and sound designers. Together, our plan is for them to work collaboratively on a film project of a young peoples' theatre production. This whole project will be fully situated in the local community, from filming on location to ensuring that costumes, catering and materials and labour for sets are sourced locally, from the paid or voluntary sectors.

Big Brum envisages related work with adults, including vulnerable adults, such as a project involving the creation of a site-specific theatre performance of the play *Dereliction* for the residents of local apartment blocks: a powerful, immersive project that will blend live theatre with film. Many local residents feel that they lack a say in things that happen locally, nationally and globally. This free project will offer them a voice.

Artists for Recovery

The plan of work to build Schools of Recovery and a Community of Recovery leads to an expansion of opportunities for participatory artists, hence the third aspect of our plan: creating Artists for Recovery. Alongside the work already outlined, the company is already beginning to produce three new TIE tours each year, targeting other areas of deprivation, partner schools ... and of course, the North Solihull schools that are central to the project.

Not only will this new body of work ensure employment opportunities for many different artists, it will also enable the company to give opportunities to people to start a professional career in the creative arts, with a particular emphasis on reaching those currently under-represented. It begins to replace an offence against the people of North Solihull with opportunities for recovery and restoration. Big Brum's ambition is that Artists for Recovery will mentor and develop a new generation of artists and practitioners for both Big Brum and for the wider arts and education community. Big Brum therefore sees the Artists for Recovery programme as both a contribution to the community and a part of its own long-term succession planning.

Together, the three programmes (Schools of Recovery, a Community of Recovery, Artists for Recovery) seek to help transform North Solihull from a place where too many people have limited opportunities – a community of neglect – to a creative and cohesive Community of Recovery.

Looking Forward

Our young people are facing unprecedented challenges. This world is a difficult place for them to live in. We began this chapter by outlining some of those challenges and difficulties in the UK and elsewhere. Big Brum has always placed itself unconditionally on the side of the young and of those wishing to defend the young. Furthermore, the company is and has always been a small organization with big ambitions. As Gramsci famously reminded us, "my mind is pessimistic, but my will is optimistic" (Gramsci,

1973, p. 159). Big Brum – and the authors of this chapter – share that disposition and recognize the tensions inherent to it.

Our will remains optimistic. The optimism is there in the power and audacity of Big Brum's work and in the company's ambitious plans for North Solihull. This optimism of organizational will is coupled with the innate positive, confident idealism that we witness, not only in the international youth movements for action on climate change or for social justice, but in our daily work with the young people of our city and beyond, where it feels that change is not only possible but inevitable. We believe that – despite the many offences and attacks on the young – this generation of young people have the power to imagine beyond the barbarism and to create a better future.

Notes

1 In economic policy, austerity is a set of political-economic policies that aim to reduce government budget deficits through spending cuts, tax increases, or a combination of both (Financial Times Lexicon, 2013).
2 Unpublished reflection notes.
3 Unpublished play text, *Over the Balcony.*
4 Unpublished play text, *Over the Balcony.*
5 Unpublished reflection notes.

References

Academy for Medical Sciences. (2024). Prioritising early childhood to promote the nation's health, wellbeing and prosperity. Academy for Medical Sciences. https://acmedsci.ac.uk/file-download/16927511.

Ball, S. J. (2003). The teacher's soul and the terrors of performativity. *Journal of Education Policy*, 18(2), 215–228.

Ball, S. J. (2018). The tragedy of state education in England: Reluctance, compromise and muddle – a system in disarray. *Journal of the British Academy*, 6, 207–238.

BBC News. (2022, 3 Oct). Jake Berry: People struggling with bills "should get a new job". https://www.bbc.com/news/uk-england-lancashire-63118022.

Big Brum TIE. (2011). Artistic policy. https://bigbrum.org.uk/about.

Big Brum TIE. (2021). *Socially distant* (teachers' resource). Big Brum TIE.

Bond, E. (2005). Drama devices. In D. Davis (Ed.), *Edward Bond and the dramatic child.* (pp. 84–92). Trentham Books.

Cooper, C. (2023). *Socially distant.* Big Brum TIE.

Cooper, C. (n.d.). *Over the balcony.* Unpublished play.

Crisis. (2022, 22 Feb). *The homelessness monitor England: 2022 report.* https://www.crisis.org.uk/ending-homelessness/homelessness-knowledge-hub/homelessness-monitor/england/the-homelessness-monitor-england-2022/.

Critchley, S. (2019). *Tragedy, the Greeks and us.* Profile Books.

Ferguson, D. (2018, 15 May). Headteachers turn to charities as families sleep by bins. *The Guardian.* https://www.theguardian.com/education/2018/may/15/headteachers-turn-charities-families.

Financial Times Lexicon. (2013, 22 Mar). Austerity measure. *Financial Times*. https://web.archive.org/web/20130322221836/http://lexicon.ft.com/Term?term=austerity-measure.

Gramsci, A. (1973). *Letters from prison*. Trans. Lynn Lawner. Harper and Row.

Holmes, R. (2023). The attack on children. *Drama Magazine*, 29(1). National Drama. https://www.nationaldrama.org.uk/product/drama-magazine-vol-29-1/.

Hope Not Hate. (n.d.). Rejecting a radical-right hard Brexit. https://hopenothate.org.uk/rejecting-radical-right-hard-brexit/.

Huxley, A. (2004). *Brave new world*. Vintage Classics.

Joseph Rowntree Foundation. (2022, 18 Jan). UK poverty 2022: The essential guide to understanding poverty in the UK. https://www.jrf.org.uk/uk-poverty-2022-the-essential-guide-to-understanding-poverty-in-the-uk.

Kwarteng, K., Patel, P., Raab, D., Skidmore, C. & Truss, E. (2012). *Britannia unchained*. Palgrave Macmillan.

Maté, G. (2018). *In the realm of hungry ghosts: Close encounters with addiction*. Vermilion.

O'Toole, J. & O'Mara, J. (2007). Proteus, the giant at the door: Drama and theater in the curriculum. In L. Bresler (Ed.), *International Handbook of Research in Arts Education* (pp. 203–218). Springer.

PA Media. (2024, 2 Feb). Experts lament "appalling decline" in health of under-fives in UK. *The Guardian*. https://www.theguardian.com/society/2024/feb/05/experts-lament-appalling-decline-in-health-of-under-fives-in-uk.

Rosen, M. (2018). The data have landed. *Michael Rosen Blog*. https://michaelrosenblog.blogspot.com/2018/02/the-data-have-landed.html.

Samuels, L. (2019). Fearriculum: An analysis of pedagogical choice and change made by Secondary level educators. The Drama in Education Hub. https://dramamtl.wordpress.com/2019/06/12/fearriculum-an-analysis-of-pedagogical-choice-and-change-made-by-secondary-level-educators/.

Settle, M. (2015, 7 Oct). Cameron: The 2010s under the Tories can be Britain's "turnaround decade". *The Herald*. https://www.heraldscotland.com/news/13807609.cameron-2010s-tories-can-britains-turnaround-decade/.

Shakespeare, W. (2004). *Romeo and Juliet*. Folger Shakespeare Library.

Sky News. (2022, 2 Oct). Online comment. https://news.sky.com/.

Wintour, P. & Watt, N. (2015, 8 Oct). Tory conference: Cameron's "assault on poverty" pledge belied by new figures. *The Guardian*. https://www.theguardian.com/politics/2015/oct/07/camerons-assault-on-poverty-pledge-undone-by-new-figures.

11

DESTINIES

An Applied Theatre Co-creation with Vulnerable Groups Producing Inter-relational Communities of Practice

Ava Hunt

> The city of lost souls rises once more with the
> voice of our mothers whispering softly
> Sleep my little angel
> Sleep my sunshine.
> And when you awake your eyes will be filled with the hopes
> and dreams of the sun
> which spills through in waves each morning.
>
> *(Lyrics, 2021[1])*

"The City of Lost Souls": Conception

Conceived in 2019, Destinies was a co-creation theatre project working with vulnerable young people in Derbyshire, United Kingdom. Working with a multi-disciplinary team of professional artists, the young people participated in writing lyrics, composing music, creating characters, singing, performing and much more. In this chapter I will reflect on the artistic working processes of Destinies, analyse semi-structured interviews collected throughout the project, reflect on the impact of the final production and propose that co-creative methods cultivated deep learning beyond the project, embracing and exemplifying the young people's lyrics:

> Hopes and dreams of the sun
> Which spills through in waves each morning
> *(Lyrics, 2021)*

Destinies comprised 26 young people aged between 14 and 19 with care experience (YPCE) or who were young unaccompanied asylum seekers (YUAS) under the care of Derbyshire Virtual School (Derbyshire County

DOI: 10.4324/9781003470434-14

Council). The partner organizations were Ava Hunt Theatre (producers), creative mentors from Derbyshire Virtual School, Sinfonia Viva Orchestra, Orchestra Live[2] and Applied Theatre M.A. students from the University of Derby. Funded by Arts Council England, the theatre and live music project was to produce a script-in-hand performance by the young people to an invited audience in April 2020, however, by March, due to Covid restrictions and lockdowns, Destinies was suspended. Over the following two years the project evolved into a fully digitalized, multi-disciplinary award winning filmed theatre piece. This chapter will highlight the importance of applied theatre theory *"for, with* and *by"* (O'Connor & Anderson, 2015, p. 91) vulnerable young people, where co-creative methods can contribute to communities of practice, well-being, pedagogy and future employability.

> Work a long day, a long night without a payday
> say yay, we did this every day day
> *(Lyrics, 2021)*

Co-creation was used in the 1990s initially within a business context to describe how customers could contribute to product design. However, since the mid-2000s the term has been used widely within the performing arts. Co-creation shares many of the values of the participatory arts as used for decades within the applied drama field (Matarasso, 2017). But specifically, it has now come to mean the curation of making theatre – participants and theatre makers together. The methodology gives autonomy and voice to marginalized communities in a powerful and creative way. But I am also interested in researching how co-creation contributes pedagogically to the acquisition of skills and how this can contribute to young people's well-being.

Important questions about the use of co-creation in the performing arts are raised by Ben Walmsley (2013) when considering the tension between achieving both "cultural democracy and excellence" (p. 12). Obviously, as artists facilitating young people to make theatre it is essential that a sense of pride and accomplishment is achieved from the finished product. Francois Matarasso (2017) suggests true co-creation is only achieved when the participants influence the piece to such an extent that the artists are also going beyond what they are familiar/knowledgeable about. This suggests that artists should not hinder the pursuit of ideas, ensuring that participants have as much autonomy as possible even if that is to the possible detriment of the quality of the theatre. But I would contest that this binary is unhelpful within the context of applied theatre co-creation, and propose that there are additional benefits when trying to achieve the delicate balance between process and product, which I shall return to later.

"We Did This Every Day Day": Method

A/r/tography research methodologies supported and contributed to the flexing and multiplying of research questions and approaches that emerged over the two-year period as artist (director and producer), researcher and teacher created a space where participants, artists and applied theatre students all operated within a multi-directional pedagogic environment. Similar to the rhizome structure, new skills, new questions and new possibilities would evolve.

The term rhizome, as described by Deleuze and Guattari in 1987 (Springgay et al., 2008), occurs when plants reproduce in multiple directions from a root origin, like for example ginger or turmeric. In research, the term implies a process that is fluid and divergent, offering a range of new interpretations, disruptions and provocations (Hunt, 2023, p. 21).

Data was collected throughout the project using semi-structured interviews with the participants. These filmed interviews were transcribed at regular intervals throughout the process. Transcripts were analysed using spreadsheets against seven thematic headings:

- Interests
- Dreams for the future
- What they enjoyed about Destinies
- Skills development
- Contribution to confidence/emotional resilience
- Gaining a sense of community
- Unexpected or long-term impact.

This data, together with regular meetings with the artists involved, enabled the project to be guided by our reflective learning, allowing new ideas to be tested and new research questions to evolve which then informed the next developmental stage.

Destinies began clearly but the middle section and end were impossible to have predicted. However, as Deleuze and Guarttari (1987) propose, the beauty and freedom of the rhizome is that it "connects any point to any other point" (p. 21). Therefore, as long as we stayed true to serving and enabling the co-creative process with the young people, we could allow the research spine to grow and adapt to change, within a shifting landscape. Research questions emerged during the initial workshops with young people: Could Destinies create a community of practice where pedagogic and skills development could evolve to empower young people, students and artists? Could the process of co-creation also contribute specifically to the confidence and well-being of the young people? Of the 26 young people involved in the project, some achieved seismic shifts, for others, for whom we maybe only worked with once or twice, impact was harder to assess. The mix of young people could not have been more diverse. Some came from war-torn Syria, Afghanistan, Sudan and Eretria. Some young people with care experience had ADHD,[3] autism, or were experiencing gender identity issues. However, for the purposes of this chapter I will focus on two young people: one YPCE known as MXX and one YUAS known as WXX.

As part of the a/r/tography methodology, master's students were also participating and contributing to the process; either within a directorial role in rehearsals, contributing to the creative workshops or participating informally by supporting young people in and around the creation period. The students reflected on their learning during additional structured sessions with myself. These reflective moments were captured in essays and portfolios, enabling students to identify the use of applied theatre, develop sensitivities around the young people's vulnerabilities and understand the importance of the role of hope and modelling for the future (Dolan, 2005; Rohd, 1988; O'Connor & Anderson, 2015).

Applied Theatre (AT) practice enables artists to create an environment where young people can participate equally, offering a clear creative structure that goes beyond the visual and physical, as Rohd suggests:

> Theatre allows us to converse with our souls, to passionately pursue and discover ways of living with ourselves and with others. We have no better way to work together, to learn about each other, to heal and to grow.
>
> *(Rohd, 1988, p. 140)*

AT practices using co-creative methods ensure that the artists are listening and responding to participant's ideas and self-expression, thus helping to shift the power balances and facilitate transformational experiences (Vettraino et al., 2017). The initial creative workshops during 2019 produced an exciting breadth of work both for named characters, such as Thief Malone and Blessing, and ideas for three songs: "Mama and Me", "New Inspirations" and "So We Will Rise". Following the introduction of Covid restrictions in March 2020 by the UK government, all face-to-face rehearsals were cancelled and replaced with online creative meetings. This was not ideal for a group of vulnerable young people who were already isolated through language, cultural identity and trauma. But when we considered the options of abandoning the project completely this seemed even harsher. So, what if we could find a way of working that supported the group to maintain connection? Would this be more valuable? What were the possibilities of creating theatre *with* and *by* young people online at a time when it was needed the most?

New inspirations, new motivations,
New aspirations, new determinations …

> And yet, the sun sets on another page
> *(Lyrics, 2021)*

"The Sun Sets on Another Page": The Context

Destinies created connections between two groups of young people who would not usually encounter each other, resulting in shifts of understanding, knowledge, new perspectives and for new opinions to evolve and thereby create a new community. Stephani Etheridge Woodson (2015) states that youth theatre offers a valuable third space within which new communities are created, where children and young people come together to experience community and environmental activities. Destinies created a third space within which young people could experience creative and artistic opportunities. In addition to working with professional artists and other young people from completely different backgrounds but who may have experiences that were similar, there was an opportunity to learn about each other – challenge refugee narratives or racial stereotypes. The concept of two different groups of people coming together to create a new community is also explored in Etienne and Beverly Wenger-Trayner's (2015) notion of interrelational space. Interrelational, as defined by the *Cambridge Dictionary* (Wooster & Hunt, 2023), proposes that it is the "way in which two or more things or people are connected and affect one another". This is helpful when also considering Wenger-Trayner and Wenger-Trayner's (2015) "communities of practice" (para. 1) which contribute to a fluid multidirectional environment where possible preconceptions are influenced safely and gently through embodied learning. Creating this safe and inter-relational space was central to every level of the project's development. Sinfonia Viva were able to bring a Syrian viola player, Raghad Haddad, into the company of musicians to contribute to the composition and performance. The presence of someone who had achieved asylum and was working professionally provided a gentle but powerful symbol of hope for us all.

In the UK there are currently 400,000 children and young people (3% of total population) in care, and specifically within the East Midlands a 15% increase in children's homes provision has been necessary to meet demand since Covid (Ofsted, 2023). Sadly, the combination of foster families, care homes and schools failing to meet Ofsted standards results in almost 50% of the young people, by the time they are 21 years old, having been "in contact with the criminal justice system" (Lomas, 2022). Similarly, many YUAS are also being failed by local authorities, outside of foster parents, where temporary accommodation in hotels is used, with recent reports of trafficking.[4] In addition to language barriers and the experience of post-traumatic stress disorder, the young people's needs are complex, and local authorities often fail to address them. Suicide rates for both young people within the care system and YUAS were increasing before the pandemic.[5] Now, post-pandemic, these figures have continued to rise, resulting in 46 different charitable organizations reporting sharp increases in levels of suicide.[6] Levels of isolation and poor levels of mental health support all contribute to YUAS's feelings of hopelessness and depression (Lammers, 2017).

Throughout the Destinies project, Creative Mentors, as part of Derbyshire County Council's Virtual School, played a critical role in maintaining and developing relationships outside of the rehearsal space. The Creative Mentoring scheme was set up by Kim Johnson in 2014 in response to some of the disproportionate disadvantages that YPCE experience as outlined above. Johnson recognized that a range of complex issues such as poor emotional development as a result of neglect and trauma contributed to low educational attainment (Johnson, 2023). Creative Mentoring offers a one to one service that provides "personalized pathways to progression" (Johnson, 2023, para. 14) – creative opportunities that contribute to educational attainment. Therefore, at different times during the project, when some young people were going through low moments as a result of isolation, communication with the young person could be maintained via one-to-one meetings, helping them to feel connected and creative in the project.

Using co-creative, participatory methods provides "a rigorous method for assessing learning in a community" (Guldberg et al., 2021, p. 97). This was achieved by the emphasis being on *process* rather than *product*. How the space is created, how relationships are managed in the space is a delicate balance of encouragement and safety. For the YUAS, the project needed to feel playful whilst also being meaningful. Perhaps supporting language development rather than re-enforcing language barriers, and skills development without it feeling like a formal learning environment, were important. The use of a/r/tography methodology enabled the research team in the room to be equally open, playful and enquiring, whilst offering a clear structure for creating music together or theatre was key. A range of theatre exercises was used that not only generated material for the piece but also contributed to developing a deep connection between the participants. WXX commented on this specifically:

> Like listening games – learning to listen to each other, learning to respond to each other's energies without talking, as in reading sign body language and all that. It's been so … It's been something that you wouldn't notice but there's something about it. I could speak to GXX by just looking at her! So, she knows what I've just said. It's a skill, I mean it's hidden.
>
> *(WXX, 2020[7])*

The Sinfonia Viva's musicians and musical instruments needed to be inviting and accessible. The musical instruments were placed around the space, creating a gentle invitation so the young people could try out different options and enjoy playing. All this contributed to a free flowing, non-pressurized and safe space in which to be creative. It was important for everyone to not feel overwhelmed with too many choices, but also to feel that something spontaneous could happen too. An example of this was when HXX, who had only recently arrived from Eretria, began to play the xylophone in a lunch break. Suddenly language was no longer a barrier. Marianne Barraclough from Sinfonia Viva reflected upon this during an interview with Orchestra Live as a key moment of the legacy and impact of the project:

> [he] just started to play this little riff and a couple of the team we clocked it ... so [we] started building this little groove up with him. We had absolutely no common language ... we were communicating entirely through the music ... we ended up making this little piece together ... and that ended up being the cityscape background music in the final piece.
>
> *(Barraclough, 2023, 1:07 mins)*

This moment illustrates the fragility of co-creation, a willingness to be open, to be creative at any moment (even in the breaks), to respond, encourage, build and honour each person's unique contribution – being responsive rather than prescriptive.

We were originally in receipt of an Arts Council England (ACE) grant for the first six months; however, as the project went beyond its original brief by working online and using animation, we needed to apply for additional funding in order to complete the project. Sinfonia Viva were also able to draw down additional funding from Orchestra Live during this period. When the first lockdown occurred ACE responded with an emergency fund which we were successfully able to apply for to ensure the project could continue. The notion of a *bridge* was useful here. Creating an artistic and structural device: bridging the project from where we were through to when we were able to perform. In the interim, like many artists, we relied upon zoom meetings. The writer produced a first draft of the script and together with our three songs that we had already written, this gave us enough material to be able to host a virtual read through and start rehearsing scenes and songs.

It was during this first on-line meeting that a new young person, MXX, joined the group. MXX was a talented drummer, but he could not look directly at the computer camera, did not want eye contact and would only speak to confirm his name. The foster carer sat with MXX and patiently held focus on behalf of them. But even for others, who had worked with us for five months, reading the script on zoom was a challenge. Either a lack of English or dyslexia created further barriers to the fluency of the reading. Even seeing themselves on screen contributed to an uncomfortable experience. As a result, some cameras were switched off, making connection and communication even more difficult, whilst others simply struggled with poor internet connection – the list went on and on. But even for the artists and Creative Mentors, the process was equally challenging; we had no idea how to run a project like this.

> There was nothing but mama and me
> But when she was gone,
> I had to go on,
> I made a new home inside in me.
> *(Lyrics, 2021)*

"I Made a New Home Inside in Me": Discovering Emotional Resilience

Both groups of young people co-created the music and lyrics for *Mama and Me*. The phrase, "My city is calling me back, but when she was gone I had to go on" (Lyrics, 2021) illustrates that both groups were expressing emotional isolation, loss, grief for family but also acknowledging the importance of development of self-efficacy. For many young people with experience of care homes in the UK where "affection is deemed inappropriate" (O'Connor & Anderson, 2015, p. 101) how do young people express feelings of loss and develop their emotional intelligence? The lack of opportunity to explore emotional affection compounds a system that far too often compounds systems of "abuse and neglect" (p. 108). But these experiences also resonated for the YUAS. Raph Clarkson (Musical Director) recalls the process by which the initial lyrics and the tune emerged:

> Words came from WXX, and then YXX just sang the lyrics on his own and this stunning folk song came out. My comment would be that a medium such as music often provides an extra layer of safety through abstraction or narrative/creative world-building – safety to be vulnerable in sharing or exploring personal experiences. So in this case, instead of asking YXX to tell us explicitly how the words related to his own experiences, he told us in a different way – through singing the words, imparting emotional information via the use of his voice – its pitch, rhythm, the melody. And in many ways this in itself says and said so much about how it related to his life, without him having to explicitly articulate it (and in a language that wasn't his native tongue).
> *(R. Clarkson, personal communication, 2023)*

By May 2020, some schools in the UK were still closed, online learning was sporadic and limited to those who were struggling the most. We continued to offer a series of one-hour workshops that would ideally maintain the connection to the project and each other. These workshops would be light-touch, playful and not product driven – meaning that developing the script and making new songs were no longer a priority. The Arabic speakers were finding it particularly difficult to engage, so a Syrian actor was brought in to work with the group using the break-out option on zoom. But this separation also highlighted the different cultural understandings between the two groups. For example, one young person identified as male and created a male character for the piece. This was a challenge for some young people from sub-Saharan countries, who were less familiar with non-hetero-normative/gender identity politics that many young people in the UK have experience of or are more familiar with. However, this only highlights in a microcosm the learning that was constantly present and multi-directional for all involved.

The makeup of the group also changed each session, which rendered carefully constructed workshop plans redundant as the young people's engagement shifted and changed. So, each session was carefully and forensically reflected upon to identify learning and planning for future sessions. But we simply did not know how to get the balance right. Being online engaged in theatre exercises not related to the script felt pointless and a waste of everyone's time. But reading or rehearsing scenes from the script felt equally meaningless when we could not rely on a full cast. And there were other pressing questions: what was it all for? Would this piece ever be performed? In the meantime, some YUAS were moved to larger cities where support and family members were more accessible. And then we had a breakthrough. A random conversation during a zoom workshop produced an exciting development. MXX said they liked to draw and had an avatar/fictional character *Rapper Man*. I invited the whole group to draw their characters ready for the next session.

WXX's painting of her character, blessing, standing alone, back turned to the rain would become the central image for the whole production. WXX's image of a young woman standing in a park environment holding an umbrella, shoulders hunched trying to protect herself from rain and adversity. As we cannot see her face it allows the viewer to only imagine what the character is feeling or thinking. The juxtaposition of beauty and pain within this single painting was perfect. The quality of the drawings fired our imagination to invite an animator to join the creative team. Perhaps as making theatre was no longer possible, the piece could use animation to produce geographic/location settings, but also offer us the possibility of creating a filmed theatre piece? One of the Creative Mentors, Nick Hersey, was also an animator and started developing ideas with the young people together with their drawing skills. This random conversation illustrates how the methodology was constantly flexing and responding to the co-creative processes, enriching the production and taking the artists in directions not originally foreseen.

Throughout summer 2020 we were able to come together to conduct socially distanced animation workshops, record the young people singing and film short scenes. Ever conscious of the transient nature of the group, we decided to produce a short documentary capturing the process which would give the young people an important sense of progress. We re-mastered the singing tracks, pulled together the animated sequences and short scenes, and then we produced a 20-minute documentary of work in progress. This was then disseminated during the October half term at Derby Theatre's Care Leavers Conference 2020. The young people had a separate screening before the piece was streamed online to a national audience of young people with care experience. We scheduled a wraparound day of rehearsal with the musicians and the young people. This meant that in addition to watching the documentary our socially distanced audience of Creative Mentors, foster parents and carers could also enjoy the young people singing together live. This was also the first time the professional musicians had been able to play together for eight months; it was an emotional moment when we realized how much we had all missed being in the presence of each other.

For some young people circumstances had changed; they had left the area or were unable to attend due to Covid, or there were other changes in their circumstances, but new young people joined us. After careful consideration by the artists involved, we agreed that we would push ahead and progress to a filmed theatre performance using projected animation backdrops against live performance. New artists would also be needed to help deliver this new technical challenge and a new funding application was required.

> So we will rise,
> Yes we will rise,
> Yes we will.
>   *(Lyrics, 2021)*

"So We Will Rise": The Role of Hope

During the spring of 2021, the Creative Mentors continued to work closely with the young people. Lin Coghlan (script writer and dramaturg) maintained a creative relationship with the participants and developed script writing exercises to help develop the characters and narrative. The animator, Hersey, continued to work on a one-to-one basis with the young people, helping to develop their visual ideas for different locations and character representation. Sinfonia Viva's composer and musical director, Clarkson, took the lyrics and music that the young people had created and worked with the professional musicians and sound engineers to produce a musically layered soundtrack.

The characters that were created sometimes directly connected to the YUAS's own experiences. But rather than focussing on the reasons why they were forced to leave their communities and families in the first place, we looked at what might be possible in their new communities – *we will rise*. By focussing on the hopes of the young people we enabled them to create characters who mirrored their dreams for the future as a living role model. Within a creative space using multiple art forms, the young people were free to set their own creative curriculum, contributing to a character that they could identify with and who they could possibly become:

> It is one of my goals to be on TV show.
> To be an actor. To be in the movies … you might become really famous.
> Singing and performing.
> A footballer. I want to be on the wing.

There is nothing new about this phenomenon, indeed for children and young people to *play* or act out a dream, to participate in something they enjoy, is a much needed distraction. The desire to escape current or past difficulties, or even oppression, is obvious; to achieve self-efficacy allows the imagination and the power of hope for the young person to be able to manage their lives. Within the context of creating the script the young people used the creative process to embody their hopes and fantasies for the future. This was clear not only from the characters they created but was also reflected in their interviews. The opportunity to *be present*, but to be *in-role* as that successful person creates a powerful template of realization – or as Boal (2019; 2002) would phrase it, "a rehearsal for life". To enact and feel empowered but still able to see the relatedness and connection with their current situation was essential. As one young person with care experience (CXX) expressed it, Destinies also contributed to their current situation:

> Well, it's just like it'll help me in school a bit better so like my education goes up a bit more, so it helps me.

> *(CXX, 2020[8])*

The desire to escape to an imagined better future was not to the detriment of remembering the past. But for some young people creating a fictional character through which they could safely explore painful events was essential. Indeed, what became clear was the interconnectedness of the young people's past experiences. Without disclosing personal details, creating fictional characters opened up new interpretations of what young people had experienced, allowing a reflective, creative and pedagogic exploration. For example, an exercise involving objects became instrumental. The group were asked to pick up an object as their character and create a short phrase that could be repeated to a rhythmic tone. One young person chose a pair of old walking boots and chose the phrase *these are my father's boots*. The use of the boots became one of the key emotional narratives for the character of Thief Malone, who was searching for his father. From this simple selection, a representation of family emerged, perhaps illustrating a hidden desire to find their real father. And even though the character, in the end, was played by a different care-experienced actor, it still resonated and produced a profound moment in the story, particularly when Thief Malone gives up looking for his father, buries the boots in the local graveyard and says:

> I think some people are too lost to be found .... This is a good place. It has angels. He will be happy here.
>
> *(Coghlan, 2021, p. 30)*

The complex issues raised here while still enjoying emotional anonymity meant that this loss and grief at not finding his father could be explored within the safety of the theatre construct. As Wooster and Hunt explore the benefits of applied drama, by

> consider[ing] issues and complex emotional problems beyond their years, but in a safe situation, from behind the protective wall of the frame or role .... Through this interaction – what has been termed scaffolding learning by Vygotsky (1987) – they develop creative, imaginative and emotional intelligence that cannot be found through normal modes of education.
>
> *(Wooster & Hunt, 2021, p. 394)*

But the character of Thief Malone also offers the story an opportunity to explore another very real challenge that some young people with care experience have, that of homelessness. Homelessness has increased in the UK since the pandemic, and combined with the cost-of-living crisis, more than half a million[9] people are currently living on the streets, of which 33%[10] are young people from care experience backgrounds. This narrative is explored throughout Destinies. Other characters are seen trying to help him, offering him friendship and encouraging him to join them in hostels, etc. By representing positive strategies to change this situation the script offers another model of hope, and at the end of the story Thief Malone decides for himself what will happen in the future:

VOICES: And young Thief Malone?
VOICES: Ended up selling windows.
THIEF: No way!
VOICES: Joined a circus.
THIEF: That's better!
VOICES: I heard he settled down and had kids of his own. He used to tell them about those boots.

(Coghlan, 2021)

This extract demonstrates beautifully how the character decides on his future by re-framing and placing new possibilities into the narrative. As Tomlin (2013) discusses, the co-creation process offers the participant through the fictional frame the power to create and transform. The participant is

> empowered to play a key authoring role in the construction of their own subjectivity through the exploration of the new ways of being together with others.
>
> *(Tomlin, 2013, p. 180)*

One young person in the group had published a short story prior to Destinies, detailing their experience of being sex trafficked; and through a process of collective creative writing, elements of this real-life experience were included in the lyrics of songs and into one narrative strand of the text. The specific detail is never disclosed within the piece, the anonymity of the person's experience is protected. In addition, the young person does not portray the character themselves, giving them a double layer of one-step removed (Baim et al., 2002). The writer, Coghlan, took this detail and gently referenced it in relation to safeguarding within the story:

> There's a lot of bad people around here and he's one of them. Don't let me see you talking to him again.
>
> *(Coghlan, 2021, p. 13)*

By working with a fictional character within a fictional frame, damaging experiences can provide powerful healing processes and positive modelling for the future. By transforming this experience into advice for others, Peter O'Connor and Michael Anderson refer to this modelling as "a teaspoon of hope" both for the performer and the community of practice. The co-creation process does not deny the experiences of young people's painful journey, the trauma of the past is there, but through *re-storying* the experience is transformed for all – the participants and audience (Dennis, 2008).

As mentioned previously, for young people the role of hope for the future is essential within the dramatic form, but how is it explored? As Frank (2013) discusses, it is essential that we are able to tell the stories that we want. To be able to see beyond the painful events that have shaped our lives and forced us to leave our homes, ensuring that the trauma that inhabits the body does not dictate the future relies on our ability to create a new narrative and avoid the potential re-traumatization of telling the old stories. It means that a theatre which offers an "intervening space where transformation that integrates the complexities of what is told, of what is unsaid and of what might be deliberately omitted" (Dennis, 2008, p. 213) can take place. However, the power to do this resides with the young person themselves. It is the very nature of co-creation that offers a flexible and empowering process that creates investment and ensures the material reflects identity and cultural values whilst still offering opportunities to gain skills and new knowledge.

During rehearsals in April 2021, the master's students took on director roles with small groups of young people. Working with script in hand young people rehearsed scenes and developed ideas for staging, including choreographing the songs. The week proved invaluable to establishing the creative team's shared vision. By now the artistic team had grown to include: animator, graphic designer, sound engineer, lighting technician, camera operator, and designer and production manager. This also allowed time for us to experiment with how to protect the identity of two of our young people who were unsure about being filmed and wanted to remain anonymous.

Rehearsals included "A day in the life" and hot seating[11] exercises, which helped the young cast to gain a strong connection between their character's daily life and themselves, and helped them to develop their character's back story. Even when we came to film in July 2021, Covid was still impacting negatively. New strains of the virus and an increase in infection levels were again starting to make it unsafe for large numbers of people to be together in a small, closed studio space. Disappointingly, this meant we could not include the musicians to play live in the studio. However, some last-minute re-casting of central characters also meant that a young refugee (AXXX) from Derby Refugee and Advice Centre (DRAC) was able to be included in the production. And incredibly, without any pressure, MXX offered to take on one of the lead characters! MXX, who had originally found it impossible to look at the camera, was now going to be carrying a key emotional narrative of the story – this was a breakthrough that demonstrated a huge leap in confidence, skill and commitment to the project.

During the final week of the filming period, the emphasis now shifted from process to product. This change in emphasis exposed the inherent tension between process and product; the young people wanted to see their hard work culminate in a performance that they would be proud of, but the amount of time we had to achieve this was limited. This put the artistic team, who were fully aware of the gap between expectation and achievement, equally under pressure.

> I quite like the rehearsal bit before you get recorded, or the bit before it all finishes, as you get to mess around a bit and change your words just so you feel more comfortable.[12]
>
> *(Unpublished assessment – reflection report)*

> I gained more confidence but I'm still not confident yet. I don't usually sing in front of people because you get judged a lot. But like these are alright to sing in front of it, you get me, so that's bringing my confidence up more.[13]
>
> *(Unpublished assessment – reflection report)*

Upon completion of the editing process a screening was held in the main auditorium at the Derby Theatre's Young Carer's Conference in the autumn of 2021, in front of conference delegates and the general public. One of the YUAS introduced the film, placing it into a wider context of the journey we had all been on – both physically and creatively.

Additionally, the completed filmed piece was submitted and won the East Midlands Mainstream Award Creativity for Good. This opportunity to further disseminate the work enabled the project to be evaluated against other productions and to be peer assessed both in relation to its artistic quality but also to the contribution of the young people themselves. The awards ceremony had an enormous impact on us all, but particularly on the two young people seeing their work achieve wider recognition against other comparable pieces of work. For MXX, who found it difficult to express emotion, their energy, pride and excitement was quantifiable. The next day at school something extraordinary happened. I received a copy of this email from MXX's teachers:

> MXX was also very keen to share the story behind the production with his peers and the fact that it was about refugees. This is a subject we have been talking about in our lessons recently, so they were all very interested. We watched a few highlights of the performance together and MXX joined in with the songs and the rap and told us that he had co-created the Rapper Man character and voiced it. He was very keen for us to see the credits at the end so we could see his name in lights too. I'm sure it won't come as any surprise if I tell you that Dxx and I were a little glassy-eyed at this point.
>
> *(personal communication, 2022)*

The semi-structured interviews, together with unsolicited emails from teachers and foster parents, as above, created significant amounts of qualitative data. This data was then entered on a spreadsheet using the research headings mentioned earlier, with Saldaña's (2016) qualitative data framework to code and identify themes. It was demonstrated that significant pedagogical outcomes had been achieved and together with the process of being able to engage in new learning processes, as a part of a community of practice, had resulted in the acquisition of new skills, and most importantly changed how the young people viewed themselves. All of the young people reported increased confidence, a sense of connection and how the project had contributed to thinking about their future goals. The project's research aim of increased connection and feeling valued as part of a community of practice is particularly well evidenced. All participants expressed strong support for being highly motivated throughout, overcoming the isolation due to Covid lockdowns and contributing to the interrelational aspect of the project:

not giving up if something happens … I'm very passionate to be doing acting and be around different people and that makes me feel very good. Because when I'm with different people and they are very friendly and I can feel that confident here and I can feel safe here and I can feel like someone.

(EXX, 2021[14])

It has built my confidence and my social life.

(WXX, 2021[15])

There are people who are different cultured and from a different part of the world.

(YXX, 2020[16])

Well, everyone thinks in their own way and like everyone puts on a front. But like it can be a smile, or you can tell that someone is like dead unsure. But people here, like they make you feel all comfortable and stuff.

(JXX, 2020[17])

This last quote is representative of being in care, the disconnect that the young person feels and how the project is contributing to greater connection. As Claire MacNeill (2015) states, young people living within the care system are

robbed of their identities, childhood spaces and imaginations. They are treated as empty vessels to be filled with dominant ideas. They live with the labels they have been issued by these systems, believing they are bad, worthless and unlovable.

(p. 107)

Interrelational benefits were created and outcomes achieved "between learning insights, practice and results that happen as a result of participation in social practices" (Wenger-Trayner & Wenger-Trayner, 2015, p. 3). The reflective skills being used here by the YUAS enables them to recognize a counternarrative to the dominant belief that they are worthless and alone. The sense of achievement from winning awards, but also through the screenings at the theatre, produced an additional aesthetic of performance. The creative outputs illustrate the developmental journey that all the participants were on. For those young people attending the awards ceremony, being in the presence of professional artists, musicians and animators working in the field reenforced the fact that their work was being taken seriously, that it had been judged to be of the highest standard.

My city is calling me back
Across the blue sea,
It's still calling me.
                    (*Lyrics, 2021*)

"Across the Blue Sea": Reflections on the Journey

The a/r/tography methodology used throughout with co-creation practices enabled me as artist, researcher and teacher alongside all the artistic team, students and young people involved to equally develop and evolve, and included multiple unexpected outcomes. Three different cohorts of students contributed and benefitted from the project to gain skills, expertise and valuable experience of working with vulnerable groups. The opportunity for young people, both YPCE and YUAS, also benefitted from the additional exposure of awards and screenings. As highlighted previously by Matarasso, my skills as artist definitely went beyond my knowledge and experience: adapting to lockdowns, using animation and integrating live performance into the filmed theatre piece. But Destinies also provided developmental experiences for both YPCE and YUAS. The longevity of the project enabled participants to not just to acquire new skills but to embed them through the rehearsal and filming process. The co-creation element enabled young people to feel connected at a deep level, to express their ideas, their hopes for the future, to explore their lived experience in a safe space and to know they had been listened to. It cannot be assumed that every young person participating in Destinies can claim to have been significantly affected, due the transient nature of some young people. However, for those young people WXX and MXX, the achievements were outstanding. This chapter has demonstrated the importance of applied theatre theory *with* and *by* vulnerable young people, where co-creative methods contributed to well-being and employability skills, where and contributing to young people no longer feeling like a "city of lost souls" (Company, 2021[18]).

Notes

1 Unpublished lyrics created by young people as participants of co-creation theatre project, Destinies, under the care of Derbyshire County Council.
2 Derbyshire Virtual School (www.derbyshire.gov.uk) provides high quality educational opportunities for young people with care experience and care leavers, using a social pedagogy model of empowering young people to reach their potential. Sinfonia Viva (www.sinfoniaviva.co.uk) are based in Derby, offering educational and inspiring opportunities for young people and all communities to write and play music. Orchestra Live (https://www.orchestraslive.org.uk/projects/destinies) work co-creatively with professional orchestras and community groups.
3 ADHD – Attention deficit and hyperactivity disorder.
4 A suspected people smuggling gang was thought to be responsible for 136 young people disappearing from a hotel in Brighton in 2023. https://www.theguardian.

com/uk-news/2023/jun/25/child-migrants-to-be-sent-back-to-hotel-where-136-va
nished#:~:text=Around%2050%20youngsters%20are%20believed,as%20far%20a
way%20as%20Scotland.

5 Children and Young People Now reported up to 2018 that suicide rates had increased to worrying levels based on cuts in UK Government support for young people with mental health issues. https://www.cypnow.co.uk/news/article/big-increa se-in-suicides-among-vulnerable-children-known-to-social-services

6 https://www.theguardian.com/uk-news/2021/jul/19/charities-raise-alarm-suicide s-young-asylum-seekers-uk

7 Unpublished assessment – reflection report.

8 Unpublished assessment – reflection report.

9 As of January 2023, a total of 271,000 people in UK were recorded as having no fixed abode https://england.shelter.org.uk/media/press_release/at_least_271000_p eople_are_homeless_in_england_today

10 33% of young people leaving the care system will be homeless within two years. https://www.stepbystep.org.uk/news/who-cares-the-link-between-leaving-care-a nd-homelessness/

11 Hot seating is an exercise where the actor has to respond spontaneously to questions from the rest of the cast (Baim, Brooke & Mountford, 2002).

12 Unpublished assessment – reflection report.

13 Unpublished assessment – reflection report.

14 Unpublished assessment – reflection report.

15 Unpublished assessment – reflection report.

16 Unpublished assessment – reflection report.

17 Unpublished assessment – reflection report.

18 Unpublished report.

References

Baim, C., Brooke, S. & Mountford, A. (2002). *The Geese Theatre handbook*. Waterside Press.

Barraclough, M. (2023, 1 Mar). *Tea Break: Ep 12 Pt 2: Working with vulnerable young performers*. YouTube.

Boal, A. (2019). *Theater of the oppressed*. Pluto Press.

Boal, A. (2002). *Games for actors and non-actors*. Routledge.

Clarkson, R. (2021). Mama and me – music. *Destinies*. Unpublished.

Coghlan, L. (2021). *The crumble house*. Derby.

Deleuze, G. & Guattari, F. (1987). *A thousand plateaus: Capitalisim and schizophrenia*. Athlone Press.

Dennis, R. (2008). Refugee performance: Aesthetic representation and accountability in playback theatre. *Research in Drama Education*, 13(2), 211–215.

Dolan, J. (2005). *Utopia in performance: Finding hope in the theater*. University of Michigan Press.

Frank, A. W. (2013). *The wounded storyteller*. University of Chicago Press.

Guldberg, K. A. (2021). Using the value creation framework to capture knowledge co-creation and pathways to impact in a transational community of practice in autism education. *International Journal of Research & Method in Education*, 44(1), 96–111. https://doi.org/10.1080/1743727X.2019.1706466.

Hunt, A. (2023, 1 Feb). Tritagonist theatre: Investigating the potential for bystander agency through three interconnected solo performances. Derby. https://repository. derby.ac.uk/researcher/8115v/ms-ava-hunt.

Johnson, K. (2023, 14 Nov). Creative mentoring. Mighty creatives. https://themighty creatives.com/creative-mentoring-a-local-authority-perspective-by-kim-johnson/.

Lammers, E. (2017). *Can theatre help? A literature review of applied theatre for the embodiment of empowerment, resilience, and other need-based characteristics with refugee youth.* Stockholm University Institute of International Education.

Lomas, S. (2022). Home for good: National statistics for fostering and adoption. Home for Good. https://homeforgood.org.uk/statistics/care-leavers#:~:text=Almost%2025%25%20of%20the%20adult,have%20spent%20time%20in%20care.

MacNeill, C. (2015). Applied theatre as reseach working with looked-after children. In P. O'Connor & M. Anderson, *Applied theatre research: Radical departures* (pp. 97–122). Bloomsbury.

Matarasso, F. (2017, 9 Mar). Co-creation: Changing relationships in the networked age. A Restless Art. https://arestlessart.com/2017/03/09/co-creation/.

O'Connor, P. & Anderson, M. (2015). *Applied theatre research: Radical departures.* Bloomsbury.

Ofsted. (2023). *Main findings: Children's social care in England 2023.* Report. UK Government. https://www.gov.uk/government/statistics/childrens-social-care-data-in-england-2023/main-findings-childrens-social-care-in-england-2023.

Rohd, M. (1988). *Theatre for community, conflict and dialogue: The Hope Is Vital training manual.* Heinemann.

Saldaña, J. (2016). *The coding manual for qualitative researchers.* Sage Publications.

Springgay, S., Irwin, R. L., Leggo, C. & Gouzouasis, P. (Eds.) (2008). *Being with a/r/tography.* Sense Publishers.

Tomlin, L. (2013). *Arts and apparitions: Discourses on the real in performance practice and theory, 1990–2010.* Manchester University Press.

Vettraino, E., Linds, W. & Jindal-Snape, D. (2017, 28 Feb). Embodied voices: Using applied theatre for co-creation with marginalised youth. *Emotional and Behavioural Difficulties*, 22(1), 79–95. https://doi.org/10.1080/13632752.2017.1287348.

Vygotsky, L. (1987). *The collected works of L. S. Vygotsky: Problems of the theory and history of psychology.* Plenum.

Walmsley, B. A. (2013). Co-creating theatre: Authentic engagement or inter-legitimation? *Cultural Trends*, 22(2), 108–118. https://doi.org/10.1080/09548963.2013.783176.

Wenger-Trayner, E. & Wenger-Trayner, B. (2015). Introduction to communities of practice: A brief overview of the concept and its uses. https://www.wenger-trayner.com/introduction-to-communities-of-practice/.

Woodson, S. E. (2015). *Theatre for youth third space: Performance, democracy, and community cultural development.* Intellect.

Wooster, R. & Hunt, A. (2021, 7 Oct). Emotional distancing. *Journal of Applied Arts & Health*, 12(3), 393–401. https://dictionary.cambridge.org/dictionary/english/inter relationship.

12

YOUTH THEATRE OF SANCTUARY

A case study on the impact that collaborative, live and digital theatre practices have had on the lives of people seeking sanctuary and the communities they live in

Rosie MacPherson and Zoe Katsilerou

Introduction

This chapter is a critical reflection on the creative work and methodologies of Stand and Be Counted Theatre (SBC), the first and leading Theatre Company of Sanctuary. Drawing on past and current projects and using theatre studies and applied theatre studies as contextual framework, we specifically focus on our work with young people to reflect on notions of inclusivity, care, listening, co-creation, empowerment and agency that can be developed through engaging with theatre and the arts.

We introduce the structure, creative work, ethos and ambition of SBC and delve into our programmes that engage with young people. We briefly outline the UK's current right-wing political structure, explicate its impacts on the lives of those seeking sanctuary in the country and elaborate on SBC's response to the government's policies. We outline our creative methodologies and expand on key qualities that constitute the roots for all our activities. This chapter is an addition to existing literature and the work of other companies and organizations in the UK working alongside, with and for those seeking sanctuary. Its aim is to offer an insight into our work and continue to advocate for excellence in artistic practice.

Throughout this writing, you will encounter the phrase "people seeking sanctuary", an umbrella term for refugees, asylum seekers and migrants. This is done not as a way of diminishing the specific circumstances and challenges of each of the above, but to highlight the need for embracing those new in the country, to offer support, care, sanctuary and to encourage practices which allow for their legal status to remain private, separate from their identity and personhood.

DOI: 10.4324/9781003470434-15

As we write, our practices continue to develop. Nothing in this chapter is rigid and finished. We evolve alongside those we work with, for them, for us. We strive for artistic practices that respect those seeking sanctuary and advocate for their uniqueness and humanity. This chapter is an attempt to highlight these qualities and to inspire you to further commit to more inclusive, empowering, playful and flexible theatre processes.

Who Are Stand and Be Counted Theatre?

Stand and Be Counted is the UK's first theatre company of sanctuary. Founded in 2010, we are nationally recognized as leaders in the arts and culture sector for understanding the needs, developing the skills and championing the rights of people seeking sanctuary in the UK. We are a collective of creatives, the majority of whom have lived experience of seeking sanctuary and immigration processes. At the time of writing we have a core team comprising of Rosie MacPherson (Artistic Director and joint CEO) Firas Chihi (Community Director), Smart Banda (Digital Director) and John Tomlinson (Executive Director and joint CEO). We have eight trustees: Inderjit Bhohal, Esther Richardson, Emily Ntshangase, Hamda Shahzad, Donna Ridland, Laura Winson and co-chairs Reem Doukmak, Trevor MacFarlane; and nine associate artists: Anan Tello, Tafadzwa Muchenje, Nahzi Nabipour, Maha Al-Omari, Hannah Butterfield, Khaled Aljawad, Alina Aleva, Mohammed Alenizi and Zoe Katsilerou. Each associate offers their unique skills to SBC's work and supports the core team to deliver and disseminate high quality work. Additionally, we regularly collaborate with a large number of freelance artists who offer specialist skills tailored to each project and our participants. Stand and Be Counted is a charity which works across the North of England with a specific focus on Sheffield, Oldham and Bradford, areas with a high placement of people seeking sanctuary, and limited resources.

SBC's work is adventurous and political, merging lived experience of seeking sanctuary with original and innovative ideas. We have always believed that theatre is a vital tool in the pursuit of positive social change and justice; for us, art is activism and by changing hearts and minds we can impact on the decisions of policy-makers and change their policies. Our work combines live and digital mediums and is wide ranging to ensure that all interests, passions and skill sets are catered for. It often includes new writing, live music, physical performance, film and video games. At the heart of each project is the participants' rich experience and the impact the work has on our audiences. Alongside making work we facilitate educational and empowerment workshops for adults 16+ and children aged 5 to 15 and their families. These include our long-term creative empowerment programmes Youth Theatre of Sanctuary, the first ever provision engaging with young people seeking sanctuary in the UK; and Soap Box, for adults aged 16+ and their families. To ensure continuity, build trust and foster community, these programmes run weekly throughout the year, offering a relaxed, social space within which participants are supported to practise English, strengthen their communities, grow their confidence, as well as gain creative and interpersonal skills. These long term workshop-based programmes include opportunities for sharing the work participants create with the public across a variety of settings throughout the year. Continuing to place emphasis on the process rather than the final product, we encourage our groups to share their work at all stages of production: early stage, work-in-progress and finished performance. Similar to all of SBC's work, the content and form of this is shaped by the interests of the participants who collaborate with a range of artists to create work that excites and challenges them.

To create this work, our team draws on our extensive experience of con-temporary theatre practices and theatre studies as contextual and practical frameworks. Using our expertise in creating innovative and experimental work, we remain available to the possibilities our encounters with participants create. We prioritize the stories they want to tell in the ways they want to tell them, and embody a flexible practice that serves their process of doing so. With that responsiveness, our theatre does not always look like traditional theatre. Our theatre recontextualizes contemporary practices and strives to reshape the public's understanding of the multiple iterations of this art form. SBC and participants have so far co-created multilingual small- to mid-scale contemporary theatre, large-scale outdoor performances, interactive films, audio adventures, documentaries, video games, site-specific performances and immersive exhibitions. Approaching theatre practices in such inclusive and responsive ways, we strive to reshape the public's understanding of what theatre can look like and encourage them to focus on the stories it serves, stories that have often been silenced, ignored and oppressed. Theatre, for us, is a living art form, one that offers new possibilities to those within it. In his book *Tip of the Tongue: Reflections on Language and Meaning,* theatre director Peter Brook (2017) touches upon theatre's ability to be a living, empowering tool and qualities which we advocate for and embody. Brooks writes:

> Theatre exists so that the unsaid can breathe and a quality of life can be sensed which gives a motive to the endless struggle.
>
> *(Brook, 2017, pp. 70–71)*

Our processes embody the principle of a theatre that is breathing both through the flexibility with regards to making processes and performances and through giving breath and voice to stories that have been marginalized otherwise. Advocating for an ever transforming, responsive, alive theatre and challenging the understanding of what it can be within the sector, we use theatre's form as a departure point to create interdisciplinary, innovative, experimental, and pertinent works. Having co-created work for 15 years, we have developed strategies that remove barriers around language, background and age and enable participants to develop skills in collaboration.

A key term throughout our process is co-creation: Creating with each other, together, with care and through play. In her blog post "Making decisions together", theatre director Anne Bogart (2018) highlights the significance of flexibility within a collaborative process and the interpersonal and leadership skills required within a collaborative process. She writes that "The best collaborators are not only creative, but they are flexible. They know when to allow others to take the lead" (Bogart, 2018). Through a joyful, exploratory, inclusive and flexible process, we support participants to remain present within their group, to be responsive and caring towards each other and to feel empowered to lead within activities.

The primary point of focus of all our work, particularly with our youth groups, is that participants feel safe, respected and empowered. We create inclusive, welcoming spaces for creativity to support participants' lives. We support those who are or wish to become artists, as well as those looking to make connections with peers and build community. We are committed to creating safe spaccs and to prioritizing the well-being, experience and needs of those shaping our work.

Each project we deliver is designed in partnership with the participants engaging in it, ensuring its relevance and responsiveness to the interests of these communities. By working closely with their needs and ideas, we offer tailored support for each individual to immerse themselves in, realize and maintain ownership of their creative journey and outcomes. This flexibility offers space for participants to develop strategies for making bold choices, finding agency, trusting themselves and the group, feeling empowered to listen, propose, experiment and share. Elaborating on the significance of using the arts to develop agency among those seeking sanctuary, Anne Smith (2014) underlines the suitability of the arts as *a context for creative agency* as participants shape the work in "individual and collaborative ways" (p. 179). It is imperative that SBC's work is led and shaped by those with lived experience of seeking sanctuary, both within the organization's structure and on each project we deliver.

Whilst the themes of our work are informed by the experiences of those making it, it often does not directly speak of the sanctuary experience. Rather, through celebratory performances, we choose to emphasize our shared humanity beyond any specific element of identity. By supporting the development of multidisciplinary, bold makers, we can encourage participants to step outside their comfort zones, develop new skills and career opportunities and build the confidence needed to speak up, share stories and change policies. The impact of our work is summarized in the words of participants who often discuss the significance of our programmes and the impact they have had on supporting them to flourish in their lives. One of them states:

> I have learned that I have to keep learning and not just one thing. I left school when I was ten and I did not realise how much I love to learn and discover new things. For a long time I have felt as though I am standing on a bridge between two banks. This [programme] is the hope I have needed to get to the next bank. I have learned the value of preserving memories but allowing myself to move forward. I know now that I have more than one option for my life and I have the power within to make positive changes.
>
> *(Soap Box Participant, 2021[1])*

There is a reciprocal acknowledgement of the value of our work and the impact it has on the lives of those shaping it. Articulated or embodied, this value continues to inspire our team and strengthens our commitment to working alongside those seeking sanctuary in the UK.

Participant care is a priority before, during and after every project. Our team of creatives and facilitators are modelling care and listening as tools for creating work, ensuring that participants have strong examples of relating to each other and are empowered to "focus on a sensitive response to the accurately identified needs and wishes" (Smith, 2014, p. 178) of their groups. The targeted cultural activities we deliver support the well-being of participants by building confidence, autonomy and resilience both through our skills programmes and the creative projects. It is SBC's priority to deliver activity that is regular as a way of countering isolation, stress and lack of statutory support available to people seeking sanctuary. This is an ongoing navigation for our charity as the funding landscape in the UK raises challenges around who can participate, benefit from and contribute to the arts. However, our work continuously reminds us of the impact of the arts on individuals' lives as it forges a sense of belonging and closeness to those in it. Through fostering creatives who feel empowered to make their own decisions, we support them in developing "emotional belonging" (Smith, 2014, p. 178), which is rooted in one's confidence and self-worth. Our participants often liken their relationships with the group to those of a family. "I feel like this group to me is the definition of family. It gives me hope, confidence, love. You don't even need to ask for love from them and you receive the love from them" (Vernon Edwards, 2023) says Kendali on BBC Radio Sheffield's *Creative lives* Programme, amplifying the ethics of care generated within and feeding our processes. For those who already face isolation and separation from loved ones, to create spaces within which such close and lasting bonds can be formed, can counter long-term isolation and offer continued investment in their ambitions and skills. As a charity, we strive to create spaces that warmly hold those within them, challenge them in gaining new skills and encourage them to find and use their voices.

Furthering our commitment to promoting cultural accessibility within communities and the arts industry, we liaise with partners, organizations and venues under the shared agreement that they will maintain agility with regards to our participants' needs. This has taken the form of allowing participants and audiences to eat, take calls, leave, re-join, or take their shoes off in rehearsal rooms and at performances. Most importantly, it has ensured that evaluation processes are as empowering as the activity itself. With the guidance of our team and participants, venues have redesigned their evaluation processes in response to the cultural and individual needs of those shaping our projects. Practically, it has meant that venues have reconsidered potentially triggering paperwork and box-ticking and have acknowledged the damaging possibilities of standardized Western evaluation processes. Extending our ethics of care to the professional artistic communities we engage with, we strive to establish new processes that consider the perspectives and well-being of those new to the UK and the sustenance of their wider local community.

Placing the priority on our audiences and participants feeling welcomed in these spaces, we strengthen our relationship with venues interested in respecting and welcoming such behaviours, and aim to provide context and support to those unfamiliar with such engagement with creative work. Venues that have welcomed our communities' specific ways of engaging with work have seen a rise of 72% of audiences new to them. This clearly demonstrates the barriers our communities face in entering theatre spaces and the potential for this to change through shifting existing Westernized habits of engaging with theatre.

Our charity's mission is focused on democratizing access to creative careers, and opportunities for people of all ages and at any stage in their lives who seek sanctuary in the UK. This commitment has shaped our work around three clear aims: to educate the public on the realities of seeking sanctuary in this country, shift narratives surrounding people seeking sanctuary and counter misinformation; to tell a range of stories without limit or expectation; to platform and celebrate the participants and artists who make the work and the wider community they choose to represent through it.

This chapter elaborates on these aims and offers a critical analysis of SBC's work in relation to hostile political narratives around migration and misinformation, and to our work with young people, and offers an insight into our methodologies.

People seeking sanctuary are faced with dehumanizing attitudes, processes and stereotypical interpersonal encounters in their daily lives. By creating accessible spaces within which these communities can engage with the arts, we support them to articulate their needs, dreams and challenges. Curating spaces for these voices to be heard ensures that negative attitudes, systemic prejudices and discrimination can face lasting change. Our programmes offer urgent support, meaningful opportunities and new skills, showcase the power of co-creation and strive for social cohesion.

Reshaping Current Narratives around Migration in the UK

Over the last ten years, the United Kingdom along with other European countries has been experiencing a rise in right-wing populism. This has resulted in a shift in narratives and attitudes around migration and has stirred "ideological questions around 'British' identity" and the characteristics of "Britishness" (Shah & Ogden, 2023). Who is British and who is not? Who is allowed in Britain and who is not? Are there any physical attributes that represent Britishness and how are they shaping relationships between migration policies and the public behaviour towards those seeking sanctuary in the UK? These are some of the questions, the answers to which have often saturated mainstream media and impacted on the voting decisions and attitudes of the public towards those arriving in the UK.

These questions inform SBC's work and our commitment to anti-racist, inclusive spaces and artistic practices. However, they are not the forefront of this chapter. The following words provide essential context for SBC's work with young people and delve into our methodologies. Both directly respond to the UK's recent migratory policies and their impact on those seeking sanctuary in this country, particularly young people.

Stand and Be Counted was formed in 2010, the same year that the Conservative party formed a coalition government with the Liberal Democrats. The Conservatives then became the sole government in 2015 and have continued in power through to the time this chapter was written, in winter 2024. Throughout our existence as a charity we have challenged their hostility to those seeking sanctuary in the UK and have fought their deliberate devaluing of the arts through offering participants tools for self-expression and critical thinking. The Conservatives' policies on migration have defined themselves as hostile. In 2023 and 2024, the Tory government increased anti-migrant rhetoric, particularly for those entering the country through crossing the English Channel in small boats. It has persisted with legalizing legislation that opens routes for migrants to be sent to Rwanda[2] and detained in barracks and offshore ships such as the *Bibby Stockholm*. The impact these policies have on young people is direct. They are incrementally adding uncertainty to their domestic circumstances and insecurity with regards to their future in this country and pressure on their identities. This is particularly true for unaccompanied minors who often arrive in the UK in horrific circumstances, are forced to suddenly step into adulthood and are expected to rebuild their lives independently.

In our work we often encounter derogative stereotypical language and aggression around those seeking asylum and migrating to this country, behaviours which are escalated by political narratives. A significant aspect of SBC's research is to challenge such statements. The government's continuous labelling of *them* and *us* to distinguish between white British and those arriving in the UK, reinforces narratives of *otherness* used by politicians as a tool for creating division and nurturing hatred of the *other*. This otherness often impacts on British global majority citizens who are falsely labelled as non-British and are treated as immigrants, creating further division within the country and amplifying misinformation regarding their colonial British identity. As part of our commitment to challenging the public's relationship with policies around migration and asylum, we have collected a number of such phrases and set out counter arguments through evidencing the facts and unpicking the misinformation that informs these claims. This both fuels and inspires us to continue delivering our work and often spark creative ideas for our productions:

Why Do They All Come Here?

They don't. The UK takes less than 1% of the world's refugees, and this group in total makes up 0.6% of the UK population. As the sixth wealthiest country in the world, 0.6% makes almost no difference to our economy and resources. The following countries' intake of refugees is greater than that of the UK: Turkey, Columbia, Pakistan, Uganda, Germany, Sudan, Lebanon, Bangladesh, Ethiopia, Iran, Jordan, Democratic Republic of Congo, Chad, Kenya, Cameroon, France, United States of America, South Sudan, China, Egypt, Iraq, Sweden, United Republic of Tanzania, Niger, India, Yemen, Austria and Rwanda (Refugee Council, n.d.).

They Are Illegal

Under international law, anyone has the right to apply for asylum in any country that has signed the 1951 Refugee Convention. It is legally impossible to be an illegal asylum seeker (The UN Refugee Agency, n.d.).

They Are Taking Our Jobs!

Asylum seekers are not allowed to work in the UK. This forces many into destitution and modern day slavery. Allowing people seeking asylum to work could benefit the UK economy by £333 million each year. Ireland, Australia, Canada and many more countries give asylum seekers the right to work. 45% of people seeking asylum would have been defined as critical workers in the Coronavirus pandemic. Among UK businesses, 66% feel that lifting the ban would improve the UK's skills shortage (Refugee Action, n.d.)

They Should Stay in the First Safe Country They Arrive in

This is not a legal requirement. Most people seeking asylum aim to arrive in places where they have family, friends or know the language, elements that offer a sense of security. Those seeking asylum are legally allowed to do this (Refugee Council, n.d.).

They Could Just Stay in France

There are many reasons why people travel onwards from France. Some will be rejoining family in the UK or communities or – in the case of Afghan veterans, for example – former colleagues. Some may speak English, others will have cultural or historic ties to the UK and others will have faced trafficking and exploitation in France (Heaven & Jessica, 2019).

They Come Here to Claim Benefits

Most people seeking sanctuary do not know about the UK benefits system. Despite not being allowed to work, asylum seekers are only given as little as £6.43 a day as living expenses, their access to the NHS is not free and they are often housed in barracks and unsafe residences (Refugee Council, n.d.).

They Don't Have a Legitimate Claim

In 2022 75% of asylum – or other forms of protection – claims were approved. However, most unsuccessful claims are appealed and subsequently approved by the courts. Appeals cost money and through appeal processes, the UK profits from asylum claims. Claiming asylum can take months and often years all the while an asylum seeker has no right to work, study, or claim any benefits other than the basic asylum support which amounts to approximately £47.39 a week. The Home Office has not provided updated data on appeals against refusals of asylum claims since March 2023. At that stage, 51% of appeals were successful. The appeal success rate has been steadily increasing over the last decade (up from 29% in 2010) (Refugee Council, n.d.).

They Should Apply for Asylum Before They Arrive

There is currently no way to do this. Individuals can only apply for asylum in the UK once they are in the UK (Refugee Council, n.d.).

They Should Come Here the Correct Way

There are currently no safe routes into the UK, which forces desperate people to take dangerous risks to get here. Legally, there is no requirement to travel a certain way and the UK government's attempt to make it so has been found to be in violation of international human rights law (Amnesty International, 2023).

We're not That Bad!

The UK government has drafted and passed a range of new laws and legislation that allow them to bypass international human rights laws and ignore evidence. The Nationality and Borders Bill gives the government powers to remove British Citizenship without notice, criminalize boats rescuing people at sea and send asylum seekers to offshore detention centres (Amnesty International, n.d.).

The Illegal Migration Bill (as cited in The Law Society, 2023a) enables the government to ignore rules set by the European Convention of Human Rights, such as Rule 39 which allows the European Court to stop the expulsion or extradition of people, the power used to prevent the government from deporting people to Rwanda in 2023.

The Safety of Rwanda (Asylum and Immigration) Bill attempts to avoid evidence-based findings that Rwanda cannot be considered a safe country to send asylum seekers to; it is a law that attempts to change facts (The Law Society, 2023b).

These laws will have grave consequences for people seeking safety and for our society as a whole as they disregard human life.

We Don't Want Them Here

Amnesty International (2016a; 2016b) has published studies that demonstrate that the general public is more welcoming to those seeking sanctuary than is claimed by the rhetoric of the current right-wing government. "GlobeScan has ranked public opinion in order of the countries most accepting of refugees – the UK comes third after China and Germany" (Amnesty International, 2016b, para. 3). The Refugees Welcome Index (ReliefWeb, 2017) shows government refugee policies are "out of touch" (Amnesty International, 2016a, para. 1) with the public. Three out of four Britons believe refugees should be allowed to live in the UK to escape war and persecution (Ipsos, 2022). 73% of British people think the UK government should do more to help those fleeing war and persecution (Ipsos, 2022).

Following the Windrush scandal, a majority polled (64%) favoured an immigration system that protected those who have a legal right to be in the UK over one that prioritizes deporting immigrants (Holloway et al., 2019, p.

5). More than three quarters of the British public would accept refugees in their neighbourhood or home (Amnesty International, 2016b, para. 11). Such schemes have only been made possible for Ukrainian refugees. 81% of people support the right to work for people claiming asylum in the UK (as cited in Refugee Action, 2022). The UK is among those European countries with the most positive attitudes to immigration (Ipsos, 2022).

SBC's work is often described as going far beyond the arts, through our direct communications with local MPs, prime ministers, our activism and campaign work alongside other charities, and our close involvement with support services and organizations who work with those seeking sanctuary. We are fundamentally committed to using the arts as a tool to provide dedicated support in platforming and empowering people seeking sanctuary, who are some of the most marginalized and vulnerable members of our communities, and we strongly argue that the arts can have profound, positive impacts on individuals' wellbeing, mental health and connection to their community. Working closely with them, our team and participants have collectively been challenging the social barriers, negative attitudes and discriminatory behaviours that people seeking sanctuary face. These challenges are numerous in the UK today, multi-layered and often compounded by intense personal trauma. However, access to the arts is often completely unattainable for people seeking sanctuary, due to their specific circumstances such as barriers to education and social engagement, challenges regarding accommodation and language, and no right to work. This is compounded by the lack of funds, support, signposting, targeted opportunities or leisure time; and is also due to the particular transient nature of these communities. To mitigate against these barriers, we work alongside statutory support organizations, often in spaces uninhabited by the arts but familiar to participants (such as places of worship, community and drop-in centres) to deliver targeted support that focuses directly on boosting the well-being of participants through developing skills, confidence and agency.

Whilst the current hostile environment is incrementally impacting those seeking sanctuary, there is an evident growth of support from within the communities we find ourselves in. The solidarity and support of the people we encounter overrides national narratives of hatred and creates possibilities for a more welcoming, inclusive, informed and caring country.

Amplifying the Voices of Young People

There is a growing number of theatres, companies and organizations working with and in support of those seeking sanctuary in the UK, particularly young people. Utilizing contemporary theatre practices as a process, we curate safe spaces for those participating to share, exchange, grow in skills and confidence, develop agency and build their lives. Faced with the current structural and governmental obstacles, this work is instrumental in providing optimal conditions for growth and resilience through engagement in creative activities. Moving beyond stereotypical, narrow notions of what a migrant is, companies and organizations strive to support people seeking sanctuary to unfold their unique humanness, find stability and integrate in their communities.

SBC are proud to be a lead partner on the rapidly growing Theatres of Sanctuary network which includes the Montgomery Theatre, Maison Foo, Migration Matters Festival, Opera North, Derby Theatre, Mafwa Theatre, Wakefield Theatre Royal, Ice & Fire, Good Chance, Tara Theatre, Babylon Theatre, Compass Collective and Journeys Festival International. Within the companies outlined above, there is expertise in artistic practice and safeguarding procedures, and an understanding that our practices evolve alongside those engaging with them. However, often within venues and big organizations, there is a lack of appropriate training across all employees, which can prove problematic when there is direct contact with people seeking sanctuary. Whilst understanding that there is further growth within our structures, we acknowledge the sector's growing desire to connect with people seeking sanctuary and their communities in meaningful ways and through their striving to make this possible through providing training, mentoring and resources that promote best practice.

Theatre Companies of Sanctuary and Theatres of Sanctuary have intentionally been moving towards creating lasting change within their provisions that will impact on the lives of those involved. Hoping for a fairer system for the future of those seeking sanctuary, through theatre practices, we regularly persist in applying pressure on those who have the power to make decisions, to consider how they might be impacting on the lives of young people. SBC's work often directly addresses policy makers, and empowers young people to advocate for a fairer future. As well as through our regular creative and making projects, this has been achieved through initiatives such as our Sanctuary Round Table events, whereby participants are supported to deliver presentations and hold public meetings with local leaders, influential decision- and policy makers and campaign theatre, creating performances that speak to a specific problem and provide tools for audiences to involve themselves in making a difference. For example, our performance *Tanja* (2016–2017) campaigned for the end of immigration detention, supporting Women for Refugee Women's Set Her Free campaign. *Have Your Passport Ready* (2020) was created as a way of supporting Refugee Action's Lift the Ban campaign.

Building on existing theoretical studies on the impact theatre can have on young people, we are drawing on our embodied experience of working with youth groups across Sheffield, Oldham, Bradford, Leeds, Coventry, Barnsley and Doncaster. Whilst SBC's work is not the only example of theatre engaging with people seeking sanctuary in the North of England, we lead the way in creating with and for young people. With the primary aim of empowering participants, we are committed to maintaining practices of high standards with regards to their artistic content, safeguarding procedures and inter-personal elements.

SBC's work with young people is wide and long-standing. We have been running creative empowerment programmes across the country since 2015 and have collaborated with over 10,000 participants in that time. Some of our past programmes include Use Your Voice (Refugee Council), Creative Activism and Leadership (Coventry City of Culture 2021) and Creative Skills for Employment (World Jewish Relief). In this chapter we will draw on our Youth Theatre of Sanctuary and Soap Box programmes and some of their specific projects, as case studies through which to reflect on our methodologies.

Youth Theatre of Sanctuary

In 2021 we launched the UK's first Youth Theatre of Sanctuary, designed to democratize access to ambitious and wide ranging arts provision, ensuring that children and young people seeking sanctuary and their families are welcomed into spaces that empower them as participants, artists and future leaders. Weekly creative empowerment sessions support our members to explore and develop a wide range of performance-making techniques for both live and digital platforms. At the time of writing, Youth Theatre of Sanctuary brings together families from Afghanistan, Syria, Sudan, Iran, Iraq and Ukraine, with new members consistently joining. We currently have 90 people signed up to our Youth Theatre of Sanctuary, with an average weekly attendance of 40. Some families attend every week, some once a month or whenever they are available. The group is open to children of all ages and their families, including members from babies to 15 years old. Sessions support participants to build on and dis-cover new skills and passions, develop language, confidence and agency, improve and personally manage well-being and present their work to the public at least twice a year. As members tend to be at different stages of learning English, we most typically find that smaller groups best function if paired based on language skills rather than age, with many younger children supporting older siblings as interpreters. However, we always plan for interpreters to be present in all our sessions to accommodate specific language needs. The activity within our Youth Theatre focuses on an age range of 5 to 15 year-olds, with our team supporting older children to take assisting roles and creative responsibilities. Co-created productions so far include live performances, digital adventures and multimedia exhibitions, some of which have been presented as part of the Migration Matters Festival and at the Crucible Theatre in Sheffield. All these projects have been multilingual and celebratory, ensuring that all members have the opportunity to experience and flourish in their own specific ways. Participants explore creative writing in a range of languages including English, Arabic, Kurdish and Ukrainian; they explore music and dance from various cultures; design props and costumes; and the technology and equipment used to create a wide range of digital work urgently addressing the gap in digital training and creative opportunity for young people seeking sanctuary. As well as our creative activities, we organize two company trips per year, often visiting the beach, the countryside and museums, offering more opportunities for the group to develop rich connections and experiences. As with all our work, we cover all travel expenses to remove financial barriers for those wishing to attend. The school holiday iteration of our Youth Theatre of Sanctuary is Family Fun Days, hosted and supported by the Montgomery Theatre in Sheffield. This programme extends our invitation to local children from the wider community who receive free school meals, ensuring that our work is consistently supporting the communities we work with to extend their networks.

Three example projects co-created with our Youth Theatre of Sanctuary are Playing with Power (2023), Secret Summer (2022–2023) and Together (2022).

Playing with Power

A collaboration with the National Videogame Museum and Biome Collective to offer our Youth Theatre of Sanctuary a term of exploring strategies for game development. These sessions offered new skills and empowered them to design and create their very own video characters, music and stories. "We get to create characters and be whoever we want … we can do everything!" (Abdallah, June 2023[3]) says 11-year-old Abdallah. The young people's creations were then exhibited at the National Videogame Museum, showcasing the learning process and project outcomes in an innovative and eye-catching exhibition. The impact this work has had on participants becomes evident through their words:

> This is what I want to do. I've been picking my GCSE's at school so I chose subjects where I can do it more … I really love designing.
>
> *(Dayanah, 2023[4])*

> I just want people to know their ideas can become real.
>
> *(Loreen, 2023[5])*

Secret Summer

Commissioned by The Space and Theatre in the Mill, Secret Summer is an app-based multilingual, immersive and binaural audio adventure using geo-tagging technology to bring the piece to life in a specific location such as a park or festival site. Youth Theatre of Sanctuary participants worked with acclaimed Syrian writer Anan Tello to create characters and narrative. Their illustrations were the basis of the app design and featured heavily in the set design. They designed their costumes, wrote and recorded lyrics and music, as well as recorded all character dialogue in each chapter, for both English and Arabic versions. The group presented a promenade performance in Endcliffe Park, Sheffield to launch the production to a live audience of 605. The production has since toured festivals such as Migration Matters and Deer Shed. Secret Summer is a project that can continue to tour, with the young people having high aspirations to where it could be presented. "We could share it around the world … they'll probably want to be like us!" (Abdulwahab, 2023[6]) says 12-year-old Abdulwahab. Secret Summer was nominated for the Fantastic for Families' Audience Impact and Innovation Award. "This is my dream come true!" (Dayana, 2022[7]), exclaims 13-year-old Dayana after recording her voice for the character of Squirrel in one of our creative workshops.

Together

Our Youth Theatre of Sanctuary co-created *Together*, a multidisciplinary live performance at The Crucible, as part of Sheffield Theatre's Together in the City Festival 2022. Participants devised performance scenes, choreographed dance sequences, wrote performance texts in a range of styles, designed costumes and set, illustrated interactive projection and directed each others' scenes. This was the first time the majority of participants had ever performed and it is the first time in UK theatre history that children seeking sanctuary have created and performed work for the main stage. *Together* was imprinted in the young people's memories, with Mustafa naming it "the best day of my life!" (Mustafa, 2022[8]).

Soap Box

This programme consists of weekly creative empowerment sessions for young adults aged 16+ seeking sanctuary. The sessions support participants to explore and develop a wide range of performance-making techniques for both live and digital platforms, with embedded advocacy and leadership training. Through our creative work and training, participants build confidence and networks and grow their language skills. This programme also supports participants to form a Creativity Council, a participants' lead space within which they can discuss creative ways of improving their lives within their communities, for example by creating street art, sharing a film, or planting trees. Co-created productions by our Soap Box participants so far include multilingual, celebratory live performances, digital adventures and immersive exhibitions. Creative empowerment in this context not only focuses on creative opportunity and talent development but on supporting and empowering young people seeking sanctuary to lead on decision making processes and on ways creativity can shape and build future communities.

One particular strand of our Soap Box programme has been the Young People Together group.

Young People Together is a creative empowerment programme for young people aged 15–29 seeking sanctuary in Sheffield and Barnsley. It was commissioned by the University of Sheffield as part of the MIMY Research project (Empowerment through Liquid Integration of Migrant Youth in Vulnerable Conditions), an EU-funded project aiming to improve the situation of young migrants throughout Europe. In order to derive evidence-based policy recommendations, researchers examined the effectiveness of integration policies in an interdisciplinary research endeavour. Together, through a co-created weekly arts project we explored how to improve the lives of young people in South Yorkshire. Utilizing creativity and skill sharing we supported researchers at the University of Sheffield to explore the circumstances of migrant young people from various countries, in the wider local population, who have encountered difficult circumstances. The project sought to understand the challenges faced and what builds empowered pathways for members and their peers. Young people co-created live and digital productions, presented at various events and conferences, delivered workshops and developed strategies for meaningful collaboration with artists, researchers and individuals or organizations seeking to engage with them. On completion of Young People Together, members continued with our Soap Box programme in Sheffield, building on this work.

The ethics and methodologies of our work are continuously driven by the openness, passion, playfulness and drive of the young people we engage with. As artists, we work in a variety of contexts outside of SBC and continuously experience a unique openness, receptiveness, creativity and joy within all SBC programmes. Our diverse spaces include people whose perspectives are vastly different to each other and who are more respectful of difference, accepting of others and open to new experiences. This comes in stark contrast with political rhetoric around those seeking sanctuary, which are based on stereotypical narratives around the countries of origin of those arriving in the UK. Building on our commitment to shifting false narratives around those seeking sanctuary, we advocate for our participants' right to occupy creative spaces, to utilize their imagination and voices and to feel empowered to build their lives. Essentially, SBC's ethos, values and methodologies grow solely out of our participants' existing qualities and of their breathtaking ability to be exemplary in their humanity.

Overview of SBC's Methodology Development

SBC's methodology has been developed over the years in consultation with workshop and performance participants, associate artists, the board of trustees and regular collaborators. Drawing on our growing relationships with communities and participants, our continuously developing artistic practices, our ever evolving experience in safeguarding and our ongoing research on immigration policies, we have compiled our methodologies and working strategies as a way of both documenting our work and continuing to advocate for excellence in artistic practice. These will culminate in *The Welcome Toolkit*, to be published in 2025, an accessible, practical guide for artists and organizations. *The Welcome Toolkit* will disseminate our methodologies, offer a useful guide to those wishing to begin their journey of working with those seeking sanctuary and complement the work of practitioners already engaging in similar practices. This toolkit outlines six key areas of practice within our work. The areas we cover are: developing welcoming spaces as a preference to the embedded creative norm of relaxed spaces; allying with white British facilitators and ways of working in coalition; well-being and emotional safety; clean language theory[9]; flexible practice; relevant and sanctuary-specific safeguarding; careful distinction between social practice and social work, working with rather than for statutory organizations. Whilst details of the tool kit are not shared in this chapter, we are elaborating on the ethos underpinning this work and the qualities that weave through it.

Our methodologies are alive and responsive to the ongoing experience of delivering our work. They contextualize, focus, guide us and offer points of cohesion in moments of re-evaluation, challenge and uncertainty. They emphasize our commitment to working in close collaboration with those seeking sanctuary in the UK and clarify the charity's working aspirations with regards to professional practices within the wider context of theatres of sanctuary in the UK.

There are three areas of focus within our work which are directly inspired by the ethos and values of our long-term charity partner City of Sanctuary. City of Sanctuary UK (2017) is an umbrella organization whose mission is to provide coordination and development support for organizations, networks and companies supporting people seeking sanctuary. Our close partnership with City of Sanctuary inspires us and offers guidance for our methodologies and work. Our three areas of focus are: *Listen, Root* and *Action*.

The distinct qualities of these areas provide the basis for all our projects and frame our relationships with participants, partners and organizations. They are the pillars of our work, wide enough to allow for the flexibility required to serve those in it and firm enough to clearly outline our ethos.

Listen

Listening is, for us, key in learning how best to serve the communities we work with. Within our processes, we encourage and provide tools for participants to develop active listening; listening that gives full attention, approaches with compassion and temporarily gives up "one's own pre-judices" (Peck, 1978, pp. 127–128) as a way of being with one another. Peck (1978) describes this "unification" (pp. 127–128) of the speaker and listener as a way of one extending themselves outwards, and states that it is a practice which always brings new knowledge. Listening is, for us, a way of reaching and connecting with others, a form of solidarity (Farinati & Firth, 2017, p. 27), a path to forging strong relationships. In a world where there is less time to listen to one another, we choose to make and give time for connecting through being present with each other and offering our full and unconditional attention.

In order to best describe what we mean by active listening, we have included a scene written by our young people participating in Young People Together (2023). Without disregarding existing research on listening within theatre practices and studies, and in line with our commitment to amplifying the voices of those we engage with, we have chosen to prioritize their understandings and experiences of listening, both within our work and their lives.

The Ultimate Guide to Listening[10]

ALINA: Before we Speak Up we're going to need you to Listen Up! So this is a simple list of tips to help you to really hear us.

OMID: Number one. Listen carefully. Allow people to speak. Don't start talking until the person has finished.

JULIA: Number two. Concentrate on the person and what they are saying.

KENDALI: Number three. Give time, take in body language. Show emotions to connect. There is more to listening than simply words.

MUETESIM: Number four. Don't assume what people mean. *Ask* if you don't get something.

ANOSH: Number five. Before you give advice, let the person say what they want to say. In this way you can really understand their situation. You can help to calm them down and offer the necessary help.

ARTHUR: Number six. Repeat. Repeat the main ideas and key words the person has said. (*To a member of audience*) Hello. Can you repeat what I just said? (*depending on response*) Good listening … or It's a work in progress …

BILAL: Number seven. Summarize what you have understood. Describe the information heard, rather than interpreting the person's feelings.

KENDALI: Number eight. Always put yourself in the shoes of the speaker. (*To audience member*) I love your shoes babe.

ALINA: Number nine. Listen to yourself, your inner voice. It is true and will never disappoint you.

ARTHUR: Number ten. Show respect and be considerate. Don't make judgements about them, us or the situation we find ourselves in.
ALL: Listen and believe.

(Theatre for Change, 2023[11])

The above scene summarizes SBC's understanding of active listening. Written by our young participants through free writing (writing without stopping or judgement), we invited them to consider the ways they want to be listened to and how they value their own listening skills, as they write. The text was performed in participants' chosen languages, creating a multilingual experience for those witnessing, and removing barriers for those inhibited by having to express themselves in English. The content of their writing demonstrates the participants' agency, collaborative skills and confidence in using their voice, all skills we nurture within our processes.

Root

As a way of further promoting excellence in the practice of working with those seeking sanctuary, we consider it integral to embed the ethics of our work in the structures of those engaging with our groups. Recognizing the important relationship between the arts, integration and empowerment, we develop, mentor and train emerging artists, local organizations and their staff to effectively support and promote the integration of people seeking sanctuary. We believe that it is society's responsibility to embrace those new in it and support them in becoming an essential part of it. Following the creative processes we facilitate, we encourage participants to extend their ideas into their chosen communities. They are supported to immerse themselves in local cultural opportunities and to utilize new skills beyond our programmes. Working reciprocally with participants and the communities they chose to exist in, young people create inclusive contexts that understand their specific barriers and can provide tangible support in their day-to-day lives. We hope that embedding empowered, strong, compassionate and playful artists in the roots of our communities will bring meaningful change to the structures of our country.

Action

It is imperative that our work does not remain isolated from other practices and processes of our industry. As we build on empowering participants to find their expressive voice and embed their work in local cultural organizations, we can no longer afford a separation between professional and community production, because in doing so we divide our stages and our audiences.

We share our work and practice as widely as possible through multiple routes:

- making work in a variety of settings.
- providing interpreters and translation across all projects to ensure that we can reach communities where English is not their first language.
- creating work that takes multiple forms to ensure its broad impact.
- collaborating with a range of organizations and communities on specific projects and deeper strategic development.
- coming in direct communication with governments, councils and decision makers with regard to the ways their policies impact on those we work with.

Listen, Root and Action are woven through all our projects, and building upon these three areas of focus, we have developed our Culturally Safe Spaces strategy, which acts as a primary manifesto of each creative space we engage with.

Culturally Safe Spaces

- *All day open door* policy; participants have flexibility to attend workshops and rehearsals for as little or as long as they are able to. This forefronts participants' day-to-day needs and ensures that they are able to participate regardless of other family, work, study and legal commitments.
- Provide interpreters and translation across all projects and resources to ensure that all communities whose English is not their first language can partake.
- All programmes are open to whole families to remove childcare barriers.
- All travel expenses are covered, with a clear part of the session marked for this so there is no need to ask.
- Hot meals of the groups' choosing are provided in each session.
- Data and devices are provided for online sessions.
- We remain in constant dialogue with participants about the types of activity they wish to undertake, skills they wish to explore, trips they would like to take and performances they would like to see. This naturally enables us to shape the delivery of each project and production we co-create. Our creative team always keeps session planning flexible so they are able to respond to the individuals joining each day.

Our Culturally Safe Spaces strategies have been co-created with our participants over the 15 years of our existence. Similar to all our work, they remain open and responsive to the experience of continuing our programme delivery. Over the years, these strategies have increased the number of young people engaging with our projects, they have supported participants' agency in choosing how they will engage with our work and they have promoted further relaxation within rehearsals and workshop sessions.

Within our safe spaces, we embody an open, welcoming, celebratory and empowering perspective. This includes a combination of interpersonal and collective guidelines around the content of our activities, both shared with our team and wider collaborators.

Session Guidelines

Welcome

We welcome participants with joy, openness and warmth. This often involves cheering on arrival, celebrating, hugging if appropriate, shaking hands, connecting and discussing with each other, and is embodied by all participants and members of the team.

Check in

To begin our sessions we offer everyone the opportunity to share how they are. We sit in a circle, give time to each other and listen. Over the years, we have noticed that the process of opening up and sharing personal information shifts as participants' language skills and confidence grow. We hold these circles with care and respect for each other, establishing the ethos of each process from its beginning and ensuring that each participant has agency over what and how much they share.

Activities

The activities of each project are meticulously tailored to the needs of each process and participant. Overall, they are playful, flexible, they embrace chaos, are creative and appropriately challenging to each group, as well as accepting of individuals' unique verbal, physical and emotional offerings. They all encourage teamwork, personal growth and collective, active listening. These activities invite participants to share their creative decisions. Sharings are flexible and celebratory, aligning with our ethos on supporting our young people to develop agency and confidence.

Check out

To conclude the session, we hold a check out circle. Similar to the beginning, we encourage a safe, encouraging space for participants to reflect on the work and share thoughts, ideas and aspirations. The opening and closing circles, reminiscent of humanity's ancient tradition of sharing standing, reciting, dancing circles, aims to further promote comfort, ease and connection within each group. We celebrate the collective and individual experience of every session by marking its beginning and end.

Food

Food is provided at all our sessions, both as a way of offering support to those with significant financial barriers and as another way to deepen relationships within the groups. Participants' cultures are often centred on food and the act of sharing food is a powerful one. Reflecting on the importance of sharing food, Soap Box participant Saud says:

> Some of us here like to cook, so when they find that someone is from another country they try to learn their food and bring it here to the session, so that's one of the things that me personally I like, it makes everyone melt into each other, breaking the boundaries between the language, the culture, the religion, the race – all of these boundaries are broken.
>
> *(Vernon Edwards, 2023)*

Saud articulately and poetically discusses participants melting into each other beyond their linguistic, cultural, religious and racial characteristics. This metaphor encapsulates the essence of SBC's work and Saud's experience proves its significance. Through attentive and ongoing development, our charity strives to promote excellence in artistic practice for those working with and for people seeking sanctuary. Our methodologies commit to this aspiration and although ever evolving, they are grounded in a fairer, more inclusive, caring and creative future.

Conclusion

This chapter reflected on the work of Stand and Be Counted Theatre for and with young people seeking sanctuary in the UK. Drawing specifically on two key programmes, Youth Theatre of Sanctuary and Soap Box, we elaborated on our creative processes, compiled and shared our methodologies. Through this writing, we have aimed to continue advocating for the significance of spaces within which those seeking sanctuary can feel empowered, develop agency and use their voices; and to promote excellence in the practice of engaging with, platforming and supporting them to lead. We are committed to using theatre as our process and are flexible when it comes to our participants utilizing it as a starting point to create innovative, contemporary and celebratory work.

This chapter has not provided you with rigid guidelines on how to make a performance and facilitate workshops. It has been a heartfelt sharing of our experiences of sharing spaces with people who inspire us, people who embody the principles of our work and people whose lives are undermined by political and hostile narratives. We hope that we have inspired you to begin your journey of meaningfully engaging with those seeking sanctuary, and if you already occupy similar spaces to ours, that we have fuelled your passion for making inclusive, ambitious and multicultural work that promotes a fairer and kinder society.

Notes

1 Unpublished assessment – reflection report of Theatre Company.
2 On 15 November 2023 the United Kingdom's Supreme Court unanimously upheld the Court of Appeal's decision that the Rwanda policy is unlawful (Claimants v. Secretary of State for the Home Department, 2023).
3 Unpublished assessment – reflection report of Theatre Company.
4 Unpublished assessment – reflection report of Theatre Company.
5 Unpublished assessment – reflection report of Theatre Company.
6 Unpublished assessment – reflection report of Theatre Company.
7 Unpublished assessment – reflection report of Theatre Company.
8 Unpublished assessment – reflection report of Theatre Company.
9 Clean Language is a counselling technique developed in the 1980s by psychologist David Grove as a way of empowering clients to find their own metaphors to resolve trauma (Paul et al., 2014).
10 Scene of Young People Together production, *Together for Change*, performed in multiple languages as part of the Migration Matters Festival 2023 and at the City of Sanctuary National Conference 2023.
11 Unpublished performance of *Theatre for Change*, 2023.

References

Amnesty International. (2023, 27 Feb). Safe and legal routes to the UK. https://www.amnesty.org.uk/resources/truth-about-safe-and-legal-routes?utm_source=google&utm_medium=grant&utm_campaign=BRD_AWA_GEN_dynamic-search-ads&utm_content=&gad_source=1&gclid=CjwKCAjww_iwBhApEiwAuG6ccEhpLll4aSEHJFFniPhM5iBnnSZ5LlBcQjY1dYvniA82VbXnet4h-BoCaUoQAvD_BwE.

Amnesty International. (n.d). Nationality & borders bill: The truth behind the claims. https://www.amnesty.org.uk/nationality-borders-bill-truth-behind-claims.

Amnesty International. (2016a). Refugees welcome index shows government refugee policies out of touch with public opinion. https://www.amnesty.org/en/latest/news/2016/05/refugees-welcome-index-shows-government-refugee-policies-out-of-touch-2/.

Amnesty International. (2016b). New poll shows overwhelming support in UK for refugees. https://www.amnesty.org.uk/press-releases/new-poll-shows-overwhelming-support-uk-refugees.

Bogart, A. (2018). Making decisions together. siti.org. https://siti.org/making-decisions-together/.

Brook, P. (2017). *Tip of the tongue: Reflections on language and meaning*. Nick Hern Books.

City of Sanctuary UK. (2017). City of Sanctuary. https://cityofsanctuary.org/wp/.

Claimants v. Secretary of State for the Home Department. (2023). UKSC 42. https://www.supremecourt.uk/cases/docs/uksc-2023-0093-press-summary.pdf.

Crawley, H. & Hagen-Zanker, J. (2019). Deciding where to go: Policies, people and perceptions shaping destination preferences. *International Migration*, 57(1), 20–35. https://doi.org/10.1111/imig.12537.

Farinati, L. & Firth, C. (2017). *The force of listening*. Errant Bodies Press.

Holloway, K., Smart, C., Foresti, M. & Leach, A. (2019). *Public narratives and attitudes towards refugees and other migrants*. ODI Country Study. Overseas Development Institute.

Ipsos. (2022). Three in four Britons back principle of giving refuge to those fleeing war or persecution. https://www.ipsos.com/en-uk/three-in-four-britons-back-principle-giving-refuge-to-those-fleeing-war-or-persecution.

Paul, T., James, L. & Rupert, M. (2014). Eliciting metaphor through clean language: An innovation in qualitative research. *British Journal of Management*, 3(25), 44. https://doi.org/10.1111/1467-8551.12042.

Peck, M. S. (1978). *The road less travelled: A new psychology of love, traditional values and spiritual growth*. Touchstone.

Refugee Action. (2022). Give people seeking asylum the right to work. https://www.refugee-action.org.uk/lift-the-ban/.

Refugee Action. (n.d.). Lift the ban. https://www.refugee-action.org.uk/lift-the-ban/.

Refugee Council. (n.d.). The truth about asylum. https://www.refugeecouncil.org.uk/information/refugee-asylum-facts/the-truth-about-asylum/.

ReliefWeb. (2017). *Refugees welcome index 2016: World*. https://reliefweb.int/report/world/refugees-welcome-index-2016.

Shah, B. V. & Ogden, J. (2023). Immigration, race, and nation in the UK: The politics of belonging on Twitter. *British Sociological Association*, 28(1), 189–209. https://doi.org/10.1177/13607804211029968.

Smith, A. (2014). Maximizing empowerment in applied theatre with refugees and migrants in the United Kingdom: Facilitation shaped by an ethic of care. *Journal of Arts & Communities*, 6(2&3), 177–188. https://doi.org/10.1386/jaac.6.2-3.177_1.

The Law Society. (2023a) Illegal migration act. https://www.lawsociety.org.uk/topics/immigration/illegal-migration-act.

The Law Society. (2023b). Rwanda bill seeks to overturn finding of fact confirmed by the highest court in the UK. https://www.lawsociety.org.uk/contact-or-visit-us/press-office/press-releases/rwanda-bill-seeks-to-overturn-finding-of-fact-confirmed-by-the-highest-court-in-the-uk.

The UN Refugee Agency. (n.d.). 1951 Refugee Convention. The UN Refugee Agency (UNHCR). https://www.unhcr.org/about-unhcr/who-we-are/1951-refugee-convention.

Vernon Edwards, J. (2023). *BBC Radio Sheffield's Creative Lives programme*. Radio broadcast.

13

THEATRICAL EVENT IN YOUR OWN PLAYGROUND

Use of Mobile Space to Enhance Theatre Productions Provision in Primary Schools

James Woodhams

Context

Schools are a key part of any community. Most young people in the United Kingdom will encounter a school at some stage of their early life. Schools can act as a key power broker to introduce a live theatrical experience to a young person for the first time. Engaging with a school environment enables producers to reach a large demographic of young people. Schools provide a key space for young people with limited cultural capital to encounter the arts. Researchers have established that increasing school pupils' access to cultural experiences can increase young people's confidence to encounter culture in different environments (Nicholson, 2011; O'Hanlon, 2019). Jacqueline O'Hanlon (2019) argues that allowing access to the arts can offer

> children and young people the freedom to develop their identities, consider ideas and alternative points of view, as well as formulate arguments of their own. Often referred to as "soft skills", these are arguably some of the most important tools in any young person's armoury, preparing them for a life beyond school and encouraging them to contribute to their communities as well as a wider world.
>
> *(p. 14)*

O'Hanlon is arguing that arts like theatre can help provide an understanding of the wider world achieved through the key skills it helps to develop. Schonmann (2023) notes that "theatre is a tool that can significantly affect children's mental development, social attitude, development of imagination, aesthetic ability, critique, analysis and synthesis" (p. 241). Schools frequently

DOI: 10.4324/9781003470434-16

play pivotal roles in helping to nurture these sensibilities and develop them as adequately as schools do for functional skills, i.e. reading and writing.

Over the past decade schools have felt a significant squeeze on their funding which has affected their ability to welcome theatrical productions. Austerity in the 2010s squeezed funds available for Theatre in Education (TiE) or Theatre for Young audiences (TYA). Since the election and formation of the coalition government of the Conservatives and Liberal Democrats in 2010 and the subsequent Conservative government, the Department of Education has put intense focus on delivering STEM subjects. This "back to basics" approach to education significantly reduced opportunities for creative education let alone engagement with a theatrical performance (Stephenson & Dobson, 2020, p. 459). Despite all the evidence proving the effectiveness of theatre to stimulate a young person's imagination, there has been a decline in the percentage of 5 to 11-year-olds accessing theatre throughout the 2010s. Figures from Statista (2023) indicate how dramatic this decline has been over the past decade. There has been a decrease of 23.3% in young people engaging in theatre from 2010 to 2020. Only 25.8% of 5 to 11-year-olds surveyed had accessed theatre activities in the year 2019–2020, compared to 49.8% in 2009–2010. Data clearly shows a growing trend of declining engagement over the past decade and the trend indicates that this issue of non-participation is not about to change direction anytime soon.

Without school regularly providing access to different cultural activities, there is greater emphasis on parents' interventions to engage with this culture. This is not unique to culture. Diane Reay (2017) notes that austerity has led to a trend where parents and caregivers have to invest in the young person's education to achieve results previously obtained within the educational environment alone (p. 15). Koustourakis et al. (2017) note that the culture young people engage in is institutionalized, meaning that the culture we engage with is influenced by the culture our family values. They observe that "the stronger the 'institutionalised' cultural capital of the students' parents was, the more cultivated the cultural choices of family members were" (p. 412). Koustourakis argues if a young person's parent does not attend the theatre regularly, then it is unlikely that the young person will attend or ask to attend. This leaves the school as a vital touch point and an essential access point for many disadvantaged young people to engage with diverse types of culture.

As an embedded practitioner working in TYA in the Bristol/Bath area of the United Kingdom during the aforementioned political period, I witnessed first-hand the effects of austerity on the presence in schools of theatre or TiE productions. There was less time and fewer visits to schools to run performances, workshops and other interventions. Whilst teachers tried to find work-around solutions, the further deterioration of funding further reduced these opportunities. Budget restrictions have even led some schools in England to consider closing early on Fridays (Pidds & Adams, 2019). Budget restrictions compounding the de-prioritization of the arts within the curriculum led to school leaderships finding it harder to justify booking a space for a performance. As this trend continues accelerate, it has been important to explore alternative ways to enable the presentation of high quality performances as part of the primary school experience. This led to a consideration of how unconventional spaces could support a performance within the 21st-century primary school environment.

This chapter examines how a mobile space might be used to engage school communities. Theatre Bath Bus is an adapted public service bus containing a black box studio space within it. How does this bus being on a young person's home turf impact their engagement with the theatrical experience? Can a mobile space be an effective performance site within a wider ecosystem of theatre performances for young audiences? This chapter will follow the journey of the production of *Beneath the Bay,* a play by Upcycled Theatre designed for young audiences. This practice-as-research study hoped to enable insight into how practitioners' creative decisions around the use of this alternative space could lead to imaginative engagement and effective use of the unconventional space. Using space theory and practice-as-research as key analytical tools, we can understand how an unconventional mobile space can effectively reach young people and provide a dynamic encounter with a live theatrical experience that facilitates their creative engagement whilst limiting the impact on a school's own limited resources. It will argue that the intimate space of a bus provides the perfect launching point for an engagement with schools, providing a theatre-going experience within school walls that enhances creative engagement, works effectively within school limitations and provides consistency for the performers.

Schools and the Theatre Experience

Beyond budgetary and contextual issues of 21st-century Britain, there are more traditional concerns with the use of school space for theatrical performance. Heidi Schoenenberger (2021) describes TYA productions pre-pandemic as mainly taking place "in a theatre venue or school space" (p. 90) indicating the dominance these spaces hold within the TYA ecology. Schools, whilst being common spaces for a young person, are also inherently complex for the young person. Nicholson (2011) notes "nowhere is an empty space and no place carries universal meaning" (p. 12). Schools are no exception. They are controlled spaces which carry different connotations for the young people who attend them. Nicholson notes that schools are "intentionally disciplined spaces in which artistic [activities] and creativity had very little place" (p. 37). These spatial signifiers are still present, creating a "negative-utopian dynamic" (p. 55) for a school's pupils. Even with changes to signifiers using scenography and other creative tools, the fact the performance takes place in a school space might not escape the disciplinary nature of the space. This disrupts the potential for generate an active climate that enables creative engagement.

On the other hand, there are potential benefits to being within a school environment. Rachal Fensham and Meg Upton's (2023) research indicates there could be significant benefits to operating on students' home turf. They indicate that being on their own patch enables some young people to have more confidence in engaging with the kinaesthetic, embodied and spatial theatrical experience (p. 259). A young person's degree of comfort with the space, a space they inhabit on a daily basis, could enable greater play. It is this dynamic between two poles that Nicholson is alluding to. I believe there is a space within both arguments that creates the potential for creative intervention. By building on those who have ownership of the space but providing difference for young people potentially stifled by the disciplined space, there is potential to generate greater creative engagement for the school demographic. The presence of a different physical space could cause a disruption that enables a slight change within the school dynamics to open greater potential for opposite poles to converge on one centre. The key is trying to find a performance space that could work with the comfortability of the school, provide a site of difference whilst generating a "theatrical event" (Sauter, 2000, p. 14) within a school environment.

A mobile space holds the potential to both simultaneously cause a disruption whilst honouring the fact you are on the young person's home turf. The Theatre Bath Bus is an unconventional performance space that has been converted from an old single-decker public service bus to host a black box performance space. A stage was retrofitted with seating appropriate to its conversion into an auditorium, with a green room built into the rear. Theatre Bath Bus is a charity whose stated mission is to provide "a place where a rainbow of thoughts can be explored and absorbed in a friendly and intimate environment" (Theatre Bath Bus, 2018).

The ability to tour a show with the same performance space and come direct to the communities, to stage a theatrical performance similar to one in theatre building whilst minimising the impact on schools was an interesting proposition. Performances can be arranged without requiring significant infrastructure or disruption to the current school's hall or other spaces. It requires little investment and after the shows the bus can drive away with minimal disruption to the host community. The combination of mobility and a small auditorium makes this space a fascinating way to engage young spectators. Small auditoriums suit TYA perfectly. Many TYA productions take place in smaller auditoria, be they studio spaces in civic theatres, school classrooms or libraries. Beyond its links to smaller TYA performance spaces, the capacity of the Theatre Bath Bus mirrored that of a school classroom, enabling performances that mirror lesson scheduling and could put less stress on teachers and timetabling of the usual school space. A mobile space could provide a vital way of aligning with the pressures of the daily school timetable whilst providing a vital site for creative engagement.

For me, the bus offered the potential to provide a theatre-going experience within a school environment. This is different to other TIE projects because the presence of a different physical space creates a slight separation between school and theatre experience. The presence of the new space itself could help generate not only a physical disruption in day-to-day activities, but a psychological one as well. Emma Miles (2018) argues that "our understanding of *the theatre* is as geographic as it is temporal" (p. 28). For Miles, theatre is not linked purely to space but to the ideas or feeling a production presents. Theatre acts in produced space that generates a *climate* for creative engagement. The combination of space and performance engenders imaginative playfulness.

Research indicates that the production must look beyond the performance space itself to generate the correct climate for imaginative engagement, to have a rounded understanding of a performance. Willmar Sauter's (2000) concept of the *theatrical event* helps us understand how a performance's reception is dependent "on the surrounding contexts" including the building and the young person's journey to the theatre (p. 14). As Emma Miles (2018) points out, for young audiences "it is not just the performance itself that is significant, but the rituals of theatre-going and the social meanings made by children about and through the theatre space" (pp. 37–38). Miles discusses Baz Kershaw's (1992) focus on the importance of the *gathering* and *dispersal* stages of the performance (p. 25). These stages are key aspects of the theatrical experience: to generate excitement in anticipation of the performance and then cement the imaginative experience after the performance has finished. Effective *gathering* prepares the young person to engage in the creative interplay with performance and thus to co-create the fictional world on stage.

Miles (2018) notes that TYA venues like the Polka often use a special configuration of theatre architecture to encourage another step before dispersal which they argue is called lingering (p. 29). Lingering is an act that can extend the performance experience through using the space for unrelated performance activity like soft play that can extend and thus deepen the theatrical experience. The act of lingering helps a young person generate familiarity with a space, thus granting them further agency within the building (p. 30). Miles notes whilst purpose-built auditoria for young audiences provide a platform for their agency to be developed, it must be activated. Theatre architecture in itself does not instigate *lingering*, this is generated by practitioner intervention.

Possibilities of generating the theatrical event in a school context became a key focus for this research project. Understanding how an alternative space could facilitate a deep creative engagement that could build on the ownership whilst the using the comfortability of the classroom space for lingering posed an intriguing proposition to research. Does the use of alternative space provide a creative engagement and a climate of playfulness in the production? Can the classroom be an effective lingering space even when it is removed from the performance space? I will argue that providing alternative space enables potential to bring more performances to a school environment. The separate space allows for creatives to generate a sense of the theatrical event within the school grounds whilst simultaneously providing a less disruptive experience for school administrators.

Methodology

This paper undertook a practice-as-research and qualitative study to understand the impact of using an alternative space within a school context. Research took place between February 2018 and June 2018. The first stage of research for this project was the development and rehearsal period, which was conducted between February and June 2018. The second stage of the research took place on 18–19 June 2018 at Shakespeare Primary School, Honicknowle, Plymouth, United Kingdom (UK) where the performance was presented to young people. Shakespeare Primary reached out as the school had expressed their wish to host more theatre and performance activities. The school only ever arranged a trip to the pantomime at Theatre Royal Plymouth every other year with a teacher noting that these were some of the only times when their pupils encountered theatre. Straight after these performances, participants took part in a rapid response session. Overall, 178 Key Stage 1 pupils (aged 4–7) took part in the research. This approach was adopted to effectively analyse how decisions about space are made by practitioners and how the semiotics engendered by the performance space affect the engagement with spectators.

Participants encountered the performance in their regular classes, with a maximum size of 34. The performance itself was 35 minutes in length. This led straight into a 20-minute rapid response session to gain young audiences' views of the production. The use of a drawing technique is key to unlocking a young person's ability to communicate with adults about their view of the production. These took place within the participants' normal classrooms. Within the sessions, participants were asked to draw in response to three questions:

- Can you draw me what the beach looked like?
- Can you draw me what the dinosaurs looked like?
- Can you draw me your favourite moment of the theatre show?

Each drawing took roughly five to eight minutes to complete. This allowed for researchers to use the drawings as a springboard to conversations with young people about their theatrical experience.

Consent was sought from parents. Participants who had consent forms had blue stickers on their name tags for the research period. If a young person was not able to be interviewed due to lack of consent, these young people wore an amber sticker so that as researchers we knew we could not interview or keep their data. The young people were still encouraged to take place in the class activity, with their teacher and teaching assistants speaking with these participants about their drawings. The performer Chloe Caddick acted as a second researcher for this period and collected the amber sticker drawings (i.e. of those who had not consented), whilst I collected the blue drawings (those who had consented). After we had vacated the classroom, all amber drawings were taken to a secure area in the school for confidential disposal. Each young person with a blue sticker was approached by the researcher and asked if they were happy for the researcher to talk to them. At this stage in the research, no young person refused to speak to us in this research capacity.

Conversations were led by the young people. These conversations were recorded by researchers using a hand-held Dictaphone. As they were drawing, participants were asked non-leading questions by researchers about what they were creating, for example: What does this mean? Why is that? and Who is this you are drawing? Using open questions enables more insightful details to be expressed as it gives permission for young people to voice their own views and not look to find the answer they think the researcher are looking for; instead they give more truthful personal reflections. These drawings acted as a common springboard to facilitate conversations between the researchers and participants. Drawings and conversation are both used independently to accompany analysis of the drawings to decode how each participant imaginatively engaged with the production. This common springboard allows for a more accurate understanding of the young spectators' theatrical experience.

A final element of this methodology was note-taking throughout the performance. I noted how the audience reacted to key sequences within the production. These notes facilitated reflective conversation with the performers about how they engaged the spectators. This was then supported by the filming of the production. Robin Nelson (2013) notes that whilst "audio-visual evidence of the ephemeral event can never be mistaken for practice itself, [it gives] insights into how it might have been visually experienced as a sequence of movements in time" (p. 86).

Summary of Performance

The production analysed in this chapter is *Beneath the Bay*, a production created by my own independent company, Upcycled Theatre. It was an adaptation of the book *Fossil Bay* by Martin Malcolm. I acted as the director, producer and writer for the project, with different performers adding to the development of the play itself. There were three other key creatives who worked on this project: Zhiyue Hu, research and development performer; Chloe Caddick, show performer and co-creator; and Martin Malcolm, author of the source material and initial dramaturg. This development took place between February 2018 and the date performances started in June 2018.

Beneath the Bay follows Dr Danielle, a professor of Palaeontology who is at the school to share her love of fossils and the story of her first encounter with one. The play follows her telling the tale of how she and her grandfather had discovered her first fossil upon a beach. She speaks of how these fossils came back to life to form a real-life dinosaur. She finds more fossils around the beach that also come to life. However, her grandfather does not see this; all he sees are rocks. After being frustrated with him, she realizes that fossils tell the story of a life. You must listen to stories all around you to learn from them; the key is to listen. The play ends with grandpa finally hearing the roar of a dinosaur, acknowledging that the dinosaurs might have been alive for Danielle after all.

Discussion

Encountering the Theatre Bath Bus

First impressions of a space have a direct correlation to how an audience member might behave within it. Choreographer Hofesh Shechter noted that using a rock venue changed the way his dance production was received. In seeking this venue for his dance production Shechter was looking for a "venue where the basic rules are different" (Jay, 2018). Shechter describes how at the beginning of the production:

> the lights went down, and the audience [didn't] know what's about to happen. And they shout, like a rock concert. That is interesting because the way we behave is connected to the room we are in.
>
> *(Jay, 2018)*

Shechter is reinforcing the idea that the space ultimately affects audience behaviour. But does this only occur if the production works within the space it's occupying? This dynamic relationship allows the performer to help the audience better connect with the piece, activating their imaginations whilst providing a variant of spectatorship. However, Shechter's perspective fails to question whether the rock concert's audience member has experienced that space's conditions outside of that performance. There is an assumption that the adult audience of Shechter's show is already familiar with the conventions that usually occupy a rock concert.

It was noted by a teacher at Shakespeare Primary School that some of the participants, especially the younger pupils, were encountering a theatrical production for the first time within the Theatre Bath Bus. Stinson and Burton (2016) note that certain people view a theatre trip as a more "risky venture than going to the cinema, because the effort, the cost, and the possibility of disappointment were much higher" (p. 72). Although it is probably safe to assume most participants had encountered a bus before, be that seeing it on the road or being in one, this was probably the first time they had ever seen one with a theatre inside.

This raises a question about how spaces engage a new audience member who has never been in that type of space before, especially as the theatre was hidden inside a bus. What we encountered when we first took the bus into the playground space was excitement. The bus generated excitement and curiosity as soon as it entered the school grounds. A remote object being positioned within their environment, their home turf, caused great interest among the pupils. The bus being parked in the playground also helped to simulate the theatre-going experience that was described in the Introduction. With the disruptive arrival of a purple bus in a school playground, it was clear something new was occurring.

A bus entering the playground, and not on a road performing its usual task, was in itself a source of playful curiosity. Laura, age 6, questioned the arrival of this different bus on our lunch break:

LAURA: What's in the bus?
CHLOE: It's a theatre.
LAURA: A what?
JAMES: You know a theatre, a place where you sit down and watch a performance.
LAURA: Oh. So, you are showing a video?
JAMES: No. There will be people performing on a stage.
LAURA: That's weird.[1]

Laura was unable to conceptualize the physical formation of this space. She was only able to picture a space that they had encountered before that was similar: a cinema. They found the idea of a cinema in a bus weird. Theatre Bath Bus holds a *duality* of two spaces, being an adapted single-decker bus that holds a conventional black box theatre within it. With the physical formation of the bus being signified but not acting as a bus, it caused intrigue. The duality of the space presenting as one thing but being another caused confusion but also drew young spectators to the space.

Laura's confusion inadvertently confirms the teachers' comments about a lack of experience of theatre performance within the school context. The probability that Laura has seen a theatre building is likely. Jen Harvie (2009) notes that within city centres "theatre is symptomatic of the civic culture not simply because of its textual references, however, but also because of its material constitutions" (p. 22). Harvie is noting that theatre buildings and their purpose have been closely integrated into the heart of cities and urban environments. Most of a city's populace could recognize their theatre by its architectural form even if they have never attended. In the heart of Plymouth city centre is the Theatre Royal Plymouth (TRP), one of the biggest venues in the country. It is a large, dominating structure that is typical of post-war, concrete, brutalist civic centres. Given the proximity of the TRP to the city centre, a substantial portion of Plymouth's citizens have probably passed the building without stepping through its doors. Six-year-old Laura could have easily done just that. Thus, for her the idea of a theatre being within a bus must have been, as she put it, "weird".

Whilst the duality of the performance space caused some confusion it did enable a greater sense of a theatrical event to be formed. Excitement grew within class groups gathering for the event. Seeing the Theatre Bath Bus produced a lot of gasps and excited conversations as the young people made the short way across the playground. This excitement continued when they entered the bus to find a different spatial configuration. Caddick noted that:

> It's a whole new space. And it's on a bus! Kids want to explore it. Even though the bus does hint at some conventions, by being like a black box space. It's really exciting like "it's a bus". And there are just curtains there, whilst in other theatres the lighting box is up some stairs and behind the wall. That's exciting and intriguing. But it's important to keep on pulling focus back to the stage.[2]

The ability to gather, get excited and then be surprised by the bus's duality enhanced it as a space of creative invention. This captured the imagination of the young spectators with its playfulness of being two spaces in one. The performance auditoria, combined with the bus's ability to cause excitement during the gathering stage in the playground, prepared spectators for the imaginative encounter to come.

The excitement caused by the duality of the performance space was shown in the rapid-response sessions. When responding to the question "what was your favourite moment of the show?" Joules, age 7, said "When the lady drew the stickman".[3] This was referencing the beginning of the play where Dr Danielle drew a stick person to try and explain the concept that something being still does not mean it is dead. What is interesting is that when depicting this moment in his drawing Joules depicted more than just the performer generating the stickman; he drew the performance event itself. The drawing included a picture of the bus, the audience and the performer in the middle of the opening scene. The picture is full of detail, with wheels and head-lights. There was even bus driver, someone not even present at the performance. Joules' drawing clearly indicates great excitement at seeing a theatre performance inside a bus. Being on a bus increased the excitement and engagement of the live theatrical experience, which in turn enabled the sense of playfulness and imaginative climate needed to generate meaningful memories from the production.

Having a performance site within a bus made it possible to generate a more creative space, ripe for imaginative engagement. Like many other TYA productions, the show could have been designed to be performed in a school hall; there, the audience could have been three times bigger per show than the bus allowed. However, as Nicholson (2011) notes, schools are "intentionally disciplined spaces in which artistic creativity had little place" (p. 37). It is perceivable then that school halls would not supply the liberating space that the arts can provide (p. 22). By moving the performance into a different space, you start to negate the disciplined nature of school spaces whilst benefiting from the large demographic pool within schools. You can provide a theatrical event within the school grounds, which is then enhanced by the space's unconventional nature. Theatre Bath Bus provided the school with a space that allows young people to access theatre at their convenience whilst simultaneously removing any negative signifiers that might emanate from school spaces. It allowed for a highly imaginative space that the young people had ownership of.

Generating Climate and Sustaining Imaginative Engagement

The above indicates that the separation of space brought enough disruption to generate the idea of a theatrical event described earlier in this chapter. The disruption caused by a bus in the playground generated a sense of gathering. To heighten this effect of gathering, each class came out separately and waited outside the bus for their turn. This was a prolonged wait to generate excitement at the impending experience. They were then greeted by a performer playing Dr Danielle's assistant, who guided them into the bus. As they entered the auditorium, they had to walk across the stage itself, giving them a chance to look at the limited scenery and other elements up close. The creation of a sense of gathering and slow entrance to the space of a performance site enhanced the curiosity that is part of the theatre-going experience. Many conversations were heard in the playground where the kids discussed what might take place insidethe bus. The plan to generate a sense of theatrical event by encouraging a gathering outside initiated an imaginative climate that could be hopefully sustained throughout the theatrical production.

Once this creative climate had been created by the disruptive presence of the performance space, it was vital to enhance the creative engagement with the production. Theatrical techniques like puppetry, which have been shown to be effective in engaging imaginations were used as tested methods of imaginative play (Francis 2012; Gallagher, 2005; Reason, 2008). Understanding how the space itself could be harnessed by the single performer and actively encourage a co-creation of the fictional world with the spectator was vital in order to maximize and sustain the excitement generated by the bus's presence.

Theatre Bath Bus, albeit in the style of a conventional black box theatre, was a very small black box theatre. Due to the unusual nature of the performance space, a substantial portion of the research and development phase for this production was used to determine how the space would be used to generate engagement. A replica of the space was used in rehearsals to explore how to best exploit the space. Through this experimentation the creative decision was made to use the whole of the bus as a performance space. Expanding the playing space encouraged dialogue between performer and spectator. This was generated by Caddick running through the audience throughout the whole play, which made interaction with the audience, in her view, "less gimmicky". Seeing the whole auditorium as a performance space enabled a quicker engagement with the audience, but it also repositioned the framing of the spectator. It actively challenged the young audience to move from spectators to co-creators in the fictional world being presented.

Due to the intimate nature of the space, Caddick had to quickly form the audience–performer relationship. Gareth White (2013) states that many audience members will only engage with a production once a simple invitation has been offered (p. 154). Embracing the whole space as a performance area helped to establish this invitation to the audience. In the first section of the production, Dr Danielle would pretend to be shy and shocked at the audience when they first walked out on stage. Caddick would then go backstage and hide. Slowly, she would re-emerge from behind the curtain as the audience slowly interacted with her, as she gained confidence. This was both intended to make the audience laugh, but also to offer an invitation to the audience to get Dr Danielle back on stage, to be a key player in the production. Caddick stated that it was "Genuinely lovely how they just laughed at the first bit. They all laughed and every group laughed. The opening happens and then they are on your side".[4] Caddick shows how using the whole space, including offstage, as a performance site enabled her to feel like she could quickly bring the audience onside. The intimacy of the space allowed for audiences to engage in the offers Caddick was presenting to them. This connection could be described as an interplay. Simultaneously the performer and spectators are sharing an imaginative energy, contributing to the game to create the fictional world of the show. Using the space's intimacy allowed for this simple invitation to be accepted by spectators, helping to generate a positive interplay that lasted throughout the show.

However, accentuating the space's configuration did not automatically guarantee success in this engagement. It requires creative decisions and a strong performer who matched their energy with the configuration of the space. A performer is key to the success of offers to an audience to engage with the show. Caddick noted as a performer in the space:

> I could tell which of the kids were off when I was talking to the audience. If I kept eye contact with all of them, I kept their interest. But I could tell about the kids right in the front, if I hadn't given them attention for a little bit, I could tell they started to look around, you would have to look at them again and look at them again. Because your instinct is to look above them, because they are so low to you. So, you must remember to come down [to their level] and pull them back in.[5]

The intimacy of the space might heighten a performer's ability to foster an interplay, but it still requires the production and performer to use their skills to engage the young person's imagination. McAuley (1999) states that there is "a degree of manipulation and control involved in the reaction between performance and spectator" (p. 240). Generating a creative climate that is conducive to imaginative play is only the first step. Next comes the creative use of space. The performer's ability to initiate creative interplay furthers the potential for a deep imaginative experience. Kim Solga (2019) notes that this combination of an intimate space with a strong performer pulls an audience "closer to the stage and intellectually and emotionally" enables a creative co-ownership of the experience (p. 54). Working with the space from the start of the development period allowed us as creatives to most effectively understand how a space could engage an audience. It helped us use the space's natural intimacy to foster an audience–performer relationship that allowed a deeper engagement to occur.

Rapid Response Results

Generation of a creative climate and the offer to participate in the depiction of the world actively combined to generate imaginative playfulness for spectators who watched *Beneath The Bay*. Evidence from rapid response sessions indicates that the use of creative techniques managed to maximize the climate generated by a separate performance space to enable creative engagement. Susan, aged 7, in response to her favourite moment of the play, drew a sequence in which it came to life. She drew the shadow puppet representing a dinosaur in bone formation turning into a fully fledged dinosaur popping its head above the projection sheet that was used to generate the shadow puppet effect. Interestingly Susan has added an imaginative image to this puppet, drawing a full body and red eyes. The puppet of the "live" dinosaur was just a head, with gaps for eyes and a green chino exterior. Susan has taken this stimulus and engaged her imagination to further the realization of the fictional character. Spectators, Gallagher (2005) argues, are constantly "soliciting both the *real* and the *imaginary*" (p. 90). Susan's response indicates how she engaged with the performative nature of the puppetry. She enjoyed how the technique was brought alive theatrically. That engagement with the playful nature of this act enabled her to apply her imagination to the semi-constructed puppet to picture a full representation of this character.

Michael, aged 6, in drawing his favourite character, drew the Petra Pterodactyl. Petra was only depicted by soundscapes as the low level of the bus ceiling made this the most convenient creative technique to give a sense of a flying creature. Looking at Michael's drawing it would appear that the lack of physical signifiers impeded his creative engagement. It was a simple blue line drawing, which maybe resembled a bird but had no colour or insight. It implied lack of imaginative co-production with this moment. On the contrary, in conversation with researchers Michael said that his drawing depicted:

a Pterodactyl … It has wings, one eye and has a beak.[6]

This conversation articulates how Michael's imagination was engaged but was unable to reproduce this imaginative experience to the full in his drawing. The creative, playful climate generated by the theatrical event allowed even this simple theatrical technique to activate imaginative agency for spectators to take part in the co-creation of the fictional world.

Rapid response sessions also indicated that this co-creation applied not just to characters, but to the whole world of the play. As part of the rapid response session, spectators were asked to draw the world of *Beneath The Bay*. Within the play, there was only a brief description of the beach. It was described as having "a mixture of pebbles and golden sand".[7] Scenography helped to reinforce these words by having a limited amount of sand and pebbles present on the right-hand side of the space within cardboard boxes. Furthermore, a soundscape of waves and a beach ran throughout the production.

Spectators seemed to seize on this limited representation as an invitation to apply their own creativity to the event. Gregory, age 6, drew a beach with golden sand and a strong grey line that seemed to be blocking the sea from reaching the sand. When asked to describe his beach he said:

GREGORY: it's the beach with the sand. It's supposed to be here, but the sand has dropped down and gone over here.
JAMES: What's caused that?
GREGORY: The water, because the water has dropped down over to here.
JAMES: So, the beach has gone back quite a lot.
GREGORY: I want to draw the water. I imagine there is a blocker here.
JAMES: What's a blocker?
GREGORY: It's something that keeps something away.[8]

Gregory added into the beach a sea wall which was something never mentioned or hinted at within the production. Plymouth is a coastal city, with the famous Plymouth Sound which has multiple beaches and docks dotted around the city. This includes sea walls in places like the Barbican, which is a small harbour on the seafront. So it is easy to assume that Gregory has been to or seen these harbours in Plymouth itself or elsewhere. He then chose to draw from this past experience to add further details to his imaginative view of the fictional world.

Stephen, age 4, also combined elements of the performance with his own lived experience. In his depiction of the beach, stretching across the top half of the page are mounds to represent the rock formations on the beach combined with golden sand and pebbles. The bottom half of the page has orange lines to represent the beach with a large orange squiggle in the bottom left. On top of the mounds are many little mounds. When asked to describe the drawing, he said:

STEPHEN: That's the sand, the grandpa and this is the water.
JAMES: (*pointing at mounds on top of other mounds*) What are those things there?
STEPHEN: Limpets.[9]

Stephen's engagement shows how the creative engagement was enhanced by the inviting the young spectator to co-create in the realization of the performance. By adding the character Grandpa (the large orange squiggle) Stephen shows his ability to combine his own impression of a beach, which depicts limpets and rocks, with a character from the play. This combination indicates the young spectator's ability to form an interplay between experience and the fictional world once they been encouraged to co-create it with the performer.

Taking the creative decision to respond to the limited space of the production by leaving deliberate gaps in the depiction of the beach combined with intentional and consistent invitations to spectators to fill them, enhanced their engagement in theatrical play throughout the show. Asking spectators to help define the world of the plays allows them to reconstruct the signifiers to generate meaning, which according to Van Oers (2007) demonstrates that young people find pleasure in this process (p. 301). This allows the spectator to not only define the fictional worlds, but to attempt construct meaning from the play and the subtext that follows from this. A separate space in which the creatives have greater opportunities and creative and consistent control generates a climate that allows imaginative engagement and thus memory generation from a production.

Generating Space for Conversations

Each rapid response session took place within each class's usual classroom. Whilst the abstraction from the theatre space might seem like a counter-intuitive creative decision, as so much focus was on generating a sense of the theatrical event, fact that the bus hosted classroom-sized audiences enabled classrooms to be effectively used to host the session. Second, it was hoped that having a separate space from the performance site would allow the sense of lingering that Miles outlined, the act of continuing the theatrical event beyond the performance, to be instigated and thus continue the imaginative expression started in the bus. Jamie Harper (2022) notes "An oscillation in play between immersion in the immediacy of action and periodic interruptions can prompt a more reflexive perspective and language is the vital link that connects primary emotions with reflexive feelings" (p. 162). Thus, as the performance only lasted 35 minutes, the remaining 25 for the rest of the one-hour lesson plan could be extended in the classroom to allow for the reflective exercises to linger in the theatrical, imaginative and playful state.

Using the classroom as dedicated space for the lingering element of the performance to occur enabled these conversations to flourish. Rapid response sessions clearly showed the lingering stage of the theatrical event carried from the bus to the classroom. As highlighted in the Introduction, schools can be perceived as a negative space for a young person (Nicholson, 2011). As discussed earlier in this chapter, the Theatre Bath Bus has signifiers of its own, and its independence from school has enabled a creative climate to form. Taking young audiences from this unusual new space back to the classroom could be seen as damaging the work generated in the theatrical event. It could actively feed back into the negative connotations pupils perceive in their place of learning.

To continue the creative climate generated by the performance, links must be established between the bus and the classroom. A decision was made to have Dr Danielle and myself in the role of Dr Danielle's assistant leading the young audience from the bus to the classroom. There was a hope that using performers who were present in the theatrical and imaginative space of the bus would help bridge the gap between the two spaces and so generate a singular theatrical event. The aim was to reposition the rapid response work as part of the event, not a separate, add-on extra.

Responses in the session indicate that guidance between the two spaces sustained the imaginative climate. It generated the state of lingering which in turn seems to have enabled greater peer-to-peer discussion. The classroom environment enabled conversations to naturally form between peers whilst guided by performers and teachers. This was demonstrated when Charlie, aged 4 and Samantha, aged 5, engaged in a conversation about a character's existence:

CHARLIE: Was it a real dinosaur?
SAMANTHA: I don't think it was real.
JAMES: Why not?
SAMANTHA: Because of the hand thing.
CHARLIE: Why did it make a dinosaur noise?
JAMES: Because it's a dinosaur, that's why!
CHARLIE: Was it a real one?
JAMES: Did you think it was real?
CHARLIE: No.[10]

This conversation indicates the power of peer-to-peer discussions. Charlie was looking for confirmation that dinosaur was real or whether it was just a puppet. Charlie's commitment to the imaginative interplay to create the fictional world was so strong that it might have confused him into wondering if the dinosaur was alive or not. In discussion with Samantha, he was able to determine if it was real or not by listening to Samantha and to integrate her view of the production into his.

Generating space for discussion allowed for Charlie to seek affirmation about his experience, opened the potential for a peer-to-peer discussion, developing not only his view of the production but critical literacy and communication skills. Elaine Faull (2020) notes that should there be many subsequent school performances like this, spectators might head straight back to the classroom space of their own accord, leaving no room for discussion. For Faull (2020), this would actively stifle creativity as the work would be "left unfinished in the minds of the young people" and thus the production "may have diminished worth" (p. 18). This was not an isolated occurrence, with many discussions happening between peers in the discussion throughout the rapid response sessions, like instances that occurred when Michael, George and others linked dinosaurs to those of the recently released *Jurassic World: Fallen Kingdom* released in 2018. Supplying a dedicated space for lingering, and using the natural resources of a classroom for extra decoding can help audience members, allowing discussion around themes. Creating the potential for peer-to-peer discussion generates the possibility for the theatre production's themes to have a wider impact. Having a classroom as the dedicated and facilitated environment helped develop discussions between peers which furthered communication, listening and critical literacy skills.

Using the classroom as a site of lingering allowed for the individuality of spectators' experience to be explored within a safe environment with peers. As each young person is different, each young spectator has decoded, embodied or imagined many different variations of the theatrical production based on the same stimuli. This difference in how they interpreted the theatrical *mise en scène* allows for a mutual topic for discussion which gives young spectators a safe way to discuss potentially difficult themes expressed by the production. The act of holding the rapid response sessions increased the probability of discussions taking place. Van Oers (2007) notes that from this can be gained a deeper understanding of the play's "ability and disposition to (re) construct and use textual representations for the purpose of clarifying meaning" (p. 304). Heidi Schoenenberger (2021) agrees with Van Oers and notes that Matthew Reason names these post-show discussions the *afterlife* of a performance (Reason, 2010, as cited in Schoenenberger, 2021). Schoenenberger (2021) continues to argue that holding workshops after a performance acknowledges performance as something that has the potential to stay with young people after they leave the theatrical space and return to their daily school routine.

Lingering within the theatrical event encourages young people to deepen their engagement with the memory of the production. It provides a space for discussion and re-interpretation. Facilitating these events can further the experience. Schoenenberger (2021) notes that this afterlife practice values the young person's voice but benefits from adults that help to frame or provoke their recollections (p. 93). Generating memories from discussion around the play increases the chances of it living on in the mind of the young person, of impacting their development in an ongoing personal and pedagogical way (p. 92). Finding space to linger after each performance is key to the extension and memory generation that theatre can provide for its ongoing legacy with a young person. Making the classroom the lingering space continues the disruption to the usual school structure and, more importantly, to the usual school space. Presenting the classroom as now a part of the theatrical event continues to slightly shift the perception of normality within the space, providing the opportunity for a different engagement for the young person. Key to enabling this shift in the perception of the classroom space is disruption. Bringing a separate space into the school, a disruptive presence that allows for a young person to embrace the difference of theatrical event can be extended between performance and school space.

Practicalities for Performers and Receiving Schools

Familiarity with the space's architecture helped Caddick and myself push performative elements to increase intimacy and spectator engagement, which this chapter has shown to lead to deep imaginative feedback. These moments would have been harder to programme if the show was traditionally touring a variety of different school halls and spaces. Mark Rylance (2017), in his foreword to *London Theatres*, notes how on tour he worried about the design features of different theatre auditoria:

> When I saw a circular pattern above the auditorium, I knew we would be alright … If there wasn't a circle, I knew we would have a difficult time.

It wasn't just that the acoustics were problematic, but it was going to be harder to convince the audience that they were in the same room as us.

(p. 6)

Rylance indicates that the simple construction and slightest changes in a ceiling could impact his ability to reach an audience and engage them in a fictional experience. Having architectural unknowns and limited time in a space could lead to a less than satisfactory experience for a spectator. Theatre Bath Bus's ability to travel to different venues provides a performer a consistent space in which to to maximize its unique architecture. This consistent space, combined with using a mock-up of it in the rehearsal space, enabled a creative understanding of space, enabling creative decisions that enhanced the space further, which is very different to the situation that Rylance discusses in his foreword.

Consistency in a venue whilst touring is most uncommon, especially within the realm of TYA. A production's lack of control over a space's architecture is compounded when delivering a theatre production within a school environment. Often schools will use school halls or libraries, which are multi-purpose spaces that might not have been designed with performance in mind, being "adaptable ... flat floored spaces" (Strong, 2010, p. 72). Like schools, if we accept that the "primary objective in the design of an auditorium is to bring as many people as close as possible to the performance area" (Strong, 2010, p. 73) then having a space that hosts multiple activities generates a complexity of signifiers for creatives to navigate in order to engage with the spectators. This complexity is compounded as the set-up for these performances is usually very short, limiting the time a performer has to acclimatize themselves to the space.

Without time to get used to the set-up, layout and features of a space, the ability to generate an imaginative interplay is limited or even negated. Spaces need to encourage a bridge between spectator and performer to allow the audience's imagination room to operate and for them to take ownership (Solga, 2019, p. 20). Providing consistency for a performer from the start of the process to the engagement of spectators allows them to be comfortable and confident within the performance space, which makes it easier to quickly establish an interplay with the audience. Theatre Bath Bus enhanced the potential for a greater audience experience by providing a consistency and an intimacy that could be exploited by the creative team designing the show.

Benefits of the bus were not limited to the theatrical production. Theatre Bath Bus's mobility of space added another dimension to engaging young people in schools. It allows access to places which do not have a dedicated theatre building to offer a community setting that provides a live performance. The mobility of the space meant the bus could go directly into the heart of communities who often have little cultural engagement. It reduced economic pressures on touring as transport for actors, lighting kit and set were already set up within the the bus. Having a consistent performance space also allowed the performer to familiarize themselves with how the space facilitated the audience–performer relationship. Economic and logistic pressures were also either negated or reduced for the school. Money is often needed from a young person's gatekeepers (i.e. parents/guardians) for a trip to the theatre. A theatre trip might require transport to be arranged, extra chaperones and other costs could force the school to seek extra funding or to be unable to fund. Having a stage physically come into the playground means that these costs are negated and pressures on critical core space reduced. This reduces the stresses on school budgets.

Mobility of the space caused less disruption to the overall curriculum delivery. Being able to use the classroom space was another benefit of using this mobile performance space. The bus's ability to perform within the school timetable was both beneficial to the school and its pupils, as it was less disruptive to school timetables. As the performance and workshop could happen within the space of an hour, only one scheduled session that week had to be changed per class. It allowed teachers to easily work the performance into their scheduled timetable with less coordination needed between the whole school schedule to find an ideal time. The balance of practicalities for the school shows that the Theatre Bath Bus has an increased potential to deliver the benefits of creative engagement that theatre can offer. The mobility of the space makes it easier to arrange for a TYA performance to comne to a school, increasing the access points for a young person to experience theatre for the first time.

Conclusion

The above research indicates that the use of a separate performance site had practical and creative benefits for theatre performances in schools. Practically it allowed for a performer to overcome issues common with TYA performance in schools and general touring. It provided a consistent performance space which maximized the ability of the performer to sustain a dynamic, creative interplay with young spectators. Limiting the demands placed by the production on the school spaces enabled the whole school to engage with the production over two days with minimal operational impact on already stretched budgets, teachers and administrators. The bus only took up a small area of the playground. Usual activities like lunch, meals and classes could continue. This reduced the resource drain that a TYA show could impose on a school. Creatively, the exterior space of the playground enabled a greater sense of the theatrical event, allowing for stages of gathering, lingering and dispersal to occur. This in turn generated a creative climate that enabled detailed imaginative engagement that could lead to lasting memories. Access to the classroom can help turn the dispersal stage into a lingering effect which helps to further the creative engagement that the young people have just encountered and to solidify the imaginative vision of the world they have just produced. This is a potent combination that could enable rich TYA engagement with the pressures of 21st-century Britain.

Theatre Bath Bus allows for a multitude of different performances, but the limitations of the performance space do put restrictions on the scale of performance. It would be naive to say this space could replace the benefits of TYA performances in school halls, community centres, theatres, libraries or other unconventional spaces. Nor does this chapter argue for this. It is instead a study which indicates that a practical and creative use of mobile space could face the challenge currently present in UK education settings. It is just one space, however. All sites for performance are vital to enable access points for young people to encounter theatre performances and workshops. Key to addressing the decline in engagement that has been persistent for the last 14 years is a variety of spaces that can generate maximum opportunity for engagement. Variety of scale, content, viewpoint, artistic style and theatricality are vital to ensure a further reach to reduce the decline in theatrical engagement. The mobile space should not look to replace any other space but to add to it. It should be viewed as potential site for certain performances, another site within the rich architectural differences in the theatre ecosystem. It provides schools and creative companies another tool for creative engagement that empowers imaginative play. This chapter is not a longitudinal study, meaning that we are unable to say with authority that this kind of of theatre space could help stem the reduction in theatrical engagement. However, this chapter's research evidence indicates that it has strong potential to add to the theatre's defences, to turn the tide and reverse the trend of decline.

Notes

1 Unpublished reflections from participants.
2 Unpublished reflections.
3 Unpublished reflections from participants.
4 Unpublished reflections.
5 Unpublished reflections.
6 Unpublished reflections from participants.
7 Unpublished reflections from participants.
8 Unpublished reflections from participants.
9 Unpublished reflections from participants.
10 Unpublished reflections from participants.

References

Faull, E.L. (2020). The impact of theatre performance in a school setting on children's learning. Ph.D. thesis, University of Exeter. ORE: Open Research Exeter. https://ore.exeter.ac.uk/repository/handle/10871/123989.

Fensham, R. & Upton, M. (2023). Post-performance methodologies: The value of memory for theatre with young people. *Research in Drama Education: The Journal of Applied Theatre and Performance*, 28(2), 253–272. https://doi.org/10.1080/13569783.2022.2097864.

Francis, P. (2012). *Puppetry: A reader in theatre practice.* Palgrave Macmillan.

Gallagher, K. (2005). The aesthetics of representation: Dramatic texts and dramatic engagement. *The Journal of Aesthetics Education*, 39 (4), 82–94. https://doi.org/10.1353/jae.2005.0038.

Harper, J. (2022). Interrupting immersive immediacy: Pursuing reflexive hypermediacy in the play of participatory performance. *TDR*, 66(1), 145–162. https://doi.org/10.1017/S1054204321000800.

Harvie, J. (2009). *Theatre & the city.* Palgrave Macmillan.

Jay, D. (Host). (2018, 10 May) *Hofesh Shechter.* Audio Podcast, Theatre Voice. Victoria & Albert Museum. http://www.theatrevoice.com/audio/hofesh-shechter.

Kershaw, B. (1992). *The politics of performance: Radical theatre as cultural intervention.* Routledge.

Koustourakis, G., Asimaki, A. & Spiliopoulou, G. (2017). Cultural activities and the family's "institutionalised" cultural capital: The case of native and immigrant primary school pupils. *Pedagogy, Culture & Society*, 26(3), 397–415. https://doi.org/10.1080/14681366.2017.1412340.

McAuley, G. (1999) *Space in performance: Making meaning in the theatre.* University of Michigan Press.

Miles, E. (2018). Bus journeys, sandwiches and play: Young children and the theatre event. *Research in Drama Education: The Journal of Applied Theatre and Performance*, 23(1), 20–39. https://doi.org/10.1080/13569783.2017.1396889.

Nelson, R. (2013). *Practice as research in the arts: Principles, protocols, pedagogies, resistance.* Palgrave Macmillan.

Nicholson, H. (2011). *Theatre, education and performance: The map and the story.* Palgrave Macmillan.

O'Hanlon, J. (2019). *Time to listen. Leaders: Association school and college leaders.* SPR, 107. Permisitmann.

Pidds, H. & Adams, R. (2019, 28 Feb). School in Stockport to close early on Fridays for lack of funding. *The Guardian.* https://www.theguardian.com/education/2019/feb/28/school-stockport-close-early-fridays-lack-funding.

Reason, M. (2008). Did you watch the man or did you watch the goose? Children's responses to puppets in live theatre. *New Theatre Quarterly*, 24(4), 337–354.

Reason, M. (2010). *The Young audience: Exploring and enhancing children's experiences in theatre.* UCL Institute of Education Press.

Reay, D. (2017). *Miseducation: Inequality, education and the working class.* University of Bristol.

Rylance, M. (2017). Foreword. In M. Coveney & P. Dazeley, *London theatres* (pp. 6–7). Frances Lincoln.

Sauter, W. (2000). *The theatrical event: Dynamics of performance and perception.* University of Iowa Press.

Schoenenberger, H. (2021). Stay at home, engage at home: extended performance engagement in the time of COVID-19. *Youth Theatre Journal*, 35(1–2), 90–102. https://doi.org/10.1080/08929092.2021.1891166.

Schonmann, S. (2023). The ecology of theatre for young audiences: Is radical theatre possible for children today? *Research in Drama Education: The Journal of Applied Theatre and Performance*, 28 (2), 237–252. https://doi.org/10.1080/13569783.2022.2091927.

Solga, K. (2019). *Theory for theatre studies: Space.* Methuen Drama.

Statista Research Department. (2023, 30 July). Children's participation in theatre activities in England 2008–2020, by age. Statista.com. https://www.statista.com/statistics/421005/childrens-theatre-activities-engagement-england-uk-by-age/.

Stephenson, L. & Dobson, T. (2020). Releasing the socio-imagination: Children's voices on creativity, capability and mental wellbeing. *NASEN: Support for Learning*, 35(4), 454–472. https://doi.org/10.1111/1467-9604.12326.

Stinson, M. & Burton, B. (2016). Keeping the stage alive: The impact of teachers on young people's engagement with theatre. *Youth Theatre Journal*, 30(1), 68–78.

Strong, J. (2010). *Theatre buildings: A design guide.* Routledge.

Theatre Bath Bus. (2018). About: Our story. Theatre Bath Bus. https://theatrebathbus.co.uk/our-story/.

Van Oers, B. (2007). Helping young children become literate: The relevance of narrative competence for developmental education. *European Early Childhood Education Research Journal*, 15(3), 300–313.

White, G. (2013). *Audience participation in theatre: Aesthetics of the invitation.* Palgrave Macmillan.

INDEX

For Product Safety Concerns and Information please contact our EU
representative GPSR@taylorandfrancis.com Taylor & Francis Verlag GmbH,
Kaufingerstraße 24, 80331 München, Germany

Printed and bound by CPI Group (UK) Ltd, Croydon, CR0 4YY
03/02/2025
01830626-0013